JUSTICE BEFORE MERCY

*A memoir about the journey to bring a sexual
predator to justice thirty-five years after the fact*

Laurie Asplund
MS., LPC, LMFT

First published by Authorhouse 7/28/2009

ISBN-13: 978-0615446653
ISBN-10: 0615446655
Library of Congress Control Number: 2009907347

Printed in the United States of America

This book is dedicated to everyone whose lives
have been affected by sexual violence.

Acknowledgements

I never could have done this without the love and support of my parents, my family, my friends and Janet and I want to thank them all from the bottom of my heart.

Of course I never could have done this to begin with if not for the Fontana Police Department, DA Phil Koss, Detective Bob Sharp and the Walworth County Judicial System. I am forever grateful for their courage, tenacity and support.

And last but certainly not least, a very special thank you to Danny who was with me daily on this heart-wrenching journey. His unwavering love and support means more to me than he will ever know.

CONTENTS

Foreword

Journals help us to reconstruct our stories – to understand differently the thoughts, feelings and experiences of the past as we reread and reinterpret those words in the present. Many journals are private, never shared intentionally by the writer.

This memoir, Justice Before Mercy, is a most personal account of life and learning. Laurie's words communicate directly and honestly the events, perceptions, and realities of horrendous teenage experiences finally brought to justice in her adulthood.

To share the story requires courage and compassion and hope...hope that through her words others will understand differently. For those who have survived abuse, that they will know that they are not alone. For those who work with the abused (counselors, psychologists, etc...), that they think and feel deeply about each person's story as it is shared and to know their potential to help facilitate healing for their clients. And finally, for all in our world to know that there is a need to work actively to stop the violence.

As you read Laurie's words you will hear her courage and compassion. I'm guessing that you will laugh – and cry – as you read her words. For those of us who are privileged to know her, we can hear her pain and her determination; I believe that you will hear that too. And from whatever perspective you enter the story as a reader, I feel confident that you will learn invaluable lessons about life and love and justice because of Laurie's willingness to share the journal that once served her privately.

With respect and gratitude for all you share in your book...

Brenda Rust O'Beirne, PhD
Teacher, colleague and friend

Introduction

The initial intent of this journal was to simply document this journey so I could have an account of what happened. However as I began to see how things unfolded over time, it occurred to me that maybe sharing this story might somehow be of benefit to others.

I had no idea what was going to happen, so you as a reader will take this journey with me. At times it may be difficult to read, but I knew that I had to be honest no matter how embarrassing, humiliating, or shameful my revelations might be. How could I help people understand if I wasn't totally honest and open about what was happening to me?

It is important to say that what is written, is what I felt, thought and believed at the time. Some beliefs turned out to be true and some didn't. I also want to apologize to anyone who might be hurt or offended by some of the things that I say. I felt it was important to keep those things in there as a "teaching tool" for others, so please accept my apology in advance if anyone's feelings are hurt or if you were offended.

One of my hopes by publishing this story is that victims of sexual abuse will be able to understand how this insidious crime has affected them and that they are not alone in their distress. I hope that this book will be of help to the family members of abuse victims as well as their significant other's in understanding the damage that occurs not only to the victim, but how it extends to people on the sidelines as well.

This book might also be of help to people who are going through the criminal complaint process so they may have a better understanding of what that will entail on an emotional level. The judicial system alone can be traumatizing no matter how wonderful the district attorney, the detective and everyone else may be.

Finally I want to try and help society understand the serious ramifications of this type of crime. There is a stigma that is attached to victims of sexual abuse and it is my hope and prayer that by opening up my story people will finally begin to realize the severity and depth of destruction this crime perpetuates. In order to do that, I have included in this book my Victim Impact Statement, which is a list of ways that this has affected my entire life. Preparing this statement is one of the requirements of the complaint process. It is excruciatingly private and though I cringe when I think that people will read it, I feel that it is necessary to convey the cumulative effects the abuse causes to victims.

I believe that society thinks that we as victims are to blame for the abuse. People ask questions such as "Why did you let it happen?", "Why didn't you tell?", "Why did it happen so many times?", "Why didn't you file charges sooner?", "Did you love him?", "How was the offender able to manipulate everyone?", "How can you look happy in pictures back then?" And the list goes on.

People often don't realize how hurtful and offensive these questions are to a victim because on some level we wonder about those things ourselves. The difficulty of a victim to answer those questions themselves is what reinforces society's message that "you must have wanted it".

The reality is it can happen to any child at any time. There is a reason that offenders pick children as their victims. That is because they are so easy to manipulate. I was a naïve, loving, trusting, and gullible child who was no match for this sexual predator. That is exactly the type of child that they target.

Society also likes to think that this type of crime happens to only lower class and uneducated people. Ruth, a friend and co-therapist says that this "belief" is a defense mechanism to protect themselves from ever believing that something this horrible could happen to "their family". It's a form of denial when people say this doesn't happen in - my community - in my neighborhood - in my parish - in my church – in my religion - in my close family - in my wealthy circles – on my sports team – in my school. Like Ruth says, just fill in whatever you want in that "blank".

Therefore it is with these intents that I lay open my life and soul so that maybe others can benefit from my journey.

Chapter 1

My Early Life

I think that it is important that readers get a brief description of who I am and some of the things that happened to me in my life before beginning this journal. To accomplish this, I decided to include a paper I wrote in 1994 for the University of Wisconsin-Whitewater. This was one of two essays that were required in an appeal to let me into the Master's program in the Counselor-Education Department. My early college grades were terrible and though I had raised my grades considerably in the latter years before graduating, my GPA was still only fair.

Life Experiences

(Written in February 1994)

I am writing in response to the request that I submit a record of my life experiences in order to be admitted to the Guidance and Counseling Master's program. I sincerely hope that after reading this you will reconsider my admission into the graduate program.

Please keep in mind while reading this that in spite of these bad experiences, I have turned out to be a warm and friendly person with a healthy and positive mental attitude towards life.

As I stated in my autobiography, my early childhood was wonderful. I was raised in an upper middle class Christian family whose members loved each other very much. Our family has always been very close and very protective of each other.

The problems began when I was fourteen-years-old. With all good intentions the adults in our community thought it would be a good idea to bring a Campus Life program to the area. This national program was intended to provide teens with a healthy program of activities that was centered on Christianity. Unfortunately the adults did not know that the man who came to run the program was a sexual predator. Through his manipulative ways, he enticed me into a sexual relationship that lasted for 1½ years. He not only took my virginity but the mental anguish he caused has remained with me. Although no one knew that we were having sexual relations, my parents were uneasy about his attentiveness towards me. They and the president of the local organization in the area met with this man, his wife and me and accused him of inappropriate behavior towards me. As a result he was fired and he and his family moved to Indiana. But he continued to come back to meet me in secret and I was so mesmerized by this man that I agreed to these meetings. Finally one night it didn't feel right. I was now sixteen-years-old and beginning to see this man for what he really was. That night I refused to have relations with him and I can still see him standing there as I drove away. I have never seen or heard from him again.

The following year after I finished my junior year in high school, my father accepted a job with AT&T working in Tehran Iran. My family moved there and I attended the Tehran American School for my senior year. I found the Middle East fascinating and very different from anything that I had ever experienced before. I found however that it was quite easy for me to adapt to the new environment and that ability to adapt has helped me throughout my life. I joined a peer-counseling program that was offered during the first summer in order to meet other kids and to learn how to help other students cope with their problems. Those problems ranged from poor home situations to poor self-esteem, difficulties in handling a foreign culture and drug use. I remained a peer counselor for my entire senior year and received four A's for that work. In doing that counseling I learned that I had a knack for helping others with their problems while at the same time I found that I was mentally helping myself.

Following high school graduation, my family and I traveled in the Far East before returning to the U.S. I got back just in time to enter the University of Minnesota for the fall semester. That school was chosen because my oldest brother was attending there and since my parents were going back to Iran, they felt that I would be safe there with my brother.

I found the University to be absolutely overwhelming. I had spent most of my growing years in Lake Geneva, WI, which is a relatively small community. The American community in Tehran was also small. With only these small school experiences, being put into a school of over 50,000 students was the wrong decision. The classes were huge-one class had over 1,000 students in it. In one psychology class I never saw the professor in person the entire quarter. He videotaped all of his lectures and the T.A.'s were there to handle any questions.

I was already struggling with the problems at school when I was stricken with a debilitating intestinal problem. After numerous trips to the emergency room, I was finally admitted to the University of Minnesota hospital for emergency surgery to have my appendix removed. However, they discovered that was not the problem and so exploratory surgery was performed. The intestinal problem remained however and has plagued me ever since. It was only recently that a new doctor determined the problem was due to a parasite that I had picked up in Iran and that it had permanently damaged my intestines.

The next two years were spent trying to cope with everything that had been building up since I was fourteen-years-old. My parents were half way around the world, our family home was rented out and the parental guidance that I needed was not there. In the college dorm, I was introduced to drugs and serious drinking. It seemed to be the "in" thing to do at the time. As a result, my grades began falling into the same black abyss that I was sinking into. This was a serious mistake since it is now affecting my current goals in life.

Things began to turn around for me after my parents moved back to Lake Geneva and helped me get my act together. In a mutual decision, we decided that I should take a semester abroad at Franklin College in Switzerland. While at Franklin I started to enjoy learning and studying again in smaller classes. Individual attention was always available and I enjoyed the learning environment.

Then tragedy struck again. I was raped while walking home from a restaurant one night. To be honest, I had had quite a bit to drink and the end result was that an Algerian man took me to his apartment on the pretense that he was going to give me a ride home. Completely trusting him I had followed him to his apartment to get his car keys. He then locked the door and raped me. It was the most terrifying experience I ever had. Fortunately he let me go and I went to the police to file a report. Then when the dean of the school refused to help me get a lawyer because of embarrassment to the school, I was devastated. It was then that I remembered that I had once written a paper on rape for a college class and that the last sentence read, "We as women have to stand up for ourselves and fight this horrible crime or it will never go away". So, after much soul searching and going against my father's request to come home, I found my own attorney and fought through the legal system. Not only was it a foreign legal system, but also all of the hearings were in Italian. I won and the man who raped me was sentenced to two years in prison. I think that overcoming what seemed to be insurmountable odds gave me back the self-confidence I had lost as a child so long ago.

After that semester I came back to the U.S. to attend St. Cloud State University. That was a more appropriate school for me and I excelled in my psychology classes. During this time I became engaged and after graduating from college, married and moved to Carbondale, Illinois where my husband was attending Southern Illinois University. I got a job with Combined Insurance Company selling insurance door-to-door. I found that I loved meeting all kinds of different people and that I was able to handle the many different situations created by that kind of selling. I have continued in the sales field selling various products until this day. I learned that I must have a career where I am dealing directly with people.

A year after I was married I found the relationship to be an unhealthy one and I filed for divorce. The next few months were especially stressful because my estranged husband broke into my parents' house and stole all our wedding presents and other possessions. Then a few months later, before the divorce became final, my husband was killed in an automobile accident. Then came the guilt and another slide into that yawning abyss. I began using cocaine on a frequent basis and as a result, quit my job, lost my money and then lost my self-respect again. After a year on a downward spiral, I hit bottom so that the only way was up. I took a trip to my brother's home in California and spent two weeks getting the drugs out of my system. After that, with the guidance of Dr. June Hadley who is a wonderful psychologist located in East Troy, I once again turned my life around. She validated the terrible experiences I had had and taught me to put things into perspective. She taught me how to help myself mentally and that is what I would like to do for others. I would like to help others be able to put their problems into perspective and as the Reverend Robert Schuller says, "Turn your scars into stars".

I must say that I did not do all this growing and learning on my own. I was blessed with the love and the constant and unending support of my family and friends. My sessions with Dr. Hadley were a source of tremendous and everlasting help. But above all I believe in God and believe that things happen in our lives for a reason. I have faith that these tragedies happened to me in order to make me a stronger and more complete person and believed that the reason for everything would be shown to me when God and I were both ready. I wholeheartedly believe that I am now ready to start my calling in life, which is to be a counselor to others.

In March of 1993 I stopped drinking and it was this final monkey that had to be removed from my back before I could begin to realize my true talents, goals and desires and be able to handle the next phase of my life – hopefully a life of helping others to overcome the problems and challenges in their lives. Even if it is only one person that I help, it will be worth all I have endured. I still have a sincere friendliness towards people and genuine warmth. It is this combination along with all that I have experienced and overcome that makes me believe that I would be a tremendous asset to the graduate program and to the counseling field.

Current Day:

Fortunately I was accepted into the Counseling Master's program and graduated with a M.S. in Community Counseling in 1996, achieving mostly A's I might add! Since graduation I first worked in a community mental health center for two years and then went into private practice where I remain today.

One population I work with is children who are involved in the Human Services Department for one reason or other. Some are children who are in foster care because of their bad behavior, because their parents were neglectful, or because some other type of abuse has occurred. Sometimes the children simply live in chaotic environments and the family needs help. Most of these clients I see in their home. In other words, I go to wherever they live whether it is in a foster home, in a group home or in their own home. As a result of working with individuals in their homes, I frequently go to bad, sometimes very bad neighborhoods.

The other major clientele I work with are clients who have been diagnosed with Borderline Personality Disorder. These are individuals who self-injure and who are chronically suicidal. I was fortunate enough to be trained early in my career in a therapy called Dialectical Behavioral Therapy (DBT). I have found through the years that this treatment approach works not only with this population, but also for people in general. There are many DBT concepts, techniques and tools sprinkled throughout this journal.

I also discovered while working with children in foster care and through the adoption of one of my "favorite" clients, that there were no appropriate greeting cards to thank his adoptive parents for their devotion and dedication to this lost boy. As a result, I started a greeting card business called L.A. Cards. These are cards that are geared towards foster parents, alternative adoptions, cards for encouragement and support, cards that can be sent to professionals as well some humorous cards.

On the personal front, I met a wonderful man named Danny and we have been together for 25 years. We have a yellow Labrador dog that we should have named Marley because at eight-years-old he is still naughty, but his name is Tucker. I have no children but Danny has two daughters, a son-in-law and two grandchildren.

CHAPTER 2

How He Did It

A sexual predator is exactly that, a predator. Their whole mission in life is to pursue their own personal deviant pleasure at the expense of someone who isn't capable of protecting him or herself. Unfortunately, since this is their life mission, many of them become very good at what they do. It is my opinion that most, if not all, sexual predators are sociopaths and one of the criteria for being diagnosed as a sociopath is "complete disregard for others" and that defines a sexual predator.

Their ability to charm others is important for many reasons because people really don't understand how a sexual predator works. I'm hoping that this explanation of what happened to me, will once and for all settle the "gripes" that society has with children who were molested.

Evil entered my life when I joined a Campus Life club in our area. Campus Life is a division of the organization Youth For Christ and its mission is to provide positive Christian activities for middle school and high school age children.

Russell (Russ) Lesser was the twenty-nine-year-old youth pastor that they chose for the job of taking over a Campus Life Club in the area. Russ was married to a wonderful woman named Jeannie and they had a year-old son, Mathew. Russ was a dynamic, handsome, charming, fun, and enthusiastic person who came into our area like a dynamo.

The first thing that happened was that Lesser beguiled everyone in the community with how handsome, fun, and cool he was. As an adult, he had the ability to interact with teenagers in a way that made us feel special and understood. Everyone including parents and children were enamored of this man. Call him the Pied Piper if you will because here was this fun young guy who we all blindly followed.

Lesser immediately began his agenda of meeting teens at the four high schools in the area by providing fun activities to get us hooked. We would have parties hosted by our friend's parents, including mine, that would include swimming and boating, movies and games that fostered building trust. I think that during all of these activities, Lesser was looking to see who his next victim was going to be. It had to be someone who was trusting, naïve and gullible, and I fit that bill to a T.

Meanwhile the parents that were involved with Campus Life and with our activities were thrilled that their children were so heavily involved with a Christian organization. They thought that Lesser was going to be able to "turn us around" and put Christ in our lives. That hope of turning around their teenagers is probably one of the main reasons they never questioned the intentions of Lesser. I must explain that we were normal teenagers of the 1970's and most of us indulged in the recreational use of marijuana and alcohol. Since it was a small community however, nothing much ever happened without the other parents finding out, so we weren't that "bad".

Approximately a month after Lesser began the group, we went to a Campus Life camp somewhere in Wisconsin and that is when he began to work on me. He would get me off alone on the pretense that he needed to "spiritually guide me" and that it needed to be private. He would talk about trust and whether I trusted him or not. I am going to go into some detail here even though it is so humiliating because I feel that it is important for people to know how sexual predators begin to groom their victims.

To prove that I could trust him, he introduced a game to me. This game had us sitting cross-legged on the ground and then first he would put his hands on the upper part of my knees and pretend like he was going to pinch me. He would keep inching up the inside of my thigh stopping to ask if I trusted him. If I trusted him, then he would go further. Sometimes he would pinch me and then he would have to start all over again by my knees. Eventually he had me playing this game with him as well.

I will say that it wasn't too many days before his hands would be right by my private area, but they never went any further. It was like he was building up the sexual tension, not only for himself, but for me as well. One of the things that I have learned through school is that a person's body automatically responds to sexual stimuli. The body gets physiologically aroused no matter what the brain might be saying. It's a natural response that you really can't stop and a child being aroused is something that they aren't able to understand and comprehend. Honestly, I thought I had to go to the bathroom. As time progressed, so did the game that we were playing.

Another characteristic of sexual predators is that they like to get their victims alone as often as possible and he certainly did that with me. He would find plenty of ways to get me alone and in the beginning it was because we had to talk "about my spiritual journey" and that demanded privacy. He would insist on driving me home from events in order to "counsel me". Little did people know that every time he would get me alone, this game would go a little further.

It's hard for me to understand why I didn't stop the game when it first got started except to say that maybe in the beginning he had beguiled me. I honestly can't remember if I had a crush on him, but he was so charming that even some of the adult women thought he was something special as one mother later told me. I think I was flattered that here was this fun, dynamic and handsome guy who was paying all of his attention to me. This type of thinking is exactly what a sexual predator wants to create, as then the child just becomes putty in his hands.

I also think that once the game started, I was too embarrassed to tell anyone. And he had told me not to tell, so I didn't. It was also hard to turn down his insistence of driving me home from events. He was such a manipulator that most times he had already set up arrangements that I would get a ride home with him. Since we had club meetings four or five times a week that meant I was alone with him a lot.

I think that I knew in my heart that this was wrong, not only because was he married, but also because it was so confusing. But he had a way of smoothing things over and I guess that helped justify what we were doing. He made me feel that I was lucky that I was getting this attention from him.

It wasn't too long into this game that Lesser began upping the ante and eventually it led to having sex. As a young girl, I not only didn't know the basics of sex or the physical reactions but I also didn't know how to process this whole thing in my brain. Lesser was just so manipulative, so smooth, and so psychologically in charge of me, I found that I was caught in his clutches. I didn't feel comfortable with this man anymore, but I didn't know how to get out of it.

That is the other thing that is important for people to know. Sexual predators have a psychological hold on their victims. They start off by gaining trust from adults and that translates to the children. If the parents trust him, then the kids believe that they should trust him and why not because he is after all a man of God.

There was a turning point in my mind however in that I knew what was happening was very wrong, but by then I was so caught in his web that I had no chance of escaping. He just kept spinning that web around me tighter and tighter by becoming more involved in my life. What started as rides home from Campus Life events evolved into him signing me up for a racquetball tournament although I had never played in my life. He not only bought me the racquet, but of course he had to teach me to play and that entailed more time with him and more rides.

As a youth pastor, he would organize events that would occur out of town, which again gave him more unsupervised time with me. Whether it was going to a hotel for a Campus Life conference or taking a bike trip out of town, he constantly set up activities that kept all of us out of our parent's eyesight. This is another tactic of a professional predator.

As the year progressed, he would drive me home from gymnastics. When spring came, he joined the girl's track team as an assistant coach. He was always around me and therefore it was like he was suffocating me. I just couldn't seem to shake him and the more I tried, the more involved he would become in not only my life, but my core group of friends as well.

Lesser was also a master in getting my core group of friends involved in his web of deceit and destruction. He would get us to conduct "practical jokes" on people or organizations he felt had crossed him. For example, when one of the high schools wouldn't provide a room for him to hold club meetings, he had us sneak into the school bus area and let the air out of the bus tires. When a resort hotel in the area wouldn't give him a free guest membership to use the pools, etc. he had us throw eggs and do some structural damage at the hotel. When the nearby ski resort wouldn't give him a free membership, he had us put one of the owner's cars up on blocks. These were illegal acts and by having us do them he created an atmosphere of secrecy among us. This was another way that he not only pulled more of my friends into his web, but tightened the web around me as well. No one could tell what we had all done because we didn't want to get into trouble.

"Why didn't you tell" is a question that haunts every victim because we wonder that ourselves. It is only after going through my master's program in counseling that I began to realize why victims don't tell. Here are some of the reasons why I didn't tell.

1. I didn't know if people would believe me. He was this gregarious, fun-loving and well-liked adult who many parents liked very much.
2. He was so entwined in my life I was afraid of him. I had seen what he did to those that didn't give him what he wanted.
3. I was afraid of embarrassing my family. My parents were very conservative and naïve. We had never discussed sex or things like that in our family.
4. I didn't know what would happen on a legal basis except that there would at least be a big scandal and I didn't want to involve my family.
5. I felt like it was my fault that it all happened in the first place and that "I must have wanted it" and everyone would think I was a slut.
6. I didn't want to hurt his wife and baby son by revealing what was happening. Jeannie was a really nice person who was obviously head over heels in love with her husband. What would happen to their marriage if I told?
7. I was just a kid and not able to figure my way out. He had such a psychological hold on not only me, but on the adults as well, that I was no match for figuring out how to get him out of my life.
8. If I told about the pranks that would get my brother and friends into trouble and I didn't want that to happen.
9. I think that I also thought about the financial aspect if my father had to hire an attorney or pay big fines.
10. It was all just too overwhelming for me to comprehend and work my way out.

These are the reasons that I can think of and they all seem to be valid reasons for a powerless fourteen-year-old. I couldn't tell what was going on and therefore I was at his complete mercy. If I refused to get a ride with him, that would cause him displeasure and I was afraid of what the ramifications of his anger might be. So I was caught in his web of deceit, and of destruction and just like an insect caught in a spider web, the more I tried to escape, the more he spun his web around me.

So you may wonder why I didn't tell once he was fired from his position for reasons other than the sexual abuse, which the board of directors didn't know about. That's because most of the above reasons would still apply.

Another question people ask is why did the abuse happen so many times. I hope that what has been read so far will answer that question as well. As you can see from all that I have revealed, I had no chance with this guy. He masterminded his agenda perfectly and that agenda was solely to give him personal pleasure.

That is how he did it.

CHAPTER 3

E-mails From Heaven

It is now about 32 years later and I have finally found a way to bring this sexual predator to justice. What follows is a journal describing my thoughts, feelings and actions during this journey. I also refer to him by his last name, as I can't bring myself to use his first name.

February 22, 2006 (Wednesday)

I received an e-mail from both David (my brother) and Rene (David's girlfriend in high school) totally independently of each other that forwarded on an article in the Chicago Tribune about this Jesuit priest, Donald McGuire. He had just been convicted in Walworth County of sexual abuse to two boys that occurred over 30 years ago.

At first I was rather taken aback that they had sent this to me, but my second thought on this was how could these now adult men accomplish this feat? I had tried various times over the years to ascertain if there was any way that I could go back and file criminal charges against Lesser and was always informed that the statute of limitations had expired. I was curious as to how these guys could do it and after a few days of thinking, I called the District Attorney's office in Walworth County to see how this case had been brought to justice.

After being transferred a couple of times, I was informed by the DA's office that I could file criminal charges against Lesser as the statute of limitations didn't apply in this case. The reason I could file charges was because he had moved out of the state DURING the statute of limitations and hadn't returned to Wisconsin as a resident since.

I then decided to call the Fontana Police Department, as they were the ones who investigated the criminal complaint against Donald McGuire. Fontana is a small community and where I grew up, so it also made me feel "safe" to call them. I took some deep breaths, said a prayer and made the call. I told them why I wanted to see them and after hearing what I said, they agreed to see me and discuss what had happened!! UNBELIEVABLE!!

February 23, 2006 (Thursday)

Today I started to think that maybe I better try and find Lesser to see if he was still alive for one thing. I went on numerous search engines today and after hours of searching, I did find his name at least. I'm not sure about his birthday, but I knew that he was 15 years-older than me so I plugged in the years of 1944, 1945 and 1946. I actually got a hit but you have to pay money for more information. I decided to spend the money and there are a couple of places where he might be. One is in Bryson City, NC or Sarasota FL. These search engines are unbelievable in that you can find out most anything you want. I think that he got a divorce from Jeannie and is now married to some woman named Margaret.

This was upsetting to look for him and I am finding that I am sick to my stomach even typing his name into these search engines. This process is going to be something else I think. I'm putting it down for a while, but at least I have a little information of where he might be for the police. Hopefully the bastard is still alive.

March 3, 2006 (Friday)

Today was the day that I met with the Fontana Police and though I was nervous, I was also convinced that this was the right thing to do. There were so many thoughts and feelings going through me as I drove the 1½ hours to the appointment but I truly felt that God was with me and was going to help me through this.

I spent about 2 hours with Chief Olson and Officer Cates telling my story; where the molestation occurred, how many times, who knew about it, why I didn't tell…the whole thing. It was excruciating describing and telling them the necessary information and I just had my hands clenched tight in my lap the whole time. I also told them that I had heard a rumor that there was a girl who had lived in Williams Bay and that Lesser might have had molested her too. I had been at a party years ago, when someone pointed to this girl and told me that Lesser had messed with her as well. I remember what she looked like, but I couldn't remember her name. I also mentioned that there might be someone from the Lake Forest area because I had heard a rumor there was, but I didn't know her name or anything about her. They said that it would be helpful if there were someone else that he had molested.

The interview was taped and they couldn't have been kinder to me as they knew how hard it was for me to discuss this with them. My stomach was in knots as this was the first time that I was telling someone in authority about what happened. The power that they emanated however was very comforting to me for some reason.

I thought it was interesting in that after the interview was over, the Police Chief asked in an offhanded manner what kind of car did Lesser drive back then. Without hesitation, I replied that it was a Renault. I'm not sure if he was trying to test me as much of the abuse happened in his vehicle, but I knew after answering that one question, after many, that this was the one that sealed their belief in my allegations.

The police chief said that he would forward it on to the district attorney's office and they will determine if they would proceed with an investigation. To say that I am excited and hopeful about the possibility of this finally happening was too much to handle and to say that I was enthusiastic when I met my parents at Chucks for lunch doesn't really convey the hopes that I had for finally getting justice. What a day!

March 12, 2006 (Sunday)

I have no idea how long it will take for the DA to make a decision or not and the anticipation and anxiety was driving me nuts. I didn't want to call and bug them, but waiting for an answer was agonizing to say the least.

Danny and I decided to go up north snowmobiling this past week to try and get my mind off what the answer was going to be, but in all honesty, for the 300 miles that we rode over the next several days, the only thing that I thought about was if they would begin an investigation or not. I thought that riding the snowmobile would help take my mind off of it, as it is important for me to focus when riding, but it didn't work. Good thing I didn't crash because usually when I "space out" while riding, that's when I crash, as I'm not paying attention.

I was even too anxious to go down to the casino at night with Danny, preferring to stay in the room and isolate. It began to rain after the third day of riding, so it was homeward bound for us and another snowmobiling season has come to an end.

CHAPTER 4

Let the Games Begin

March 15, 2006 (Wednesday)

I finally screwed up my courage and called the Fontana police chief to see if he had heard back from the District Attorney. It has been almost two weeks since I had given them my statement and patience isn't my best virtue. Lo and behold he said that the DA believed me, believed we had a case and that it would be assigned to the Walworth County Sheriff's Department for investigation! There was a flood of emotions that went through me when I heard those words and they included incredibility, excitement and yes, fear. It's like when I sent in my video application to "Survivor." Once I had sent it in, fear set in because what would happen if they actually did select me? I would have to go through with it no matter how scared or full of self-doubt I was and it's the same with this. I just know that this is something that I HAVE to do, scared or not.

Captain Olson told me that Captain N. from the Walworth County Sheriff's Department was going to be assigning it to a detective to follow through. I had heard Captain N.'s name before and Danny reminded me that she was involved with "Prisoner Pete". Prisoner Pete is a man who worked for Danny when they were both with this insurance company. He had transferred in from CA where he had been some big producer. To make a long story short, Pete was a bit wild and unpredictable. We knew that he could be volatile and was into drugs, but since he was producing a lot of business for the company, everyone basically looked the other way.

Well, one night while he was driving back to Janesville from Milwaukee, he got pulled over by a Walworth County Sheriff for suspicion of driving drunk and that was pretty much the end of Pete. He freaked out and ended up hitting one of the police officers knocking him out and then kicked the other one in the privates. He then stole the police car and took off down Hwy. 43 with the police lights blazing, as he didn't know how to turn them off! He eventually exited near Delevan crashing the cop car in the process.

He of course got caught and through the Walworth County's investigation, it turned out that Larry P./Pete B. wasn't who he said he was, but rather his name was Pete B. and not only was he was a fugitive but he is part of a well known mafia family!

Needless to say, the Walworth County Sheriff's Department hates Pete, as he has been nothing but a pain in the butt as far as the judicial system. He is constantly harassing Walworth County by using the judicial system to his advantage. Now, the captain in the Walworth County Sheriff's Department that dealt with Pete is going to have my case in her hands and I am afraid that if she knows that I know Pete, the detectives won't want anything to do with me.

I did finally screw up my courage once again and called her to see what happens with this now. Captain N. was absolutely wonderful to me and validated that this is a crime that needed to be investigated even though it happened so long ago. She said that she would be assigning the case to Detective F. for the investigation and that he would be in touch with me. There was also no hint that she knew that I was connected with "Prisoner Pete" thank God. I don't know how she would, except that I have my name on his visitor's card, so if she ran a check on me through the Sheriff's Department that might come up.

After talking with Captain N. I decided to e-mail my friends who were involved in this process to tell them that it was going forward to an investigation and that I might need some help from them in the future. Rene immediately e-mailed me back with some names of people from Lake Forest who might know more about a rumor she told me years ago that he had maybe messed with someone there. She told me the name Joanne C. thinking she might know something, but she didn't know her married name or where she was. The detective work continues.

March 20, 2006 (Monday)

I think that it is important to begin looking for the adults who were involved in this case as well. I thought the more information I could gather for Detective F., that's less that he has to do. I began by calling Mr. and Mrs. H., as that would probably be one of the harder calls. It was difficult talking to them about this and they were flabbergasted to say the least about my information. Mrs. H. was the one who remembered however that she had been concerned about Lesser's attention to me back then and had even said something to my mother and that's when my mother got wise. Mr. H. states that he doesn't remember anything about Campus Life and that he doesn't remember even serving on the board. I don't think that is true as I think he is protecting his family as he did back then but I don't know for sure as memories fade as we get older.

Mrs. H. happened to have the P.'s address and phone number as I said that I would have to call them as well. I also needed the F.'s phone number and she had that too. They are both going to be difficult calls not only because I haven't spoken to them in over 30 years, but for what I was going to have to tell them as well. I think the P.'s will be the hardest because they were close to Lesser and of course they were.

Mr. and Mrs. P. were surprised by my phone call and shocked by my news and we actually talked for quite a while. They are sick about this happening and that they had believed Lesser when he said that he wasn't messing with me. Mr. P. also told me that he had asked Lesser directly if he was screwing around with me and Lesser had told him no.

I think this news has rattled their faith somewhat as they continue to remain very religious. It is my belief that they are going to have a difficult time reconciling the fact that someone they trusted and were friends with, could deceive them in such a way. I know EXACTLY how they are feeling and tried to convey that to them. I was literally shaking throughout the whole phone call. I'm glad that is over.

I then called Mr. and Mrs. F., someone else I hadn't talked to in over 30+ years, and told them what as going on. Mr. F.'s first words to me were "I knew I smelled a rat"! He talked about not trusting Lesser from the start and though he didn't know about Lesser molesting me, he remembered that Mom and Dad had expressed their concern about his attentiveness towards me. He was really very nice, validating and so sorry that this had happened to me. He is willing to do whatever is necessary to move this case forward. What a friend he is!

March 30, 2006 (Thursday)

I have waited for quite a while to have Detective F. call and since he still hasn't called, I decided to contact him myself to see how this whole process was going to proceed. He was very nice on the phone, but informed me that there was a stack of cases on his desk and mine is in there somewhere. To hear that mine was "somewhere in his stack" was disappointing to say the least, but I didn't want to say anything, as I certainly didn't want to be pushy with the detective who is going to be conducting an investigation that might change my life and others. I honestly do feel badly that he has to investigate this case when there are many others that are more important and that need his attention. I said as much to Detective F. and he said that mine was just as valid as his other cases, but that it was going to have to wait for at least 3-4 months.

Hearing this news was crushing to say the least, but I just have to somehow learn to accept the reality of the legal system. My emotions are all over the place and I find it difficult to think about anything else but this investigation and case. I think this is going to be a long, long process.

April 10, 2006 (Thursday)

I have decided that if I could find out a lot of the information that Detective F. will need, then maybe we could move forward quicker as he wouldn't have to do all of that legwork. I am the one who knows the people that were involved and if I could find them, it would be of help to him and therefore to me. As I said, patience isn't one of my virtues. Looking for all of this information also gives me something TO DO and something to focus on. I am already going crazy!

The person that I need to find the most is the girl who Lesser might have molested in Lake Forest, so Rene and I have been e-mailing back and forth this past month, different names of people in the Lake Forest area who might know what happened there. What is also interesting, is that I can see this girl in my mind as I think I saw her at Lesser's house one summer. She had long dark hair and was tall. I think she is the one that he had been messing with because when Lesser and I pulled away from the house one time, I remember her having a really sad look on her face.

There are quite a few names that she has given me and I have been calling a couple of them to see if they were involved with Campus Life. I kept hitting a dead end; especially trying to find someone by the name of Joanne C. who Rene was sure would know something.

I confess that I did many devious things in order to try and find her! I won't say what they are as I'm sure I could get into trouble. I also tried to get into the Lake Forest alumni website, but couldn't because I wasn't an alumni. So then I called Lake Forest High School to find out if they could locate her name and address through their records. The lady wouldn't give me any information about her, as I'm sure the whole thing sounded fishy. All I had told her was that I needed to find out where this woman was, as she might know some things from years ago that I need to know. Didn't work and I struck out again. I feel like this is going to be impossible and I'm sunk if I can't find someone else to verify that he did it to them as well. I am feeling despair at this point.

Today I had to give a workshop at University of Wisconsin – Whitewater on DBT and then meet a client, her daughter as well as the father of the child in Williams Bay. As I was heading home after our session, I had to drive by Williams Bay High School and I thought that maybe I should go in and try and find out the name of the girl who lived in Williams Bay and who might have also been a victim of Lesser's. My stomach was churning to say the least as I asked for permission to go through the yearbooks. I told the staff that I needed to find out the name of a girl I was looking for from years past. I explained that I knew what she looked like and the possible years that she graduated. I just couldn't remember her name and thought I could find out what it was through the yearbooks. I was directed to the library and the old yearbooks and it didn't take more than 20 minutes to find out her name! It is interesting to me that when I did find her picture and name I felt excitement, but at the same time I felt sick to my stomach. A dialectic in how can I feel two opposite emotions at the same time.

I was fairly excited to have discovered her name so easily and went back to the front office. The school staff asked if I had found who I was looking for and I said that I had and did they have any information about this particular girl. The ladies in the office looked at each other kind of funny and said that she had died a long time ago. She had medical problems through high school and about two years after high school she had a heart transplant and then died a couple of years later.

I was devastated to say the least as here was a possible lead that wasn't going to go anywhere. On top of that, I felt sorry for her as a person and that she died at such a young age. As I thought back to her and the times that I had seen her in high school, she did always seem very quiet. I remember her as being off to the side and kind of a wallflower and that if Lesser had indeed messed with her as well, then he was going to pay for her too.

I swore to her right then and there in the parking lot of the Williams Bay High School that I would nail him for both of us and would try as hard as I could because she couldn't. The school staff had given me the names of her siblings and parents who were still in the area, but I am hesitant to call them, as I don't want to upset them if he had indeed assaulted her.

I called Detective F. with the devastating news and I then knew that my only chance to prove that there are others is to find this girl from Lake Forest. I discussed with him the possibility of talking with this girl's family to see if they knew anything, but that I really don't want to open that can of worms if necessary. The last thing I would want to do is hurt her family more than they have already suffered as a result from her death. He agreed, so this was a dead end.

I am devastated and really upset to say the least. I cried for almost the entire hour and a half drive home grieving not only for that girl, but for myself as well.

June 27, 2006 (Tuesday)

It has been a long time since I have written and that is because NOTHING is happening with the investigation. I have continued to search for this Joanne C. but haven't had any luck whatsoever. It is so disheartening to keep coming up with dead ends trying to find another victim and I'm afraid that my case is going to be dead in the water if we can't find someone.

I am trying not to be too depressed about how long it is taking for Detective F. to begin his investigation, but it is difficult. I find that all I do is think about this case and how I can get it moving, but I'm at the mercy of other's, not something that I enjoy. I have decided that it would be in my best interest if I try and forget this for a while, but it is difficult.

November 1, 2006 (Wednesday)

I have felt that I have been patient for a long time and therefore decided to call Detective F. to see what is going on or not going on. I think that he understands how difficult this is for me and so he actually set up a date where we could finally meet and discuss the case. I haven't even met him yet and it's been almost 9 months since the criminal complaint was registered. The date is for December 4th and I am thrilled as FINALLY I have something to look forward to in regards to this case.

December 4, 2006 (Monday)

Today I finally get to meet Detective David F. in person, to discuss the case. It has been almost a year from the beginning of when this started and I was finally meeting with the detective. It has been a long year, but I feel that it is maybe, finally going to begin.

Met with Detective F. and to meet him in person was great. He seemed like a big Teddy Bear and was very kind and thoughtful as he led me through his questions. We talked about the incidents, when it happened and everything in between. I tried to stay strong during his questioning, but found that tears sprang to my eyes on more than one occasion. The fact that I got tears in my eyes bothered me, as I didn't want him to think I was a sissy, but rather was a strong enough person that I could get through this process.

During the interview, I reminded him about the rumor that there had been a girl from Lake Forest that he had been involved with. I told him that I didn't know anything about her, including her name, but I was working on it. I told him I was trying to find someone with the maiden name of Joanne C., as she might know the name of the other possible victim. He has better resources for finding people than I do, so I thought that maybe he could help find her.

There were also questions that he asked in which I didn't have any answers, beginning with the exact timeline of when this all occurred. I had to know when he first moved to the Lake Geneva area and to help me figure things out, Detective F. said that the courthouse would have the real estate information in their files, so I went over there to get the information.

I feel like this is starting and it felt good to be doing something active on the case. I was able to obtain his buying agreement as well as his selling agreement and it turns out that he closed on his house and moved to the area in June 1974. There is then documentation that the house was sold by him on October 31, 1975. I couldn't believe my eyes when I saw that he had only been in the area for that brief of time. It seemed like it should have been longer due to the destruction of lives that he caused in his wake.

I then met my parents at Applebee's in Delevan in order to tell them what had happened. They were as surprised as I was that he had only been in the area for that brief of a time, as it seems like he was here forever. I truly think my parents are doing all right as far as this investigation as the last thing that I want to have happen is to upset them to the point of having a stroke or something. Mom is overjoyed that this is moving forward as she has wanted to nail Lesser from day one. Dad is a bit more conservative about this whole thing, but I also think that he is ok with me doing this.

December 6, 2006 (Wednesday)

One of the things I want to document during this ordeal is how it is affecting me on an emotional level. Since the beginning of this process, I have been on edge so to speak. I have begun to hibernate at home and don't want to go out. When I do go out, I rarely find any pleasure, whether I am around friends or not. It seems like my mind and my body are just somewhere else, and I can't focus on what is going on in the here and now. Maybe more importantly, I don't really care what is happening in the here and now with friends, or with anyone.

I feel more comfortable listening to the 70's music that I grew up with and still find comfort in today. Fleetwood Mac, John Denver, Hall & Oats. They seem to represent a time when life was easier for some reason, although that was the time that this whole debacle happened.

Lately I've been feeling extremely emotional about everything. I can't watch television and certainly not the news as I cry at every sad story. I'm thinking dire thoughts about being killed in an accident, or losing my parents to death. I think about losing Danny and Tucker and what life would be like without them. I can't seem to help these terrible thoughts that keep running through my head. I'm scared driving home at night that I will have an accident, hit an animal, see an accident, all sorts of things. Therefore my stomach is in a knot for the entire hour to hour and a half drive.

That knot in my stomach began when I read the story about the Jesuit priest and now it seems to be a constant presence. That alone is interfering with my life as I can't eat, can't relax, am sick to my stomach and feeling like something bad is going to happen at any moment. I'm hoping that by writing this down, not only will some people be able to identify, but also in hopes that these feelings and thoughts go away…at least for a little while.

CHAPTER 5

The Search Continues

December 19, 2006 (Tuesday)

Since talking with Detective F., I knew that it was important to try and find this Joanne once again therefore there has been a lot of e-mails flying between Rene and I. Rene, bless her heart, was finally able to find the last name of Joanne's older sister Susan, so I now had her name to try and find Joanne. The problem was that Rene didn't want me to use her name with Sue or Joanne, as she didn't really know them that well nor did she want to get into trouble with them if they were angry with me finding them. I find that interesting in that people want to help, but don't want their names included. I wonder if it will be like that down the road and therefore we won't be able to get anyone to testify for me.I was able to find Susan's phone number off the Internet, but unfortunately it was an unlisted number. The number that was given in the phone book was only a fax, so I thought that I would write a letter to Susan to ask her if she knew this Joanne C. that I was looking for. It was a difficult letter to write, as I didn't want her thinking that I was some crazy person or something, but I finally finished it, faxed it off and prayed.

Praise the Lord as later today Susan called me to find out more about this situation. It had worked!! I explained who I was and that I was looking for a Joanne C. who might have been involved with Campus Life back in the 70's. She was rather cagey in her response but said that she would get back with me. My heart was just pounding wondering if I had FINALLY found the person who could tell me if there had been another victim or not.

It wasn't too long before the actual Joanne C. called me and I explained to her what was happening with my situation and why I needed to talk with her. Joanne did remember Russell Lesser and said that in fact Joanne and some of her other friends, actually confronted Lesser about having an inappropriate affair with their friend. Her friend's name was Janet P.! FINALLY!! I asked if she would have her married name or if she could find it for me, and she said that she would try. I am forever grateful to her that she has finally given me a name as she could have lied about the whole thing.

While I am elated that I finally have confirmation that Lesser had done this to someone else, Joanne's words were like a direct punch to my stomach. When I hung up I just cried and cried and cried. I also threw up. I feel badly for myself, but also for this Janet P. who was also so injured by him. I am somewhat surprised at how crushed I am hearing this news and all I want to do is hide from the world. Maybe why it hit me so hard is because now I KNEW that he was a sexual predator, not simply a young man whom had been attracted to a girl who happened to be underage. I finally KNEW that he never did have feelings for me as a person, but rather was used solely for his pleasure and entertainment. I can't stop throwing up and feel like taking a shower.

January 13, 2007 (Saturday)

It has taken a while to process this information about Janet P. and I simply couldn't do anything but lay on the couch for the past couple of weeks. It was so upsetting to me that I just had to leave this whole thing alone for a while.

But I have gained strength once again and so I spent the day trying to locate Janet P. Since that is her maiden name and I really have no other information about her, it is difficult because as I am discovering, there are many Janet P.'s in this world. I have been using different search engines on the Internet and wrote down a couple names of people that live in IL. that sounded promising. Then with a knot in my stomach, I screwed up my courage and began to call.

I had to come up with some script so that my call didn't sound threatening at all and what I devised was something along the lines of "Is this the P. household?" When they would answer in the affirmative, I would say my name and that I am trying to locate a woman by the name of Janet P. who lived in Lake Bluff and graduated from Lake Forest High School.

Most people are friendly, but I can tell from their voice that they are rather taken aback by my request. One woman in Springfield said that she has gotten a lot of calls looking for a woman named Janet P. Not sure if that is the same one that I am looking for, but if it is, that is interesting. After a long day of being on the Internet searching and phoning most of the ones that looked promising, I called it a day and fell into a disturbing nap on the couch. I have two left that didn't answer who might hold some promise.

What is also weird to me is that after talking with Joanne, I haven't heard back from her. I have e-mailed her a couple of times, yet got no response and I'm not sure why. Of course now my paranoia is kicking in as I'm thinking that she doesn't want anything to do with this whole thing. Today I left a phone message for her to call me as I have a couple of questions to ask her. I would like to know if she knows anything more about Janet such as her middle name, her parents' names, her birth date and if she will talk with Detective F. I don't think people have a choice about talking to the police when it comes to criminal investigations, but I'm not sure. I just hope she doesn't crumble somehow.

January 15, 2007 (Monday)

Finally heard back from Joanne and that was great as I was worried that she didn't want anything more to do with this after thinking about it. But she e-mailed me that she had been busy with the holidays, work and moving her daughter into an apartment. Joanne said that she hasn't been able to find out any more information about Janet, but will continue to work on it.

She also expressed that she was a bit worried about how Janet was going to handle this if we found her. She claimed that she wasn't her "best friend" or anything, and just to be careful how I presented this to her if we ever found her. We talked for a while about whether I should call Janet or let the detective talk to her. I'm concerned that when we do find her, Janet could just lie to me, while if a police officer is asking her questions, she might be more apt to tell the truth. In all honesty, I have no idea where Janet is at in life or how she will feel about this whole thing if/when we do find her.

CHAPTER 6

Healing Old Relationships

January 16, 2007 (Tuesday)

I e-mailed Detective F. to tell him that I hadn't been able to find Janet and had been searching the Internet and calling different "Janet P.'s" in trying to locate her, but none of them knew anything about her. It is so discouraging to continue to come up empty handed, but he assured me that we would find her.

This is also the day that my parents and I met with Mr. and Mrs. P. for lunch. We haven't seen each other or been in contact with them for over 30 years, but they are in town visiting their daughter-in-law, so I thought this would be a good time to meet. My parents said that they weren't nervous, although I was. I really didn't know what was going to "happen", but it turned out well.

Much of meeting with the P.'s was because I wanted my parents to begin healing. They have so much guilt over not being able to see what was happening, and they need to know that all of the adults were "duped" by him. All of the parents that I talked to are completely mortified that this happened and that they didn't see it, and Mom and Dad need to hear that.

It was a little weird being with them as it has been so long, and the reason we are together is because of a nasty event that occurred in our lives, but they were lovely and we talked about family. Mr. and Mrs. P. had lost their son Jeff to Lou Gehrig's disease and we talked about him. We talked about their daughter Wendy and their grandchildren. We talked about my brothers and their families and what they are doing. It was a fairly easy conversation as we were good friends in the past.

At the end, we discussed the case and I told them all the things that Lesser had done with us kids. He had bought us alcohol, condoned my brother and his girlfriend sleeping together, ditched out on a dining bill (although in retrospect, I think us kids did it without him and he was mad about it). How we had let the air out of the school bus tires, egged the Abbey, put Mr. G.'s car on blocks and such. We discussed a trip to Fort Meyers Fl. we had taken with him and that I remember all of us drinking 10-cent beers with him.

They were horrified that all of this had happened and that they had no clue about any of it. Mr. P. even got tears in his eyes because of how badly he felt. I felt so sorry that I had to reveal to someone who considered him a friend and a confidante as well as someone who they completely trusted to be around their children, all that he had done with us.

Mr. P. talked with me about having 3 options here. One was to do nothing and walk away. Another option was to continue doing what I was doing, which is to try and criminally charge him. The third was to call him up on the phone and confront him about what he did. Do something along those lines and then do a Christian thing and walk away. Even though I listened respectfully to him, my gut was churning and my mind was saying "no way in hell is this guy going to walk". I think I heard him say after giving that advice was that he didn't know if he would be able to do the third option and that he would want some type of justice. My father later confirmed that that is what he said.

They offered to do anything that they could and said that as of yet, Detective F. hadn't called them. They didn't know if they were supposed to call him or if he was going to call them. I told them that I would contact him to ask about what they should do.

As my parents and I were driving back to my car, we discussed how things went. They both felt that things went excellent and were glad that we had all done it. The fact that Mr. P had cried, reinforced to my parents that they truly cared about me and that had they have known, things would have been done differently.

While driving home that afternoon and thinking about everything that had been said at lunch, I had quite an epiphany about something. Recently, two boys who had been kidnapped by this pedophile had been found alive. One boy, Shawn Hornbeck had been kidnapped 4 years ago and this disgusting pervert had kept him for his own perversions that entire time. The media as well as the public were asking questions as to why this boy didn't run away from his kidnapper when he had the chance.

These questions by the media had been pissing me off as no one who hasn't been in that position can understand the complete mental control that the pedophile has over his or her prey. Therefore it wasn't fair that society was jumping all over this poor boy. But societies outcries and accusations against Shawn as well as the meeting with the P.'s got me to thinking about why I never told and what had I been afraid of. I had a loving family and people who were beginning to ask questions, so why didn't I tell?

My epiphany today was that he had me under a type of fear as well, although it wasn't overt. He had us kids do vengeful things to people as well as organizations that he felt "dissed" him. When the school wouldn't allow him in, we let the air out of the bus tires, causing a lot of havoc. The Majestic Hills thing with Mr. G.'s car and we egged the Abbey when they wouldn't give him a free membership.

He was vindictive and I think in some way, I was afraid of what would happen if I told or at least told him to go away. I think one of the things that finally released me from that fear was what was happening in my family. My mother was so distraught over the whole thing and the nervous breakdown that she had in the winter/spring, scared the hell out of me. I couldn't see my mother suffer in that way for something that was happening.

That and the fact that we were moving out of the country and halfway around the world, finally gave me the strength to get rid of him. To me, the realization that he did have me in some type of mental hold was huge in that it validates to me, why I didn't tell. I sent Shawn Hornbeck one of my L.A. Cards telling him and thanking him that it was through his awful experience, that I finally realized why I never told. I don't know if that was appropriate to do, but I felt I had to tell him that he had made an important impact on my life and for him to stay strong and know that there are many people who support him completely.

January 17, 2007 (Wednesday)

I called Detective F. right away in the morning to tell him about the P.'s and they didn't know what to do in regards to speaking with him and I gave him their phone number so that he could call them right away. I want to get this thing going as I don't want it hanging over my head any more than it already is/has. That is one of the reasons why I have done so much preliminary work...so that he could hopefully start working on putting the case together, and not spend valuable time looking for people and contacting them. I have been making up a list of all the names of people who were involved back then, their phone numbers and addresses, as well as what they knew or remembered about Lesser.

He sent me back an e-mail that said he was meeting with the P.'s the next morning and that "We will begin looking for Janet P." For some reason, that statement right there hit me in the gut and of course I went and threw-up. It is finally starting in earnest and I am hopeful that maybe Lesser will finally be held accountable for the destruction that he has caused in numerous lives.

January 19, 2007 (Friday)

It is Friday and I'm dying to know how it went with the P.'s, but the last thing I'm going to do is bug Detective F. and I'm not going to call the P's. to ask as I think that is inappropriate for some reason. It is now time to let him do his job and it is terrifying in some ways to know that in some way, my fate is in the hands of someone else and I have to give that up. It is scary to put the control of such an important situation into the hands of someone you have met only once. The good thing though is that hopefully God will help all of us in this endeavor.

Chapter 7

The Meltdown

February 3, 2007 (Saturday)

Today I finally experienced a "meltdown". It's been a long time in coming and I just finally broke down into sobs. It was the kind that comes from your gut and just won't stop until all the pain is out and there are no more tears to shed. It was exhausting and energy-sapping.

Today it seemed like there was just too much bad news and though I haven't heard anything from the detective, life continues to throw emotional curve balls. Last week, my boyfriends' brother-in-law, Charlie, his 85-year-old mother fell outside and ended up laying there all-night and freezing to death. She was a lovely woman who did good things for other's all her life. Helen didn't have an exotic life as someone said at her funeral, but rather her life was totally fulfilled in what she did for her family, her church, her friends and her community. It doesn't seem fair that she had to die such a horrible death. It was an emotional week on top of an already emotional week and tragic in many ways.Another sad thing that happened is that a longtime friend had finally lost her fight with cancer. She died at 2:00 last night. That is yet another emotional blow.

Finally on this day, I decided to write a letter to Peter S., a young man who was greatly involved with myself and Lesser. I don't remember a lot about how emotionally involved Peter and I were, but I think the whole relationship with him was a ruse that Lesser had set up. I remember being with Peter, but then meeting with Lesser and going with him. I think that Lesser used him to get more time with me, and unfortunately, I guess I went along with it. What hurts me is how much my behaviors hurt Peter, as he was a really nice guy and truly a friend no matter what. I called him when this thing first started to appear like it was going to happen. I hadn't talked with him in over 30+ years but my gut was telling me that something bad had happened with him after that conversation. In other words, I think that he was seriously hurt as a result of Lesser's deception and manipulation and I guess you could say mine as well. Of course I was also being seriously manipulated, but I still feel badly about Peter, as I do know that he was a good friend despite how Lesser twisted our friendship.

After talking with the detective in person, I once again called Peter to let him know that the process might be beginning and he didn't call back. The following weekend I left another message for him and he still hasn't called me back. As a result of that, I had to reach out to him in a letter to share with him what I was feeling. I felt like I had to apologize for any past hurt and pain that I had caused him. Since my "wise mind" (DBT term) or intuition is telling me that something isn't right here, my belief is that remembering all this is once again hurting Peter and I feel terrible about that. He has every right to be hurt and angry, but all I want to do is make it right.

In talking with my parents today and telling them about writing this gut-wrenching letter to Peter, Mom gave me a great analogy about why I felt so strongly about reaching out to Peter and making any amends necessary. She imagined this process and my life as a piece of rope and there are knots all along the rope and what I am now doing is untying each knot as I come to them. That is so true!! Every challenge in this process is just a knot that needs to be untied and smoothed out. I need to do this for Peter as well as for myself because once again, the worst part of this whole debacle is that there were many people hurt and I don't like people hurting in this life. Furthermore, it was my actions and the fact that I never told, that compounded all the hurt in everyone. Once again, if I had just told, maybe the hurt and pain wouldn't have been so pervasive for everyone involved. But I just couldn't at that time.

I also received a letter today from the P.'s in response to my letter thanking them for meeting with us. I am certainly blessed to have friends such as them and I thank God for putting them into my life so long ago.

February 10, 2007 (Saturday)

It seems that things are just continuing to pile up and today is a day for me to regain some emotional strength. It is so difficult dealing with my client's issues as well as all of my own emotions, and it is wearing me out. I think often about drinking to find some relief from this constant sense of "foreboding". I think that I am finally beginning to understand a little about the clients who are overwhelmed with emotions and just can't seem to "shake" their anxieties. It's like my body and mind are on constant "alert", I'm worried about every little thing, my body is tense and ready for flight so to speak. It is a very "discomforting" feeling, something we call "dysregulated" in DBT. Dysregulated is a state of being where a person feels a cacophony of emotions and thoughts all at once, usually in response to a "dialectic". A dialectic is having two extreme and opposite emotions and thoughts occurring at the same time. These opposing "forces" cause vast turmoil emotionally, physically and cognitively. It's more than simply "being upset" and I use the term dysregulated a lot as I am finding that I am dysregulated a lot!! I simply want some peace in my mind as well as my body. The only way it seems that I can achieve that, is when I've had too much to drink because then I just forget about everything but what is in the moment.

The problem then becomes that when I do indulge in drinking too much, I usually end up throwing-up and feeling like crap the next day, emotionally and physically. I have learned that drinking isn't the answer for trying to control my emotions and thoughts, but it does seem to alleviate everything for a little while. I can now understand why I turned to drinking and drugs and it was to blot the emotional bombardment that I had been experiencing for most of my life and that I am currently experiencing again.

I try to utilize some of the DBT techniques that I teach my clients and they do work. I'm pulling things out of the "distress tolerance skills" set such as playing with the dog, writing this book, going to a musical with my family, watching TV., reading, doing Sudoku puzzles, baking and feeding the animals outside. These things do help in that for a little while, I am thinking about something else, and that is the goal of the distress tolerance skills. To just get through the emotion, rather than letting the emotions control you. It is an exhausting endeavor as you are constantly trying to keep your mind and body occupied while at the same time, it seems that the mind and body just need to find peace.

Today therefore will be a day for movies and catching up on all of my magazines. Danny is gone for the day, the dog is tired from being at the kennel last night and I'm going to snuggle under a blanket and try to decompress.

February 16, 2007 (Friday)

I am so sick of everything and today I had to have another one of my teeth pulled. I hate losing body parts and of course I started crying even before they pulled it. They must think that I am nuts. But it was either the tooth, or another $2,000 spent for a root canal and a crown. I have now had to have 4 root canals and four crowns in the past year alone! The fact is that the tension and anxiety that I am feeling as a result of this case is causing me to grind my teeth at night, which then results in cracks in the tooth. I blame it all on Lesser.

March 9, 2007 (Friday)

More stress in that today is the day that I have to have a cyst cut off my rear end!! Not only was it embarrassing but also it was upsetting to me because I had to bare my private area. Something that I am not comfortable with at all and once again, a fall out from Lesser! What was further upsetting was that Dr. M. finally showed up about 1½ hours late to perform the procedure, so my patience was wearing thin.

I then went down to the bar to meet Danny and my friend Julie but unfortunately Julie and I ended up getting into a fight. I have been on edge as it is because of everything and so I knew that I wouldn't be able to handle it if she started to complain about anything. I knew that if someone "crossed me wrong" or pissed me off for any reason, I was going to blow.

I handled it okay when she spent quite a bit of time ragging about her ex-husband who is still my friend as well, but when she was going to repeat everything she had just said again to Danny, I told her that I couldn't stand to hear it all again. At that point, she blew up and then I blew up. It was an ugly scene and she ended up leaving the bar in a huff.

I feel badly about our argument, as I know that her nerves are always frazzled, but I just couldn't take one more thing. See what this is doing to me?!

March 30, 2007 (Friday)

Tried to find Janet P. again and so far, all of my attempts have been futile. It is so depressing to keep running into brick walls and right now I feel like I will never find her. I really need the police to help me out with this as they have much better resources than I do. The other problem is that I don't know if she is married or what her married name would be. This is so frustrating and I just wish that we could get started on this piece.

I ended up with a sick headache again as this is so upsetting to do the research and just find dead-ends all of the time. I think that I'm going to leave this alone for a while, as it is too overwhelming emotionally.

CHAPTER 8

Sick and Tired or Just Sick

April 16, 2007 (Monday)

Haven't written for a while and that's because nothing is happening as far as the case. I e-mailed Detective F. a couple of times before he finally replied. Waiting to hear from him is nerve-racking to say the least. Your mind just wanders as far as imagining what is going on, or at worst, that nothing is going on. After hearing back from him, it appears that that is what is happening…nothing. He has had to take on another detective's cases and therefore hasn't been able to spend any time on mine. As disheartening as that was to hear, it is understandable as there are serious crimes that have occurred to children now, and they need to be addressed first. I just wanted and needed to know that I'm still "on the list" as he has said.

This whole situation is interesting in regards to my anxiety levels and how they are fluctuating dramatically. When the case is "on the front burner" so to speak, as it was in January with meeting with the P.'s and looking for Janet P., my stomach and nerves are in knots. It's like my body is "on high alert" and I'm overly sensitive to everything. The slightest thing that contains emotion will bring immediate tears. It could be television commercials, news reports, a dead animal lying in the road, a client in misery…it doesn't matter.

Due to that high level of anxiety, my stomach has now been causing problems again. I have an intestinal problem that has plagued me since living in Iran, and it flairs up at times and major stress is just one factor that makes it flair up. As a result, I've had to again have numerous medical tests, such as a colonoscopy, CAT scan of my abdomen and a camera down the throat to ascertain if there is anything else going on. During this process, they found out I have at least two hernias and will need surgery on those.

They also found that I had a severe case of gastritis or what I call "gut rot". My gastroenterologist is wonderful and since there is nothing wrong with any major organs, his next question was, "What is going on in your life?" I told him a little about this case and he suggested that I speak to a therapist. I probably should, but I won't.

People have wondered why I won't go to a therapist, especially since I am one. My doctor has even suggested that I go as she doesn't try and heal herself when she is physically ill. I think the reason why I'm not going is that first of all, I know what is happening to me and why. I don't believe that there is any therapist around who could interpret what is going on any better than I could.

Since I am also a trained Dialectical Behavioral Therapist, I am utilizing a lot of the skills that I have taught clients for years. Those skills have proved to be invaluable as far being able to keep some type of sanity throughout this whole thing.

I also utilize my parents A LOT as I talk with them about EVERYTHING that is going on. I'm not sure if that is healthy for them, but they assure me that they are interested in "this journey". Besides, there is no one in the world who knows me like my parents so they are more apt to be able to help me put things into perspective. Like the rope analogy that Mom gave me. They have done this all of my life and it only seems natural to talk about all of this with them. Of course the more personal things I don't share with them, but I do share with you my journal.

I have also been using Danny as a sounding board to express some of my thoughts and feelings. He isn't as empathetic as my parents, but he listens to me and supports me when I'm at my lowest. He is very helpful in not only suggesting activities that keep me sane, but insists at times that I go and do things to get my mind off of this case. What I am learning is that I couldn't do this without his love and support and I appreciate that more than he will ever know.

Lastly and probably the most important reason why I haven't gone, is because it is my belief that I need to "experience" all of these emotions from the past. For most of my life I have tried to submerge all of my emotions about this incident and that has not been healthy at all. This time I feel that I need to experience the highs and lows of the entire process so that I can work through them instead of just stuffing what I am feeling. These might seem like excuses to people and maybe they are, but I just don't feel that a therapist would be a good idea for me right now.

Back to what is upsetting me now, if my poor health wasn't bad enough, Tucker had to have surgery to remove a fatty tumor. I can handle most anything, but when it comes to my animals, I turn into a complete ball of nerves and worry. Lately I can't even go to the vet with Danny and the dog as that is way too upsetting for me. It always has been, but right now I can't even fathom going to the vet, as I would be a puddle of emotion and anxiety.

I can really relate to people who are so overwhelmed by the stressors in their lives that they can't attend to normal everyday living with full concentration. It is difficult to separate it all and you feel like you are just drowning. It is a very helpless feeling and not one that I am used to at all.

May 21, 2007 (Monday)

Another root canal with Dr. Copeland in Lake Geneva! Pretty soon all of my teeth will have root canals and hence crowns! The stress from this case is just killing me and I am so pissed off.

June 11, 2007 (Monday)

More health problems as a result of this case! I went to see Dr. K. who is affiliated with Aurora Health in Elkhorn to see what he thinks about my hernias. Dr. M., the "butt surgeon", has been so wishy-washy about it, that I want/need a second opinion to alleviate my anxiety. While I was there, I also had him feel my neck as it continues to feel weird although all the doctors say there is nothing wrong. He did so and said that he felt that it was "tender" but didn't need to be addressed quite yet. He said that I should make another appointment in about 3 months to see what was up with my hernias and my neck.

I didn't really understand what he meant about my neck, but I decided that rather than wait 3 months for another check-up (again patience!), that I will follow up sooner, so I made an appointment with my primary physician. The problem is that I really can't tell if all of my ailments are psychosomatic or what. I do have poor health and it has been so difficult lately to tease out what is stress related and what if anything is wrong.

June 29, 2007 (Friday)

Had my appointment today with Dr. K. and she sent me for an X-ray on my lungs as I have some difficulty breathing. I was really there for my neck, but she wanted an X-ray of my chest. Add another thing to the list. Turns out that I have pneumonia!

July 10, 2007 (Tuesday)

I finally went for the ultrasound on my neck and they did find a fairly large mass, so now I need to see the Head and Neck surgeon Dr. R. I feel very validated as I had been complaining about my neck being sore as well as not feeling well in general, but all the tests had come back negative. As a result, I felt the doctors thought that all of this was in my head. See, it wasn't!!

July 18, 2007 (Wednesday)

Went to Dr. R. to have a biopsy done of the mass on my thyroid and not only did he do that, but he also took off a little cyst by my eye that had been bothering me!! It's funny how "little things" are causing me such "upset" in life. I had wanted a plastic surgeon to do it, but my primary physician had told me there wasn't a plastic surgeon on staff at the Monroe Clinic. I was looking at Dr. R.'s credentials however while waiting for him and they said that he was a plastic surgeon, so I asked him about doing it. He said that he could do it right then and there!! Yeah!! I am so thankful to get that thing off as it was bugging me. I told him that I considered that a wonderful birthday present as my birthday is tomorrow!!

Then I took off for Lake Geneva to see about possibly needing ANOTHER root canal. Dr. Copeland said I did and even worked me in at the end of the day to do it. Thank God!! I don't think anyone is as grateful as I am to get a root canal as then the pain in the tooth and everywhere else is finally going to be over. Thanks to Dr. Copeland!!

Even though there have been health issues, I am thrilled that some of these "issues" that had been bothering me were being rectified. The feeling that things are finally going in the right direction has been very comforting to me at this time. I consider this moment of peace and happiness in my life on this day, is a birthday present from God. I haven't felt this happy in a long time and just wanted to let you know journal!!

CHAPTER 9

A Little Slice of Heaven

August 1, 2007 (Wednesday)

Tomorrow I take off to go on vacation up in Ely MN with my brothers and nephews! I am so excited that once again, I am invited to go with the boys on their trip. We motor way up into the Boundary Waters area, set up camp somewhere and spend the days fishing! This time, I am going to set up my tent on the "lakefront property" that Sue claimed the year before, as she won't be with us on this trip!! I hope that no one has claimed that campsite, as it is perfect for all of us!

I am so excited about going and I know more about what to expect this time around as far as being with a bunch of testosterone-laden teenagers and my brothers.

There is just something about Ely that is so calming and relaxing to me and I have some friends up there I look forward to seeing. One is Sue who is our fishing guide, another is Cliff at the bait shop and then there are the owners of the resort where we rent our boats.

I am hoping for some peace in my soul on this trip!

August 8, 2007 (Wednesday)

Just came back from a great trip to Ely with my brother's, David and Richard, their boys and David's nephew-in-law Michael. It is so cool up there and so relaxing. There are no computers, phones, radios, telephones or ANYTHING up there. The Boundary Waters is in the middle of nowhere and the scenery is beautiful. It is God's country as there is nothing but trees, water, loons and various other wild animals. Once again I asked LaTourell's, the outfitter that we use, if there was a job for me!

It is so fun to be in such a place with my brother's and my nephew's as I really get a chance to get to know them without the distractions of society. For many years I stayed away from my nieces and nephews because I didn't want to expose them to me when I was doing drugs and drinking a lot. As a result, I don't have the closest relationship with some of them and that bums me out. At least in Ely, I get to spend some quality time with my precious nephews. I also think the boys are impressed with my camping and fishing skills and overall "survivor skills" as I pretend that I am practicing for when/if I ever apply to "Survivor" again.

Last year I spent most of the time fishing with our guide Sue and we caught more than the boys. Of course they say I have an unfair advantage because I'm with Sue, but like she says, she doesn't put them on the line for me. I also had to laugh as Sue has the best job.

It was also last year we were sitting in Sue's boat and the black flies were biting me like crazy so she told me to grab the fly swatter that was on "her desk". Well her "desk" is just a big plastic container that has all of her fishing and camping gear in it. I laughed that she called it a desk and she said something to the effect of "yeah, and how do you like my office" and gestured around the Boundary Waters area. At times I would love to do her job, but of course in reality I couldn't because I have such anxiety and fears.

One of the things that does scare me out there is not the bears or other animals, but rather humans. It would be so easy for someone to come up on your campsite and do whatever they want to you. That to me is terrifying and I don't sleep the best while being in the wilderness due to the nighttime noises.

The other thing that is a shame is that I haven't gone swimming with my nephews on any of the trips up to Ely, as I feel uncomfortable being in a swimsuit around them. The reason is terrible to admit, but I don't want them to "look at me" so to speak. Another fallout from Lesser and it just breaks my heart as I can't tell them the real reason why I don't go swimming with them.

But despite that, I was able to get away from the case and the worries about Lesser for a little while and that is golden in my mind. I really didn't even think about him when I was up alone in the early morning and sitting on the shore looking over the lake. I thought about a lot of things and he wasn't really one of them. I tried to stay mindful of where I was and to enjoy this wonderful experience and soak in the beauty of God's creation.

CHAPTER 10

Back To Reality

August 14, 2007 (Tuesday)

More health problems! I had a CT scan done on my lungs and my liver and my doctor said that I have Emphysema! Not only that, but I have a spot on my lung and on my liver. They don't seem cancerous to the radiologist, but they will have to keep an eye on it. She also wants me to go see a pulmonologist in the clinic to having breathing tests to determine the severity of my Emphysema. This is just too much to bear and to say that I am scared doesn't even cover it. Of course, though, when I left the doctor's office, I lit up a cigarette. Go figure.

August 17, 2007 (Friday)

Had an appointment with a pulmonologist and he told me that the spot on my lung wasn't serious looking, but that I do have Bulious Emphysema!! That isn't as serious as Emphysema, but if I don't quit smoking, it will turn into the bad Emphysema.

Let's just add another thing to my list of health problems. I know that years of smoking have taken their toll on my lungs, but this diagnosis does scare me. Not enough however to quit smoking on the spot!! I also wonder about the "death wish" I've seem to have been on for the last 30+ years and the fact that I still don't want to grow very old. Maybe smoking will shorten my life, but I don't want to be old and senile in some nursing home where someone could hurt me. I'd rather go fast.

August 20, 2007 (Monday)

Had to go to the hospital and stuff to do all the paperwork for my surgery on the 4th. This just sucks!! I shared my fear with the anesthesiologist that I might not wake up after he puts me under and he assured me that that wouldn't happen. Still, it does happen and I JUST HAVE to wake up so that I can continue working on nailing Lesser to the wall.

I also saw Dr. R. when I was leaving and he is going on vacation next week. I told him to take very good care of his hands, as he had to operate on me when he got back. He laughed; I didn't, as I was serious!

September 1, 2007 (Saturday)

Danny and I are feverishly cleaning the house as I expect that my parents will come out the day after my surgery. I do like them to come out, but anyone coming to the house, initiates a cleaning frenzy. It's not that I keep a dirty house, but rather I have a tendency to clean "around things" instead of moving things. I am such a nerd!!

September 4, 2007 (Tuesday)

Today is the day that I go in for surgery to remove the mass on my thyroid. I was able to sleep last night, but I am so afraid that I won't wake up from this and then I won't be able to get Lesser. Please God protect me, help me to contain my fear and guide Dr. R.'s hands.

September 6, 2007 (Thursday)

Had my surgery and thank God that the mass that they removed isn't cancerous for sure. It was so weird being in the hospital and I really didn't get any sleep at all.

Surprisingly, my wound didn't hurt so I refused pain medication. I don't want to take something that might make me sick and since there are many medications that make me sick, I didn't want anything. I think the nurses were surprised that I didn't want anything, but that's ok. Honestly, I also didn't want to be "out of it" while in the hospital. It's upsetting enough to be there and I wanted to stay in reality so to speak or maybe to stay in "control".

Mom and Dad had come to Monroe the day of my surgery and spent the night. I was bummed when Danny and my parents left my hospital room to go to dinner, as I wanted to go!! They did spend the night however at a motel and the next morning when I got discharged, we went out for breakfast and then they came out to our house. The first time in probably 8 years that they have been invited to come out. I'm weird when it comes to people coming to my house, even when those "people" are family.

As far as my wound, I have weird stitches up and down on my neck and it looks a little scary. It actually looks like someone slit my throat, which in actuality is what happened!! I am not feeling any pain, just tightness in my neck and difficulty swallowing. I called Dr. R. to ask about these things and he said that it was perfectly normal and that I should be feeling back to normal fairly shortly. He also called me his "Star Patient"!

I am soooo thankful that this piece is over as it was just another worry on top of all of the other worries I have going on in my life!!

September 15, 2007 (Saturday)

Today Danny and I met up with David and Julie to attend a Badgers game with them and Bobby. It was really a lot of fun and the Badgers won!!

It is wonderful to have my nephew so close and going to school, but I have instructions from David to give him some space. I think that has been the problem all these years is that I have given him space…maybe too much and that's why I don't know him as well as I would like to. I did get to know him a lot more from our Ely trips and that is one reason that I wanted to go so badly with them.

Bobby seems to be adjusting to college and we went to a fraternity party before the game. It was only 11:00 a.m. and already some guy was puking by the garbage bin!! Way to go Wisconsin.

For me, it was a break from constantly thinking about the case.

CHAPTER 11

The Pass-Off

October 4, 2007 (Thursday)

It's been a while since I've been in touch with Detective F. because of the surgery and dealing with all of my other health issues these past couple of months. Therefore I e-mailed Detective F. to see if anything is going on and much to my surprise and dismay, he has had it transferred to a Detective Sharp. He said that he couldn't find the time to work on my case and that Detective Sharp was an excellent detective who would do his best for me. I'm not sure how much these guys really want to work on a case like this, and who can blame them.

There are times when I vacillate back and forth about the benefits of going through this process and though I recognize that there are more important cases happening right now, I still can't help but think that this bastard needs to be nailed and I deserve some attention as well. That might be selfish on my part, but I feel that I have been waiting as patiently as possible for a very long time and this waiting is wearing me out.

It is difficult to deal with not knowing what is happening and actually not having anything happen with the case is getting so depressing. It simply hangs over my head and it seems like I am reminded of the abuse much more frequently than before this process started. It will be "interesting" to see how I feel when things start rolling. I just hope they start rolling soon.

October 29, 2007 (Monday)

Just got back from a much-needed vacation in Bar Harbor, Maine and it was great to get away. I wasn't however able to let go of my tension or nervousness so it wasn't a vacation for the soul as I had hoped. It was however a vacation of the "senses". We stayed in a cabin right on the ocean, so we could hear and smell the water all of the time. We had a huge fireplace so of course I loved that. I ate lobster and had clam chowder everyday!! We went out whale watching and finally found a whale about 40 miles out. I would love to swim with whales someday so it was thrilling to be able to find one in such a vast amount of water!! I like to think that God sent him to me because seeing these amazing animals up close is one of my most favorite things to do in life!

We also found a bar where the owner was previously from Wisconsin and we ended up having a blast with the locals. There were some local lobster fishermen in the bar drinking who were definitely of the "salty" type. We had so much fun partying with them and they invited us back the next day for a REAL lobster feast. We were too hung-over to go back the next day, plus it was about 1 hour away from where we were staying, so we didn't go back. I did send them a thank you card though for the great time!! It was so fun to laugh and laugh with them!! It was a nice change of pace, as I haven't found anything to be funny as of late.

The trees were also still in full color so we drove through the Acadia National Forest and the scenery was gorgeous. We ended up rescuing a mother, daughter and her daughter's friend who had tried an adventurous hike to the top of the mountain, not thinking about the cold or how far it was. We ended up touring the top of the mountain with them and then gave them a ride back down to their car. This lady was originally from Wisconsin!

Since coming back from vacation, I felt strong enough to contact Detective Sharp. I had previously e-mailed him, but never got a response, so this time I thought I would call him.

He answered immediately and sounded very nice. Once again, I feel badly that I am taking their time away from cases that currently are active and need their help, but at the same time, I NEED for something to happen. It's been almost two years since this process got started and there is rarely a day or it seems a moment that I don't think about it.

Detective Sharp said that he had just finished up with a burglary case he was on in Rock County and hadn't had a chance to look at my case, but he would. Surprisingly, he called back a couple of hours later and he had already contacted Detective F., the Fontana Police Dept., and Lowell S., the family attorney!

He asked a couple more questions about whether I knew where Lesser was at and I said I thought FL or NC. That was surprising to me as Detective F. stated at one time that he might have found him. At any rate, it is good to have at least some movement on this and Detective Sharp was very validating about my need to prosecute and my rights as a citizen.

Once again, my stomach is now in knots and I ache for the peace and quiet I felt while in Maine. So much for that!

November 18, 2007 (Sunday)

Just when you think things couldn't keep happening, they do. Danny and I were watching church this morning on television when there was a loud bang. Tucker went and hid behind the chair while I got up to peek around the kitchen and living room to see if something had exploded because that's what is sounded like. Danny made some smart aleck comment that the noise was probably a hunter shooting the house. Ha Ha.

After church, he went upstairs to get dressed as he was going into town while I did some paperwork before going to meet with Julie later in town.

When I went upstairs to get dressed myself, I noticed that there was "stuff" all over the bed. I immediately thought it was Danny that made a mess and I of course cursed him not only in my head, but out loud.

I then noticed that there were bits of glass all over the bed as well and I thought that that was weird as why would there be glass all over the place. That is when I remembered what Danny had said earlier about a hunter shooting the house. I looked at the bedroom window to see what happened and when I pulled up the blind, I saw a hole in the glass and some splintered wood in the upper right part of the window.

I thought if that was a bullet then it should be across the room and when I looked across the room, there was a bullet stuck in the wall!!! Talk about freaking out!! I didn't really know what to do except to probably call the Sheriff's Department, so that's what I did.

A really nice officer came out and he was as amazed as I was that this bullet went right through the window and was sticking in the wall. He did his investigation and left, so I then went into town all freaked out.

We found out later it was a guy who was hunting on his property, which backed up to our neighbor's land that's behind our house. This guy was actually in the cornfield next to our house waiting for us to get home and apologize. He was so upset about shooting through our house and immediately gave us $500 for repairs. Just another day of drama!!

Not only that, but the next day a reporter showed up at the door asking if he could interview me about what happened as well as to get a picture of the window. I really didn't want to do it, but since I was a reporter in the past, I knew that it would be a good story. I agreed to talk with him as long as he didn't print the guy's name that did it to spare him any embarrassment and that he didn't print my last name. I am very cautious about my name and address being easily available to people because of my job.

November 28, 2007 (Wednesday)

Had our normal Thanksgiving at Deanna and Richard's and it was a tough one to say the least. Deanna's sister-in-law Kay, who we all love dearly, was diagnosed with lung cancer about 3 months ago. It is so advanced that she most likely will not live long, so this might be our last Thanksgiving with her.

I didn't really know what to expect as far as the atmosphere of Thanksgiving, but Mark (Deanna's brother) and Kay are so wonderful, they wouldn't let it bring down the day. This might be the last time that we would be with her and she wasn't moping or anything. She even took off her wig after dinner and was able to joke about her bald head.

Mark and I went out to have a cigarette (real smart) on the porch and he did break down as far as what it will be like living without her. They are the most romantic and loving couple that I know and despite being married for a gazillion years, they are still affectionate with each other.

On the way home, I just cried and cried, as I knew that this was the last time that we would see her. Danny was mad at me that I was just giving up on her, but I knew in my heart however that prayer wasn't going to heal her.

A tough, yet beautiful day. That's sure a dialectic!!

December 13, 2007 (Thursday)

I have decided for the most part to leave the investigation alone during the holidays. So much has been going on and I don't want to begin bugging Detective Sharp right away, so I have found myself backing off a bit as far as working on it. There is really nothing more I can do as I have now given them all the information that I have gathered. Now it's simply waiting for Detective Sharp to really begin investigating this.

Patience is still difficult for me, however with the holidays, I don't want to think about this whole thing. Having said that, that's all I think about.

January 3, 2008 (Thursday)

I e-mailed Detective Sharp in order to keep this case in the forefront, as I hadn't heard anything for a while. He immediately got in touch with me and asked quite a few questions about the information that I have already provided. He also said that he had a call in to Campus Life and was hoping for a call back soon.

Detective Sharp has really begun to start the ball rolling it seems like and I am so thankful that he is now a part of this case as hopefully it will finally get started. Just the fact that he has contacted Campus Life is freaking me out so to speak, as I'm interested to see what they will say.

January 4, 2008 (Friday)

Detective Sharp called and said that the Campus Life people had called him back, but they have no record whatsoever that he worked for them. They said something to the effect that they don't keep records that long, but then again the guy told him that they do go back to the 70's.

Of course my immediate reaction is like I was kicked in the stomach. I'm bummed that they don't even have a record of him, and that makes me suspicious as well. Why would they have no record of that...unless they expunged all of his data for a specific reason?

I was also terrified that this was going to be the end of the investigation, but Detective Sharp says that he will continue working on the case, as there are plenty of people who confirm that he did indeed work with Campus Life in Lake Geneva. Detective Sharp has also talked with Mr. F., although I don't know what they talked about except whether or not Mr. F. had kept any information on him. Unfortunately, my father and mother threw out all the information that they had kept on him for years. One strike...bummer.

CHAPTER 12

Baiting the Hook

January 18, 2008 (Friday)

When I got home from work last night, I discovered that Detective Sharp had left a voice message for me saying that they had found Lesser in N.C. and that the police there had already gone out and confirmed that this was the Russell Lesser that lived in Wisconsin in the 70's!! I couldn't believe my ears and was so excited that I could barely get any sleep last night. I was dying to talk to Detective Sharp.

I immediately called this morning and Detective Sharp is intending on going to NC to interview him! What a switch from nothing happening on the case, to all of a sudden he is going to go interview him! We discussed the possible options of what might happen while interviewing him. Detective Sharp said that if he confessed, he would be arrested immediately and extradited to WI. If he didn't confess, then Detective Sharp would continue with preparing a case against him.

This information has really turned me upside-down and I'm shaking all over and of course threw up. I am thrilled that Lesser has now been contacted in some way about this case, although what the NC police said to him, I don't know. I would hope however that he is beginning to shake in his boots wondering what is going on. This is a wonderful day as finally he is aware that there is a "game" that's been being played and that he is somehow a part of it! Ha Ha.

After talking with Detective Sharp about him going to NC to do this and me being all excited, he e-mailed me back that after talking with his supervisor, Captain N., he has to wait until at least April of '08 to go out there. He has recently had foot surgery and has been placed on light duty until the end of March. As a result of that, he isn't allowed to travel.

My emotions immediately went from exhilaration to despair. To hear that is very discouraging for a number of reasons. One is that I have to continue waiting until the next step and that is difficult at best. It also means that I will be able to do nothing else, but think for the next couple of months and worry/wonder about what his reaction is going to be. On the other hand, my Pollyanna side says that this might be good in that hopefully Lesser is worrying and wondering what this is all about and if he does think it relates to me, then let him wonder what is going to happen to his life.

The shoe is now on the other foot and I just pray that he is really afraid of what is going to come down the pipe. I've always wanted to turn his world upside down, just like he did to me 34 years ago, and that he will have to suffer for the rest of his life. It's about time that he pays for what he has done not only to me, but most likely to other girls as well. To say that I am sick to my stomach, shaking, nervous, happy, scared and completely emotionally dysregulated (DBT) doesn't sum it all up. I am a complete mess, but thank the Lord that I don't have to work in the field today, as I wouldn't be of any help to any of my clients. I have a terrible stomachache and I alternate between crying uncontrollably to acceptance of where it is right now. I feel like in some ways I'm going through the Kubler-Ross grieving stages.

In order to keep myself sane today, I am going to utilize DBT distress tolerance skills and watch the movie "Birdcage" yet again. I find that movie so funny that it helps me take my mind off of this whole thing for just a little while and therefore just one of the DBT tools I utilize to stay as regulated as possible.

I also "meekly" encouraged Detective Sharp to maybe step up looking for Janet P. during this "break time" so that he might have more "ammo" when he does interview Lesser. I certainly don't want to tell him his job, but I want to keep this ball moving.

January 21, 2008 (Monday)

It has been a very emotional weekend for me and what started it is that Danny asked me yesterday morning what the effects were to me as a result of the abuse. I was immediately offended and looked at him in disbelief, as he knows how weird I am about a number of things. Not only that, but he has been living with me and observing first hand the tears, rage and depression that I have been experiencing for the past 2 years!

It then however occurred to me that he had a point. From the outside I look and act normal, but it is the inside of me that is a mess. He had asked a good question and therefore I thought it was important at this time to begin listing the effects that the molestation had on me.

I really didn't want to do that, as I knew it was going to be upsetting to say the least, but I had known in the back of my mind that I was going to have to express the effect that this has had on my life at some point, and I guess this is now the time. To say that listing these things was excruciating doesn't even seem to do it justice. I spent hours writing the list and the more things that I listed, the more upset I got realizing how significantly this has impacted my whole being. It is a list that is so private to me, but also liberating in that I could see how everything was entwined. I also got a major sick headache as a result of writing the list and had to spend the rest of the day on the couch.

January 22, 2008 (Tuesday)

I e-mailed Detective Sharp as I had talked with my brother's this morning and we all had some questions for him as to what might begin to happen now. Detective Sharp had told me that when the NC police went to his house, only his wife was there and though they were vague in why they were asking the question of whether or not he had lived in Wisconsin, she kept asking the police questions.

It is also my understanding that Lesser did show up, however, while the police were there and Sharp told me that when the NC police asked him if he had lived in WI, his wife then asked him why they were asking him this question. I guess his response was very nonchalant and he said to her something like "Oh, someone must be looking for me", but he did verify that he lived in Wisconsin at one time.

My family and I believe that he will most likely figure out why the police were asking these questions, and if that is true, then what is going to be his next move. Being the "person" that I believe he is, he might think that he will be able to talk his way out of whatever problem might be coming his way. I'm also sure his wife is continuing to pester him about what is going on, as I know that I would, but we'll see.

I also think I found Jeannie, his ex-wife, this morning and so I sent that information along to Detective Sharp. I had offered to call her and in one of his e-mails to me, he suggested that it might be best for me from an emotional and mental standpoint to take a step back from the investigation. He wasn't trying to offend me but rather was nicely telling me to back off. Even though I was taken aback by his words, I didn't take offense to that, as he is exactly right. This thing seems to be taking over my life at this point as all I can do is think about all of the possibilities.

I'm making references to this investigation as "a game", although it's really my life on the line and therefore extremely serious to me and most certainly not a game. However it finally hit me today, that after playing "this game" by myself for so long, Lesser has now finally been drawn into it. I can't believe it and I thank God for all that He has done to make this possible. In between my tears and extreme anxiety, I am now also able to "enjoy" certain things…such as the thought that he might be nervous…and he should be. He doesn't know what is going to hit him, but I hope it's a tsunami to say the least.

I tried to calm down today, but found it impossible to calm my physical anxiety, upset stomach, pounding heart and racing thoughts. I have to take a break.

January 26, 2008 (Saturday)

I recognize that I need to do something to try and alleviate the physical symptoms that I am feeling. My heart still starts pounding when I think about the case and it feels like a motor is running inside of me that just won't quit.

Fortunately there were snowmobile races today and I went and raced the snowmobile. It felt so liberating to be "free" of my thoughts for a second as you HAVE to concentrate on what you're doing or you might crash…and by the way, we are going very fast. The highest I clocked today was 98.6 mph in 1,000 ft. and I won 2nd place in the races! Only Jr. beat me and that's because he is lighter than me and his sled goes faster!! The rush of adrenaline that you feel while racing helped to calm down my body and by nightfall, I was not only mentally exhausted, but physically as well.

This is going to be a long and hard journey and I hope that I will be able to keep it together emotionally, mentally and physically. We are already making plans on going up north snowmobiling as that is one activity that helps me to calm down. I like being in God's country and to see the beauty of this earth, as I'm so tired of all of the "bad stuff" in this world.

January 28, 2008 (Monday)

Started this day with a couple of e-mails. One was from Joanne C. who I had e-mailed earlier in regards to Janet P., and the other was from Detective Sharp asking some questions about Janet.

It's amazing how fast my heart started pounding just seeing that I had mail from them. So much for the "peace" I had been feeling. It was good to see however that Detective Sharp is pushing on by beginning to look for what might be a big piece of this case and that is Janet. The beginning of this investigation in sincerity is just incredibly emotionally and physically draining.

January 30, 2008 (Wednesday)

Even though I've decided to "sit back" and let Detective Sharp take care of business, I e-mailed him and asked if it was possible for him to tell me when/if he found Janet P. He e-mailed back and said that he would. He also said that he was playing phone tag with Joanne C. but hopefully would talk with her soon. This is exhausting!

CHAPTER 13

The Search Ends

February 1, 2008 (Friday)

Got an e-mail from Joanne saying that she had spoken with Detective Sharp and that she was going to look for someone else that might know more about the case. I checked back later in the day and I was shocked to see an e-mail from Detective Sharp saying that he had gotten Janet's married name from Joanne and that he had found her!!! He also had given me her address and phone number!!! I can't believe that after all of this, I finally have a name, address and phone number!!! Unbelievable and probably the happiest day for me since this whole thing started!!

Detective Sharp and I had previously discussed the possibility of me talking with Janet before the police if/when we found her and he was okay with that. I wanted to do this for a couple of reasons, but the most important reason was that it was going to be difficult for her as it was, and maybe me breaking the news to her myself might be "easier" for her.

After receiving Detective Sharp's e-mail, I immediately wanted to call her, but knew that I should stop and think before doing that. I wasn't sure what to say, how to say it and knowing me, when I'm nervous, things come out of my mouth the wrong way at times. I literally had to force myself to stop and think about what the next logical step "in this game" should be. Finally I called my parents to help me figure this out as I was beginning to think that maybe I should write her a letter. I am much better writing things in this type of situation, so after processing my thoughts with them, that is what I decided to do.

For the next 2 hours, until 11 p.m., I wrote Janet a letter and it was difficult and gut wrenching to say the least. I had to be careful about how to address this situation because I knew that if she was a victim, this was going to turn her world upside-down. The last thing I want to do is hurt her or cause her anguish of any kind, but I have no choice. I did the best I could and I am emotionally exhausted from the effort. Besides that, I now have a massive headache.

February 2, 2008 (Saturday)

After basically a sleepless night and terrible dreams when I did fall asleep, I polished up the letter this morning and sent it along with one of my L.A. Cards that says, "I believe…we are kindred spirits".

Today I'm feeling a little more in control and maybe that is because what I had to say to Janet has now been said, and it is in the mail. I can't turn back now and besides, this whole thing is in God's hands anyway and always has been.

But I guess the thing that has concerned me the most about filing charges in the first place, is what might happen to the other victims if we ever found any. In some ways I feel that it isn't fair to drag her into this if she was a victim as well, but then again, maybe she wants/needs justice for herself too. Hopefully I'll find out in a couple of days. I figure she'll get the letter either Monday or Tuesday and am praying that she will call me. It will be in her hands though at that point as to what she wants to do and what is best for her and I totally understand that.

To say that I'm anxious about this "next piece" doesn't really describe the feelings appropriately. I am scared, worried for her, sad, sick to my stomach and throwing up. On the other hand, I'm happy, comforted and resigned but still fully committed to seeing this thing through. Once again, this is a dialectic; feeling two extreme and opposite emotions at the same time!! I had invited Janet to join me in this fight and in some ways it might be easier for us to do this together. I just don't know.

February 4, 2008 (Monday)

I am now starting to feel really guilty about sending Janet a letter. What right do I have to drag her into this and bring up memories that might not be the best? I wish I hadn't sent this letter now and dread what might happen.

The weather here today is rainy and might get icy, so I have made the executive decision to stay home today. I am so worried about this letter and when/if Janet will call me, that maybe I should have gone to work so I don't ruminate all day about it. I think now what I did by contacting Janet might be wrong and I can't stop crying. All I can do is pray about it and try and let God handle this situation that I have caused her. I am so very sorry Janet.

February 5, 2008 (Tuesday)

I had to call my parents yesterday due to having such major doubts and guilt about writing to Janet. I even e-mailed Detective Sharp about the fact that I was feeling this way. He said that he would have contacted her regardless if I had or not, but the point is that maybe I never should have brought her into this at all.

My father had the best advice telling me that I wasn't reminding her of anything that she didn't already remember. That is true and it did make me feel better talking with my parents about this. Mom's advice was to just STOP tormenting myself with all of these thoughts, but it is so hard to do. I vacillate between "emotional mind" and "reasonable mind" (DBT) and it is difficult. On one side is "the victim" side that is beginning to cower and doubt every move (emotional mind), but then there is the "clinical side" or (reasonable mind) that realizes exactly what is going on. Unfortunately it seems that most of the time emotional mind seems to "win" more.

This is such a difficult time and it is affecting me in so many ways. I simply want to stay home and isolate from everyone and everything. I don't want to have to deal with anything and work just seems to make things worse. It is so hard to concentrate on helping other's when my thoughts are scattered and I'm not really able to focus 100% on my clients. I find that I'm also losing my patience with them and being a little more "direct" in clinical advice and directives. I also have a lot less patience for Danny or for my more needy friends.

I am also beginning to have bad dreams again, although not necessarily about the investigation or Lesser. This morning I was up at 5 a.m. and already began thinking of all sorts of things. Clients, Janet, Lesser, Danny and his job, my new client, the huge snow storm that is going to hit today and tomorrow and money. By 7 I was already exhausted and fell back asleep for ½ hr. That was when I dreamt that Tucker had swallowed some kids sucker and was choking on it. Good thing he was laying right next to me when I woke up so that I could see that he is ok.

I am also worried about safety and the people I love getting hurt. I can't stand the thought of my parents driving to Chicago to my brother's house, my driving in this weather, Danny and I snowmobiling and of course Tucker and his health. I feel like something bad is going to happen and it's a constant nagging thought that something will happen. I know this isn't rational and it is taking its toll on me not only mentally, but physically as well, but I can't help it. The one good thing about when I do work is that for a little while, I can forget about my problems. I really have to make an effort to focus and lose myself in my client and when I can accomplish that, we usually have dynamic and productive sessions.

Janet didn't get a hold of me last night, but then again, maybe she didn't get my letter yesterday. The other thing I was thinking is that if I was she, I would like to maybe e-mail the other person before talking with them on the phone. I just don't know and it's fruitless to worry about it.

CHAPTER 14

A Kindred Spirit

February 6, 2008 (Wednesday)

What a day it ended up being yesterday!! I called Danny last night to tell him I was on the way home and he said that there was a message from Janet on the machine. I took that as a good sign as she wouldn't have called immediately if she didn't want to talk with me. I was driving home in a snowstorm and all I could think of was that I better not crash and die before I have a chance to talk with Janet! Honestly!

I got home and immediately called her and she is wonderful!! She was also a victim of his unfortunately and she had it so much worse than I did. She was involved with him for over 6 years, I think, and she actually was head over heels in love with him. He had insinuated himself so terribly in her life as well as her family's life, that it is scary. He provided family therapy with her entire family, and even performed the marriage ceremonies for her brother and her sister!!

Janet couldn't have been more wonderful and unfortunately, she seems to be more screwed up than I am due to the vast betrayal that she suffered at his hands and I feel really badly for her. We talked for a long time and I think that this process could be healing for her as well. She has much more guilt than I do due to the fact that she was involved with him for so long, but he is such a conniving predator, she really didn't have a choice in the matter. Once he focused his attention on someone that was pretty much it. She even talked with me about us being at the same Campus Life camp together. She remembers seeing him interact with some girl while there and thinking to herself that "that girl is going to be in trouble". She thinks that girl was I and I'm sure that it was. I told her that I thought I knew who she was as I remember this tall girl with long dark hair who watched Lesser and I drive away one day. She thinks that she remembers that as well.

Janet is willing to talk with Detective Sharp and I called him immediately this morning to tell him what happened in the call with Janet. Since Lesser molested her in Williams Bay, he is going to add more charges onto this!!! Whether Janet wants to pursue this or not, will be up to her, but I think that if she has someone to do it with, she will. She and I are definitely kindred spirits in more ways than one and I adore her to say the least.

There was so much that we talked about, and much of it personal, but it was so validating for me and I hope for her as well. She said that she had a lot to digest after talking with me last night and I'm sure that she does. I'm sure she didn't get much sleep last night while for once, I had a good nights sleep. I did dream, but I didn't remember the dreams when I woke up, so that is a good thing.

I can't tell you the relief that I feel after talking with Janet last night. I was so worried about her and dragging her into this mess and it turned out good. I think God has got her in a place where she needs to do this and is ready to do it now that she knows she has support. I am totally creeped out as to the level that Lesser was working on and how he was molesting at least two of us at the same time. It makes me sick, but he is a sick bastard himself and the web that he wove so long ago, is beginning to encircle him and I couldn't be happier!

Like I said to Janet, years ago it was like we were his marionettes and he was pulling the strings. Now he is my/our marionette and WE are pulling the strings and I'll tell you what, he is going to get so jerked around, that I hope he will be destroyed.

I feel the best right now in life than I have for a long long time and it feels so good to know that he might finally be revealed for the person that he is. There is so much I want to say about this but what I think is most interesting is that I feel that it is important for me to try and help heal Janet and her issues.

I don't mean to counsel her per se, but to help her understand how this has affected her life, help her to see that it wasn't her fault; no matter how long she was with him or what her feelings were towards him. I also want to help her heal the relationship with her old friends in Lake Forest as the thing with Lesser ripped their friendships apart and Janet feels badly about that.

I had promised Joanne that I wouldn't tell Janet who told me her name and I didn't, even though Janet asked how I had found her. I felt bad not telling Janet who gave me her name but since she isn't angry about that happening, maybe Joanne would let me tell and they could reconnect.

I e-mailed Joanne after hanging up with Janet and explained to her that Janet wasn't upset by my phone call at all, and that maybe Joanne could e-mail her as Janet had said how badly she felt about losing her friends.

I guess how that happened is that the first time that Lesser molested her, she went to school still freaked out and told some of her girlfriends. She then went and told Lesser that she had told them, and he made her go back and tell her friends that she had lied about it. Janet said that when she did that, her friends began to pull away from her. Hopefully Joanne will find it in her heart to e-mail Janet and reconnect after so many years. I pray that that can happen.

Later:

Just got an e-mail from Janet and since she was 18 when the abuse happened in WI. we can't file additional charges against him. Detective Sharp did say that she collaborated some of my testimony and that will be helpful to my case. Janet had also told me that she would testify for me and I hope that she will continue to feel that way in the future. Janet also said that this has gotten her thinking about looking into filing charges in Il. I wish her the best of luck in everything and encouraged her to call me at any time for any reason. I can't tell you how good it makes me feel that I have a "friend" who understands exactly what I am talking about as well as experiencing and thinking. Thank you God for including her in this journey.

February 11, 2008 (Monday)

It's been almost a week since I've talked with Janet and I haven't heard back from her. I had sent her an e-mail in response to the e-mail that she sent to me, but she hasn't replied to it. I certainly hope that she is "ok" and hope that her family has rallied around her. I imagine that it would be like an old wagon train deal where they would circle around her and help her through this difficult time.

I go back and forth about contacting her either by phone or mail, but not sure what to do. It's my belief that she is probably having some type of "breakdown" and rightfully so as her world was once again "bombed". I think the betrayal that she feels is so much greater than I felt and it will take her a while to process through that. She had said that she had been totally in love with him back then and for her to find out that he was "involved" with others at the same time, was quite a blow. She now truly realizes what a lying, deceitful man he really was and that most likely the whole thing was just a "game" to him. Talk about destroying the soul and I feel very badly that I was the one who had to "give her the news".

February 18, 2008 (Monday)

I was STILL debating about calling Janet to see how she was doing for at least a week now, and I finally felt strong enough to call her this morning. She is such a wonderful person and I'm so thankful that I called, as she seems to be doing as well as can be expected. She talked about all of the emotions that have been going through her since our conversation, but she hasn't been destroyed by the news, which I am so thankful for.

We talked about many things this morning, but the thing I most wanted to impress upon her was that she was in no way at fault in this whole thing. Lesser is a sick man who in my opinion is a sociopath, and it was/is unfortunate that our paths crossed with this evil person. I also talked with her about the sense of betrayal that she must feel discovering that everything that man had said and done with her was a lie. Thankfully she is emotionally stable enough in life to be able to handle this situation without it "knocking her back down", and we both thanked God for the role that He has played in this pursuit. Neither of us has lost our faith in God, which is also a good thing. I personally have always believed in God, I just don't trust the "messenger" anymore.

I just can't say enough about how much I really like Janet even though we have never met. She seems like an open, enthusiastic, intelligent, well bred, centered and fun person who didn't let bitterness take over her life. We both hope that someday we will be able to meet.

February 21, 2008 (Thursday)

Janet and I have e-mailed back and forth the last couple of days, as she wanted to know about the sexual aspect of the case. We got personal in our e-mails as I think it is easier to discuss it that way, than on the phone or something. She confirmed that he would also "pull out" for her too and that he even had a name for it…the Delta Method. I don't remember that and after hearing that, I thought that we better be careful what we talked about from now on. I don't want to do ANYTHING to screw up this case and so we made a deal that we wouldn't talk about anything that could screw up the case.

He is certainly a very sick man and the more that I think about it, I am a bit scared about what he might do in retaliation. A person like him isn't going to go down without a fight and I expect nothing less from him. He will also play dirty if he has to, so it is beginning to scare me the closer we get to Detective Sharp going to interview him.

Janet and I also wonder about Jeannie and what's up with her, so I e-mailed Detective Sharp about it. We would both like to know if she ever suspected or "knew" that something was going on. Detective Sharp said that he wasn't going to talk with her until after interviewing Lesser because he doesn't want Jeannie to tip him off in case they are still on good terms or whatever.

It seems like therefore things are on hold until at least April, when Detective Sharp can go to NC to interview him. I'm sure he's working on the case, but I don't know exactly what he is pulling together. I would love to know simply out of curiosity. I will leave him alone though to do his job, as the only part I really want to know about next is Jeannie.

This is going to be another long wait and the only pleasure I can derive from waiting again, is that I'm hoping that Lesser is sweating it out everyday wondering why the police came to his house. I can only hope and pray that he is getting anxious, nervous and yes - scared. Hopefully that is just going to be the beginning of an emotional and mental nightmare that he will be in for the rest of his natural life. God will decide what to do when he dies, but I hope that he will continue to suffer for eternity.

Janet is a wonderful person who I have grown very fond of and I am going to make sure that he pays for what he did to her as well. She seems like such a lovely, fun, positive person and I see us being friends and kindred spirits for a long time. I really admire her spirit, courage, honesty and attitude and I'm glad she is with me in this. She has given me such a lift in the process as the stress was really wearing on me. Due to her, I feel re-energized and more committed than ever to nail him. Let's hope and pray that happens.

March 4, 2008 (Tuesday)

I have been e-mailing Janet to see if she has heard from Joanne, but she hasn't e-mailed back yet and it's been a week since the first one. I just hope that Joanne isn't angry with me for giving Janet her e-mail address.

This has also been a frustrating time these past couple of weeks as once again, we are just waiting for things to happen. The end of March is when Detective Sharp goes back to the doctor to see if he comes off "limited duty". If he is released, he will then go to NC to see Lesser and continue the investigation. I had e-mailed him earlier about what the time frame might be for this whole thing and he really couldn't give me one.

He said that once his investigation is done, he will turn it over to the DA, at which point it is in their hands. Knowing a little about how the judicial system works, that will take a long time as well. It is too overwhelming to think how much longer this might go on, so I'm trying to get back to life. Detective Sharp had recommended that I just keep moving on with my life while this whole thing shakes out, and though that hurt my feelings for some reason when he said it, I think that he is right.

I am back to taking clients again…even the difficult ones. I need the money as well as maybe the distraction and again, who knows how long this will take. The only solace I can take in this continued "wait" is knowing that at least Lesser has been "visited" by the police, so I hope that he is feeling anxiety of some type every day! The longer that it takes Detective Sharp to get out there, the longer that he has to wonder what that visit was all about. The good thing is that most likely he doesn't know who is now circling him like prey. I imagine myself as a bird and he is my prey. I am circling around and around waiting for the moment to strike, while my prey is unaware that danger is present. Just like he did to me so long ago.

March 12, 2008 (Wednesday)

Nothing has been happening and Janet hasn't yet responded to my last e-mail. I'm really hesitant to call her because if she isn't answering my e-mails, then obviously she doesn't want to talk with me. Of course, my mind goes to the negative where I think that something has happened to her or she is angry with me for some reason. I should just call to check it out before my imagination runs away, but I don't want to intrude on her and her life any more than I have already.

I haven't heard from Detective Sharp either, but that isn't surprising, as I don't know what he is working on. He's most likely put the case aside until he can interview Lesser, which won't be for at least the rest of this month and maybe April. We're in a holding pattern right now and though this case is constantly on my mind, I am once again able to focus on my clients.

March 25, 2008 (Tuesday)

Janet finally e-mailed me back and the reason it has taken so long is that she has been really busy. Her mother was in a car accident, so she has been helping her among other things. She is such a sweetheart and it is amazing the bond that I feel with her. I honestly had been wondering if Janet had been in a car accident and that was why she hadn't e-mailed back. Once again, worrying about nothing, although there was an accident in the family.

Janet was also wondering when Detective Sharp would find out about whether or not he will still be on light duty, and I said that he goes sometime at the end of the month, but I will e-mail him again and ask him.

Joanne still hasn't e-mailed her back and that's really a shame, as I feel sorry for Janet. Janet did say in her e-mail however that she has found a new friend in me and I would have to agree!

March 26, 2008 (Wednesday)

I e-mailed Detective Sharp to meekly ask when he would find out about his duty assignment and he is going to the Dr. on March 31. I really hate bothering him all of the time.

April 2, 2008 (Wednesday)

I have been "patiently" waiting to hear what happened with Detective Sharp's appointment and finally I just couldn't wait any longer; so I e-mailed him to see what the news was and he is off light duty!! At least that piece is over! Now however, Captain N. is on vacation, so he won't be able to talk with her about what to do next until she gets back. So we'll wait a little more. This is just agonizing!

April 9, 2008 (Wednesday)

I haven't heard yet from Detective Sharp and though he told me that he would contact me when he had talked with Captain N., I still e-mailed him and asked what they had come up with. Unfortunately, he and Captain N. couldn't get together yet as he had jury testimony on Monday and Tuesday and on Thursday, he had to attend his uncle's funeral. Therefore, nothing will happen until next week at the earliest. It is impossible to describe how excruciating it is to wait for every little step in this process. I have so many questions once he tells me that he's going.

April 12, 2008 (Saturday)

I got the terrible news on Thursday, that Deanna's sister-in-law Kay finally lost her battle with lung cancer. That just sucks to say the least. Kay was such a wonderful person, inside and out, and it is a tragedy for her whole family as she was the glue that held them together. That mantle will now most likely pass to my sister-in-law Deanna who is also a wonderful person. We were very lucky that Richard married into such a warm and loving family. Our two families were happy that we did get along so well as many in-law families don't. We all loved Kay and she was the shining example of how to love your husband as they were in love until the day she died.

She also made an interesting comment to Mark the day she died. I guess she had been floating in and out of sleep for much of the day and she woke up one time and said to her devoted husband "I left you for a while". Mark then asked her "Where did you go"? Kay responded "It was beautiful" so Mark asked, "Why did you come back?" to which she responded, "I don't know. I must be crazy" and that was the last words that she spoke as she slipped away a little while later. Leave it to Kay to try and comfort and reassure all of us that the place she was going to was "beautiful" and that she had wanted to stay.

Although we are going to miss her presence on this earth for a long time and in many ways, we also know that she is safe in the arms of our Lord now and happy there. Isn't that what we want for all of our loved ones? It's going to be a very sad week ahead with the memorial service and everything. Deanna has already lost her younger brother when he was like 21 and her father when she was young. She has had a lot of tragedy in her life too and this is so sad for her as well. She considered Kay a sister as Kay had been around Mark and the family while Deanna was growing up.

April 14, 2008 (Monday)

It is Monday evening and the first thing I did when I got home was check to see if Detective Sharp had contacted me about his plan. Nothing there! This anticipation is just unbearable at times and I was sick to my stomach driving home thinking about it all and now there is still no news. It's been 2 weeks since Detective Sharp has found out he could travel, so why hasn't there been any news? This is so frustrating but then again I have to stop and remind myself that my case isn't the only thing going on with Detective Sharp. This is such an emotional roller coaster.

I also had an opportunity to talk with my best friend in the whole world, Lisa about what was going on. It is very nice to be able to vent some of this stuff to someone who loves me, who remembers more about that whole time than I do, and just someone to "vomit" it all to. Maybe I should get a therapist, but I have my friends. They aren't acting as therapists as I already "treat myself" so to speak, but rather they are people who love me and support me. What more can you ask for in life than that?

Hopefully, Detective Sharp will call soon but until then, I will have to continue to wait.

Kay's funeral service is tomorrow night and I'm most certainly not looking forward to that. The one good thing about working today is that I was able to keep my mind off Kay and the extreme sadness that I'm going to feel when it finally registers that she is gone. I did send her one last e-mail however to tell her goodbye and that I loved her.

CHAPTER 15

Hurry Up and Wait

April 18, 2008 (Friday)

Well, today was the day that I finally got some news from Detective Sharp and boy, was it good news. He had talked with Phil Koss who is the District Attorney (DA) in Elkhorn and it turns out that instead of the police interviewing Lesser, they are going to just issue a warrant for his arrest!

There are a couple of reasons why, but it seems that the NC police haven't been responding to Detective Sharp's requests for some type of paper that I think proves that they went out and did confirm that this was the Russell Lesser that we were looking for. That has made Detective Sharp wonder if the NC police are "friendly" with Lesser. The other thing is that maybe Lesser might flee when he finds out about this whole thing, although Detective Sharp doesn't think so. Detective Sharp thinks that Lesser has too much invested in his life to just take off.

I immediately called my parents, my brother's and then Janet. To say that I'm exhausted today doesn't really describe how depleted I feel as it's just been an emotional week all the way around.

Everyone was so supportive, but Janet was absolutely wonderful. She asked me how I was feeling and in reality, I'm a little scared of what is going to happen in the future. I have no idea what is going to come down the pipe, but she was encouraging by telling me that she was confident that I could handle whatever will come my way and to remember that it is in God's hands.

To be honest, I am so exhausted that I will have to finish this tomorrow, but just wanted to let my "journal" know, that the web is beginning to close in on him and even if the NC police want to "protect" him, Detective Sharp and the DA on my side aren't going to allow that to happen. The protectiveness that I feel from the DA and Detective Sharp feels very comforting and finally, we might be able to get him.

April 19, 2008 (Saturday)

What a day it was yesterday and I am still coming to grips with the news that an arrest is imminent. There are so many feelings and thoughts rushing through me that it is difficult to focus on life in general. Last night I just had to go and pull the covers over my head. I wanted to be alone and feeling safe somewhere as that feeling of security and safety isn't here right now. I feel very vulnerable for some reason.

Danny and I talked for quite a bit this morning, which I think was helpful to him. I haven't really discussed "specifics" with him, as I know that it is upsetting to him. I also wonder how much he thinks this is my fault. I've questioned him about this in the past as I think he is from the old school where things like this didn't happen and if they did, why didn't you stop it. That is the question that many people are going to ask once this gets out, and it is a difficult question to answer on many different levels.

It's so hard to explain to people about the mind control that someone can obtain over other people, and it's difficult for people who haven't had that experience to understand. Danny was very nice this morning as he can get "pissy" himself with all of this and who can blame him. He is the one who has to put up with my sultry moods, my tears, my need to isolate, not being interested in sex and in general, pulling away from him.

Now that this is coming to a head so to speak, the fear of the unknown is causing me to once again begin to withdraw from people and society in general. I just want to stay in my little house and not even leave the property. I am afraid of how angry Lesser is going to be, and wonder if he is going to retaliate in any manner. He could easily hire someone to bump me off, and though my brother David doesn't think that he would come after me, I don't think he knows how twisted Lesser really is.

April 21, 2008 (Monday)

Yesterday was Sunday and therefore church day. Danny and I have been watching the "Hour of Power" for years. I understandably have difficulty believing "pastors", but years ago we found Dr. Schuller and his program the "Hour of Power". He was an older man who mixed psychology in with religion and I found that this might be a man who I could trust to relay God's word. I now consider him my pastor and the Crystal Cathedral my church. Danny and I have been fortunate to not only visit the Crystal Cathedral a couple of times, but also to personally meet Dr. Schuller. That was one of the highlights of my life I must say, as he is the one who helped me begin healing so long ago.

I was hoping that there would be a comforting message from church that could help me in the weeks to come and there was. The message was about the spirit of fear and that God has given us the spirit of power and love and a sound mind, in order to counteract fear. I relate this to my situation in that I AM scared about the future and what is going to happen as well as how Lesser is going to react to all of this. But what I need to remember is that I now have the power in this situation as a result of the judicial process; I have the love of my friends and family; and I have the sound mind, which I absolutely HAD to have in order to go through with this whole thing. I NEVER could have done this before and I am so thankful that I am of sound mind as that is what it is going to take to beat Lesser.

I also had a long talk with my parents yesterday about this whole thing and while talking with them, I shared my apprehension about what is going to happen in the future. We also talked about how formidable of an "opponent" Lesser is going to be and they agreed that he will be. It was then that the slogan from the television program "Survivor" popped into my head. The goal of "Survivor" is to "Outwit, Outlast and Outplay" all of the others, and that is exactly what has to happen here. I've always wanted to be on "Survivor", even applying for it, and I guess in some ways, I will be "on Survivor" as I'm going to try and "Outwit, Outlast and Outplay" Lesser. I LOVE having this slogan to remind me of what needs to be done.

The next couple of weeks are going to be anxiety producing…at least until he is arrested. What is interesting is that I am beginning to feel kind of badly that his life is going to be so turned upside down, as I'm not really a vengeful person. But then again, he didn't feel badly about screwing up Janet's life or my life, so why do I feel badly? I think it is because I know what it's like to have someone screwing up my life and it's not very fun to say the least.

April 25, 2008 (Friday)

I've been anxiously and nervously anticipating this week after hearing that an arrest warrant is going to be issued, but it is now Friday and I haven't heard a word! This is SO difficult to wait and wait and wait. I know that we are nearing the part where Lesser is fully aware of what is happening, so maybe that is why this wait is more agonizing than ever. I want and need to have him know that it is ME who is after him. But then again, every step and every word in this process over the last two years has been agonizing, so maybe it just gets more and more agonizing. I don't know, but I do know that this is excruciating right now. I wake up every morning with a knot in my stomach and then usually throw up at least a couple of times.

I will call Detective Sharp later this morning to see if there is any news, as I find myself being very dysregulated over the weekend if I don't know where it ended for the week.

I am also still obsessing about what Lesser's reaction to this is going to be and the more I obsess about it, the more scared I become. I finally realized last night driving home from work that the pit in my stomach that I have felt since this whole thing started, is my intuition or "wise mind", warning me that he is a dangerous man. I think that even back then, there was some inner "niggling" that kept me from telling, and that "niggling" was I believe my wise mind warning me that I needed to be careful.

I am not only becoming afraid for my safety, but for my parent's safety as well. I realize that this fear probably isn't rational, but I can't help it. I can't begin to imagine how wrecked his life is going to be…starting the minute that he gets arrested. His whole life is going to go down the tubes, and I would be stupid to think that he is going to take this lying down.

Detective Sharp had said that Lesser had some money, so he definitely has the means to hire someone to do something to me. An "accident" could easily happen due to me working in some extremely dangerous neighborhoods. A "drive-by shooting" might not seem like anything to the police but me being in the wrong place at the wrong time. I am definitely going to tell Detective Sharp that if something "weird" happens to me, to look squarely at Lesser.

If he is convicted of a crime, he will be forever ruined, and that will piss him off. I feel like I have ripped open a huge beehive so to speak and the fury that is going to come at me, is going to be scary to say the least. Oh well, "so let it be written, so let it be done". That's one of my favorite lines from the movie "The Ten Commandments".

April 26, 2008 (Saturday)

Yesterday was a difficult day hoping to hear from Detective Sharp and finally about noon, I e-mailed him asking if there is any news. In the meantime, I had taped a "Dr. Phil" program about this woman who was accusing her father of sexually molesting her as a child as well as possibly abusing his own grandson, her son. It was a rather emotional show and the ending was today. I asked Danny to watch it with me so that he could listen to this perpetrator and try to get an understanding of how they act and think.

It was so emotional and in the end, the father's denials on a polygraph test came back as "deceptive". Needless to say, his daughter just lost it. Somehow though during her "meltdown" she was able to verbalize to her father how he had screwed up her life. She named off numerous areas in her life that were a train wreck as a result of what he did to her so long ago. She cited many of the same things that I have listed earlier in response to Danny's question to me. I felt validated by what she was saying and that she was just as "screwed up" as I was. Hearing her speak about how it has negatively affected her life was hopefully reinforcement to Danny about how the same thing had happened to me.

After watching the show, I thought I should check to see if Detective Sharp had e-mailed back and he had! The case is now at the DA's office and he gave me a number to call to find out what the disposition is! I immediately called, as I was concerned that they would be closed already for the day, but this wonderful woman helped me to find the case and explain what will happen.

This woman said that it is in a pile of papers waiting for some lady (who was on vacation this week!) to make a "charge determination". I'm not quite sure what that means, but I think it means that they have to figure out what to charge Lesser with. I then asked how long it will take for that to happen and when would hopefully a warrant be issued. She said that it could take anywhere from 1 day to 6 months! I exclaimed "6 months" and I think she could "feel" my dismay and despair as she tried to validate that it was a long time, but maybe because of the nature of these charges, they might do it sooner. She was so nice to me and said to possibly have a glass of wine to help alleviate my disappointment. I had to laugh as I was going out to celebrate my friend's birthday so I most likely would have a drink or two at which point she said that I better have a designated driver as I didn't want to end up with a DUI or something. At least when I hung up, I was laughing…a little.

So here we go again…hurry up and wait. I will have to send Detective Sharp a thank you note as I think that basically, his work is done. He has been a wonderful asset to this case in regards to the rapidity of his progress as well as his support to me as a human being. He truly was God sent!

I then talked with my parents to relay all of this information, as I'm sure they were on pins and needles themselves.

We ended up having quite a conversation as I shared with them some of my fears about the case, as well as all of the other fears that pop into my head. When I have expressed these fears in the past, they have kindheartedly tried to tell me that sometimes my thinking was "far-reaching" and that message always felt invalidating to me. When that began to happen this time, I finally told them that their "dismissal" of my fears hurt my feelings and that yes, I have had some far-reaching thoughts in the past but it's just what I feel and think. I usually don't share those thoughts with anyone as I realize that they are thoughts and beliefs that are "out there", but I have shared them with my parents because I felt they wouldn't invalidate them. This time however, I actually started to cry and told them how that statement of being "far-reaching" felt very invalidating and that when they said that to me, it really hurt.

We discussed our "different sides" for quite a while and I think they finally came to the understanding that these thoughts, beliefs and feelings are real for me whether they are rational or not. This validation is something that I do for clients on a regular basis as a result of my DBT training; validating their thoughts and feelings, while at the same time challenging them to change some of the more irrational or unreasonable ones. The most important piece here is to validate what you can about their thought or behavior, even if is just a "nugget" so to speak and THEN and only then challenge it. My parents will most likely deserve their own counseling degrees by the time this is done! Ha Ha.

I called the DA's office today to see if they could answer a couple of questions for me and I ended up being referred to the victim's advocate program. A woman named Evelyn helped me and though she was very nice, the conversation didn't start off very well. I had some questions about whether or not they will tell me when he is arrested and more importantly, what happens to the case now that it is at the DA's office.

Evelyn told me that at this point, the DA would decide if he himself will take the case or if he will assign it to a prosecutor who "specializes" in these types of cases. She also explained that there are many cases on their desks and when they get to mine, they get to mine.

The prosecutor will then look at the case and determine if they can prove beyond a reasonable doubt that this crime occurred. She talked about the legal difficulties that might arise due to the nature of the case and the fact that it happened so long ago. She also said that they might decide that the case needs more investigation, and if that is the case, then they will give it back to Detective Sharp

I'm afraid that I didn't take all this news very well and started to cry due to my disappointment. I had thought 2 weeks ago that an arrest was imminent, and now I'm learning that there might not even be an arrest at all! All I felt was complete and utter despair and I couldn't really comprehend anything else she was saying after that.

Evelyn was as sweet as possible and despite my tears at hearing this news, I had to laugh when she asked if I had someone that I could talk to about this. I then explained more to her about what I do for a living as well as the fact that Detective Sharp and I communicated quite a bit. I told her that I had heard from Detective Sharp that he had been in discussions with DA Koss and that it appeared that this WAS going to happen. At that moment, I didn't know what or who to believe, but Evelyn stated that I should trust in what Detective Sharp and I had talked about.

After explaining my case more to her and some of the things that Detective Sharp and I had talked about, I think that it will still go through, but all of the negative possibilities that could happen, was sure a reality check. This is by no means done, but I am going to continue to trust that this is in God's hands and that it wouldn't have gone this far if nothing was going to happen. God wouldn't do that to me.

I have very mixed feelings right now as to the future of this case and maybe I was being too confident in the fact that Lesser might finally be held accountable for what he did. This is such an emotional roller coaster.

P.S. Detective Sharp hasn't called back yet and that is rare for him.

I got an e-mail from Detective Sharp this morning and I just can't explain how good it felt to see his name. I have really come to trust that man and he is of more comfort to me than anything.

He hasn't been to work since last Tuesday and that is why he hasn't gotten back to me. He confirmed that he would tell me when HE decided to arrest Lesser, which is confusing yet again. I'm just not sure anymore who has the power/authority to arrest him and when. It seems like in all of these crime television programs, that people get arrested without a real cause all of the time, but then again, that is only television.

I had sent Detective Sharp a great thank you card that simply said that I thanked him from the bottom of my heart. I couldn't have found a more appropriate card to tell him how much he means to me. Right now, his word is the only thing that I am going to trust and listen to.

From a clinical perspective, it is really weird to me how I have emotionally connected with Detective Sharp without ever meeting him. It is the same with Janet in that I feel a real connection with her, although we have never really met. When I see an e-mail from Detective Sharp, I not only have a physical reaction of being sick to my stomach, but I also feel something in my heart as well. It is like he is my guardian angel, as I know that he has my best interest in mind and that he will keep me "safe". What that exactly means, I'm not sure, but I just know that I can trust in him and that feels really, really good.

It is also interesting in that I feel that same kind of connection with Janet. I truly feel that she is someone who is totally and completely on my side, and will do whatever she can to "protect me" so to speak. She was so comforting in her last e-mail to me about keeping my strength up for this process and reassuring me again that not only does it have to be done, but that I am capable of doing it. Both she and Detective Sharp really have no idea what they mean to me as I'm finding it difficult to convey to them their importance in my life.

Late Afternoon:

I had a "light bulb" moment right now about what it is that Detective Sharp does for me and that is…He's my reasonable mind! According to the therapy DBT, and maybe I've explained this earlier in this journal, but DBT states that people operate in 1 of 3 minds.

First is "emotional mind", where a person looks at things and reacts to things from an emotional context only.

Second is "reasonable mind" which is where a person looks at and reacts to things from a totally unemotional standpoint. This is when only "facts" are important and there is no emotion factored in at all.

Finally, there is "wise mind", which is when you make decisions and act through a combination of reasonable and emotional mind. I like to call it the "gut feeling" that a person has.

My light bulb moment is figuring out that Detective Sharp is my reasonable mind! I approach much of life while in emotional mind and that isn't healthy for anyone to base everything on emotions. I've had to learn how to utilize reasonable mind to achieve a more appropriate and balanced approach to problems and life.

In this current situation, I'm much more apt to slide back into emotional mind and the reason Detective Sharp's communications are so comforting, is that it is reasonable mind making me come to wise mind. Coming to wise mind about things therefore enables me to put things into perspective and to able to calm down. He is the calm amidst this raging storm that I find myself in and he is the one who is keeping me grounded by his sensible responses. And even though he is ALWAYS in reasonable mind, which is what is calming, there is sometimes an "empathetic tone" that are in his responses. He is the perfect match for my personality!! That is my light bulb moment! God is definitely planning this almost perfectly right now, except He could move it along a little faster!

May 18, 2008 (Sunday)

It's been a couple of really difficult weeks for many reasons, yet a lot has been taken off my plate as well.

I recently have been having health issues again in my neck. It has been really hurting for quite a while and it's not just the salivary gland and that area that hurts, but now it feels like there is something in there pulling at things. It is really painful and therefore my Ear Nose and Throat doctor's assistant and I felt that we should take a CT Scan of it to see if there was something going on.

Since it is close to my 6-month check up for the spot on my lung and the spot on my liver, I asked if we could just do them all at once. Thankfully neither spot on my liver or lung has changed and there was nothing in my neck. As happy as I am that they didn't find anything, it also makes me wonder if everyone thinks I'm a hypochondriac. It really does hurt, although there was no evidence of what could be wrong.

Brian did say however that it might be muscular/skeletal issue and that got me thinking about whether or not it could be from grinding my teeth during the night. I decided to try my mouthpiece again and I could immediately feel a difference. Therefore, it must be that I am grinding my teeth so badly at night, that it is affecting all of my muscles in my neck. Why didn't I think of that before, although honestly, it is very comforting to know that there is nothing wrong.

Another issue that was resolved was that Danny finally went to the orthopedic surgeon for his shoulder injury and it ended up being an A/C Separation. Sounds serious, but he got a cortisone shot and hopefully that will be all that he needs. I was so worried about what was wrong and if he would have to have surgery or not. That was another huge relief and worry off of my plate.

Finally, Danny took our dog Tucker to our new vet to have her look at the lumps that he has on his side, and just thoroughly check him out. He limps after being outside for a while and he grunts and groans while lying down. It sounds like the air is being pushed out of his lungs. Dr. Thayer who had been our vet and just retired, had previously told me that Tucker has an enlarged heart, so I worry about the stress and strain that is put on his heart while playing hard outside.

It turns out that he is ok as well. The lumps are fatty tumors and they don't need to be taken out. There is also nothing in his chart about having an enlarged heart and she thought that his heart and lungs sounded fine. Sometimes I truly think that I am losing my mind as I KNOW that Dr. Thayer had told us that when I requested an X-ray of his heart and lungs while he was under anesthesia for having the other growth taken off.

Maybe all of my anxieties and worries are exaggerated as Danny always tells me, but to me, they are real and I can't help them. There are reasons to be worried about the health of the three of us, let alone the state of the economy, our stupid ass government and all of the terrible things happening to people around the world. It does affect me and I can't help it. I think that is why I was such a drinker, in that it helped to not worry about things for a while.

Having those things off my mind has been very helpful and I found that I've been able to focus better on my clients.

Then Thursday night I found an e-mail from Detective Sharp that he has talked with DA Koss and that he wants Detective Sharp to interview my parents, my brothers and Jeannie and then come back to him. Just like Evelyn, the victim rights lady said, that it might need more investigation, and that is exactly what happened!

This news was another blow in that everything is not only delayed once again but my family is now going to be pulled into this cesspool that I have been living in for the past 35+ years. They will now have to relive it and regurgitate it all over again. I feel so badly that they have to do that, although my whole family said that it wasn't a big deal and that it wasn't a problem at all. They have all said from the beginning that they supported my decision to go after Lesser, but it is still upsetting to me that they finally have to join in this "game" as it's not a fun game.

I called my family Thursday night to tell them that Detective Sharp wants their personal information (even though I had already given it to him) and they all sent it to him right away. I thought that he might start interviewing them on Friday, but he never called them nor responded to my e-mail, so once again I was disappointed.

Needless to say, all of this, plus life events with friends and Danny's family, sent me over the edge yesterday and I ended up with the sickest headache I can remember. At least it wasn't caused by alcohol. I was physically ill for most of the night and just puked my guts out. I really don't handle this stress very well and it all comes out of me in a physical manner.

Today, hopefully, I am going to be able to lie down and relax. It's Sunday and starting right away tomorrow morning, I have to start taking care of everyone else once again so it is important that I take care of myself today.

CHAPTER 16

A Rolling Stone Does Gather Moss

May 20, 2008 (Tuesday)

Today is the day that Detective Sharp finally called my brothers and parents. I was able to talk to Richard, my oldest brother, while on the way home from work. Richard really doesn't know much about the whole business as he was in college when all of this was going on. He said that he spoke to Detective Sharp for approximately 10 minutes and that he apologized for not really remembering some stuff...such as where we were when I told my family. I don't really remember although I think it was while we were in Persepolis, a city in Iran.

David is currently traveling somewhere, plus it's his son's birthday today, so I left him a message asking him to call me tomorrow.

Detective Sharp also called my parents and Dad sent him an e-mail with all of the things that they had written down in regards to the situation back then. Mom and Dad want to meet face-to-face with him though so they will meet next Tuesday at his office. Both of my parents feel that it is important that Detective Sharp see how this whole thing has affected them. They have felt such guilt over the years for what has happened that it has literally torn my mother apart. Dad is more stoic, or tries to be, but I can see the pain that they have also been in for many years. Maybe that guilt is what keeps them "enabling" me for all of these years, and I feel terrible about that. I should be able to take care of myself in all instances and in all ways, but that takes a kind of emotional energy that I just don't have, and I don't know why.

While driving home though last night, I realized that rather than still being really upset about my family being involved now in the legal process, I now found it very comforting. It kind-of feels like there is a protective circle beginning to form around me and I can actually breathe for once.

For so long it has just been me in my misery and in my memories, not only since this case started, but also for 35+ years. One by one, God has added the people that I will need in order to do this. But I also think that they are also people that need to find their own type of justice and comfort through this process.

The first one to really join with me in this "game" was Detective Sharp. He was the first one that really began the fight for me and through all of his e-mails, he showed that he was going to be a formidable player to have on the team. He also gave me a sense of "safety" in making me feel like he wasn't going to let Lesser hurt me ever again.

The next big "player" was Janet and the fact that she immediately rallied to my support was more important than anything in this whole process. It's not so much that she will testify and everything, but that she also knows how it feels to have her life destroyed by Lesser. The fact that she is such a kindred spirit as well is amazing to me.

Now Richard, David, Mom and Dad are involved as well and it feels very very good. I finally feel that I am totally surrounded and will be protected. It feels like my whole family is that "Mama Lion" who will do anything to protect her young. That is such a comforting feeling and I will hopefully carry this with me for quite a while, as I like it. I personally have still not heard back from Detective Sharp, but hopefully he will contact me when/if he interviews Jeannie, Lesser's ex-wife, as she is on the list of people DA Koss wants interviewed.

While Danny and I were talking this morning, I thought of another analogy to describe this whole process. This analogy is about the saying "A rolling stone gathers no moss". In this case, it's about the rolling stone GATHERING moss instead. The image involves a stone rolling down a huge mountain and I'm that rolling stone.

This stone is rolling and crashing down this rocky, cragged mountainside taking a new shape and form along the way with each crashing hit on the rocks. This ever-changing stone finally finds some vegetation and slowly begins gathering moss while still pelting down the mountainside. The moss slowly begins to form around the stone providing protection from the sharp blows of the rocks while on its continued tumble down the mountainside.

This moss represents the people that I am meeting along this journey that also need some justice of some kind. Only they know what they need to gain from this prosecution, but they are jumping onto the stone. It's like the stone is being layered which brings me to another analogy.

A long time ago, all the protective layers around my soul were peeled away by Lesser's actions towards me. I have been this bare "onion or bulb" so to speak that has been vulnerable to everything. Now those layers are being "put back on" and though I still feel very vulnerable and most likely always will in life, I feel like that huge tear in my soul is at least beginning to be "super glued".

May 21, 2008 (Wednesday)

Quite a day today in that David left a message that he and Detective Sharp talked about the bad stuff we had all done together and just "standard questions". It was obvious from the tone of his voice and his message that he really didn't want to talk about it, so I will leave him alone. I know that this process is extremely painful for him, so I will leave it for him to contact me when he feels the need. That has been pretty much the way it's been between us since this whole thing started and fine with me.

I then called Mr. F. (one of the parents) to relate where we were on the case and that hopefully a warrant for his arrest will be issued in the next month or so. I also told him about Janet P., as he didn't know about her either. As usual, he was supportive and kind.

I also called the P.'s and talked with Mrs. P. for quite a while. I brought her up to speed on what is happening with the case and we talked further about Lesser and the Williams Bay Campus Life group. Lesser didn't want to "mix" the two groups, so I'm not sure what if anything happened there, but I have my beliefs and I shared those with Mrs. P.

Detective Sharp called later and said that he had interviewed Jeannie and although she had her suspicions and even confronted Lesser about me, she really didn't know. She further told him that neither she, nor her oldest son even talks with him, one son rarely talks with him and one son does.

It is now comforting to know that Lesser's family won't be devastated by this information as both Janet and I were worried about how the boys, (who are now men), would take it. Now we don't have to worry about that as they have obviously somehow suffered at his hands as well and therefore already know that he is evil. This whole thing is just incredible and God is certainly taking care of things.

1 hour later:

I called Janet to tell her about Jeannie and what Jeannie had said to Detective Sharp about knowing what happened. I also shared with her that I wanted to call Jeannie, but that Detective Sharp had left for the day, so I wasn't sure if I should or not. Janet said that if my heart was telling me to call her, then I should. Janet also said that she wanted to talk with Jeannie and ask for her forgiveness and that shocked me. I wasn't thinking along those lines at all, but Janet felt it was important for her to do. Jeannie had done so much for her in the past and Janet felt that she owed it to Jeannie to apologize. I decided to call.

Jeannie answered and I think she was shocked that I had called, as she was a little apprehensive at first. My intent on calling her was to mainly see how she was doing emotionally as Detective Sharp had said she was extremely upset when he talked with her. I wanted her to know that I wasn't mad at her at all and to explain to her why I had to do this. We weren't on the phone too long for a number of reasons, but mainly because her middle son was calling her. Jeannie apologized for not knowing and not protecting me and seemed sincerely distraught about the whole thing. She said that she and her children had had a rough road with Lesser and that he had hurt her and the boys terribly over the years. I'm not sure what he did, but I know that I don't want to know.

Jeannie remains very religious and said that after talking with Detective Sharp, she immediately called her husband as well as two of her children who interestingly enough, work for Youth for Christ. She then met with I think the VP of Youth for Christ as well as Jeannie's mentor. Jeannie said they all needed to process this crushing news and that they needed to figure out how they were going to handle this as a family.

I apologized for creating this chaos within her family, but Jeannie reassured me that I was doing the right thing and not to apologize for filing criminal charges. Thankfully, her son called while we were talking and that gave me a reason to hang up. I did ask her though if it would be ok to give Janet her phone number so that those two could talk and she said that would be ok.

I then called Janet back and told her how it went. She said she would call me later.

I then called my parents and Richard, as I always do after any movement on the case and told them what happened. I was also able to articulate that since I have talked with Jeannie, I don't worry anymore about how she is going to take it. It sounds like Lesser has already put her through the mill and that everyone already knows what type of person he really is, so this won't be "that" big of a shock. It also sounds like they are an EXTREMELY religious family as Jeannie had told me that she hoped that this road that Lesser will have to go down, will bring him once again back to God.

Actually, I hope that he instead will burn in hell, although I didn't tell her that! What I also find interesting is that I feel no emotional ties to Jeannie whatsoever. While I worry about Janet's mental health, her marriage, how her family is handling this, I will not worry about Jeannie and her family. Right now I do feel a little anger towards her as she said that she had heard rumblings about both Janet and I, but believed Russ when he denied it.

Now, I have to e-mail Detective Sharp, confess to what I did and hope he isn't mad that I called her.

What a day and needless to say, I've now got a sick headache and of course, threw-up.

May 27, 2008 (Tuesday)

Today is the day that my parents go for their interview and actually, it is happening right now. I am so anxious and nervous for it to be over for them and I'm having a hard time keeping it together. I don't know why today is affecting me so much, but I just hope and pray that nothing happens in a physical manner to my mother. I am so afraid that she is going to have a stroke or something and if that happens, I'm really going to be pissed at Lesser then.

My heart is pounding and I have all of this nervous energy. I've been utilizing DBT distress tolerance skills all morning to try and stay distracted and for the most part, it does help for a while and at least stuff gets done! It's only 11 a.m. and I've already dusted and vacuumed my whole house; took the dog out to play while I weeded my gardens; done a ton of paperwork; made client appointments for tomorrow and Thursday; and sorted some clothes and shoes for St. Vincent De Paul.

I'm smoking endlessly, throwing up and will begin to cry now and then. I've also prayed that God watch over them while they go through this interview. I don't care what anyone says, it is extremely dysregulating to be at a police station and being interviewed by police officers. The "power" that you feel that they have over you is scary to say the least and then to discuss and open old wounds in front of someone you don't know, is also upsetting.

Last night I also called Janet, as I haven't talked with her since I gave her Jeannie's phone number. This past weekend was Memorial Day and I didn't want to bother her over the weekend in case she had some fun plans, but finally called her to see how it went.

She seemed to be happy with how their conversation went, although she admitted to being nervous in the beginning because Jeannie wasn't saying anything. Janet said that she did begin to "warm-up" however…maybe in response to seeing that Janet wasn't going to "blast" her either. We both feel badly about what this is doing to Jeannie and her family and both Janet and I feel that it was helpful for Jeannie, as well as for us, to talk with her.

Janet also seemed to be a little disturbed by the same statement that Jeannie had made to me about maybe this experience would lead Lesser back to God. I thought I could hear a tone of disgust from Janet…just what I had thought and felt. Janet is really something and I am so thankful that she is the person that she is, as I just adore her. She is such a comfort and a great sounding board at times.

Just got off the phone with my mother and she reported that their interviews went well. Mom adores Detective Sharp and says that he reminds her of Dad in his presentation. He is cool, calm and collected, is soft-spoken and was kind to Mom. Detective Sharp interviewed them separately, which was fine for Mom in that she said no one would interrupt them. I think she meant that if she had been with Dad, he might have interrupted her. Ha Ha. She didn't cry, although she said that her voice did shake at times indicating that it was still difficult to talk about after all of these years.

I will call later in the afternoon to check on Mom as I want to make sure that she is still doing still doing ok!!

CHAPTER 17

Hurry Up and Wait Some More

June 2, 2008 (Monday)

It's a new week and I feel like this is going to be the week that an arrest warrant is issued. I don't know why, but I feel it is going to finally happen this week. Dad however cautioned me that the wheels of justice move slowly and not to be disappointed if it didn't happen.

The rest of last week was busy as far as clients and most weren't acting like "good clients". It ended up being an emotionally draining week and the weekend was busy as well.

Saturday I got a lot of my nervous energy and frustration out by doing paperwork, running the never-ending errand runs and mowing the yard. It helps to get physical when I am so dysregulated as that has a tendency to keep my mind busy. It also has the added bonus of being physically tired from all of the outside work that I do. The final benefit of this is that the yard looks really nice right now.

On Sunday I went to see my parents as well as to attend a graduation party for a long-time friend's daughter. It was interesting in that while driving over to Lake Geneva to meet with my parents and attend the party, I felt like I was having an anxiety attack. My heart was pounding, my stomach was upset and I couldn't calm down for some reason. I was very anxious to see Mom and Dad as I hadn't seen them since they talked with Detective Sharp. I think I was nervous, as I wasn't sure what frame of mind I would find them in. They both were actually doing very well emotionally, mentally and physically and my mother was thrilled to have gone, so I need to let it go.

It was very comforting to be around them and though we did talk a bit about the case, we also talked about politics...one of my mother's favorite subjects. It is the one thing that she has total recall on, so it is comforting to me to talk politics with her. I love both of them so much and they have been such a source of comfort, validation and unconditional love.

June 7, 2008 (Saturday)

Well, it's Saturday and once again, I didn't receive a call from Detective Sharp that a warrant had been issued. I was so sure that it was going to happen this past week and I am disappointed to say the least that it didn't happen.

I have been so nervous/upset from anticipating an arrest that I have a cold sore that extends along half of my lower lip. It is so painful and just goes to remind me how dysregulating this experience is.

It's been a long week and though I am anxious during the week to find out any news, when the weekend comes, I do tend to calm down a bit. I think that it's because I know that nothing will happen over the weekend, so then I don't worry about it hourly.

Today Danny is going to his daughter's house to help her with a boat that she has purchased. His other daughter will be there as well with her young daughter, so I will have a couple of days to myself. I really do like having this time lately as then I don't have to talk with anyone, take care of anyone or deal with another person's emotions of any kind.

June 17, 2008 (Tuesday)

A lot happened last week, although I'm just getting a chance to write about it. On Wednesday of last week, I e-mailed Detective Sharp to call Danny's phone in case he heard something about an arrest warrant being issued. We were going up north to help his sister, Linda and brother-in-law Charlie with their cabin that they're remodeling and I didn't want to miss the news.

Detective Sharp e-mailed back that I could call DA Koss directly to find out the answer, so after much debate in my head, I called him last Thursday morning before taking off. The last thing I want to be considered is a pest by everyone at the DA's office and I certainly don't want DA Koss pissed off at me for bugging him even before the case started, but I couldn't help it.

The secretary who answered the phone was nice, but I didn't know the case number and she put me on hold. Then she came back and asked if I had more information to which I replied no. She put me on hold again and then came back on and said that they had been expecting my call and that she was going to put me through to DA Koss. To say that I was shaking in my boots doesn't quite explain the nervousness that I was feeling. I have never talked with him, so I have no idea what he is like.

DA Koss turned out to be really nice and didn't seem to mind me asking some questions. I didn't want to come right out and ask him when he was going to make his decision, so I mentioned that I had talked with Evelyn in the victim advocacy program and she had told me that it might take the court up to 6 months to figure out what they are going to do. DA Koss said that it most definitely wouldn't be that long and in fact, he should make his decision within the next two weeks. I now have a possible date from right out the horse's mouth so to speak!! I did tell him that we were going to be up against a formidable opponent, although I forgot to tell him that I am also scared about what Lesser's reaction might be.

I'm sure that I will call him again before "the event" as I have now thought of other questions to ask him. I'm actually dying to call him today, but again, I don't want to be a pest. I could call Evelyn, but I'm not sure that she would have the answers to my questions and anyway, my personality dictates that I have no patience going through a middle man so to speak. I think that DA Koss and I will have to be in collaboration to get Lesser convicted and therefore it is important that we be able to work together. I hope that we will be able to do that, as sometimes I can be rather "controlling and demanding". At least I've finally talked with him on the phone and was able to tell him that I am a nervous wreck waiting for an arrest warrant to be issued. Hopefully knowing what a nervous wreck I am, will hasten his decision and hence the arrest.

After talking with DA Koss, I quickly called Mom and Dad as well as Richard, so that they also would have a date in their heads as to when there might be an arrest. I am so worried that something will happen to my parents and they won't be able to see justice finally done. For that matter, I'm afraid that something might happen to any of us involved with this case.

Immediately after talking with all of these people, Danny and I left to go up north, but unfortunately, I was a wreck from talking with DA Koss. I felt like I was having a panic attack as I couldn't catch my breath and couldn't stop the tears. Danny made a comment that he hoped the entire ride up north wasn't going to be like that and then I blew up at him. He has to allow me to vent after receiving this news and since he is the only one that I feel at all comfortable with doing that, he is going to have to do it. As I'm saying that, I also want to say that he has been very supportive of me this entire time. I'm sure that he gets sick and tired of what this is doing to me emotionally and physically.

Danny had to stop at his office on the way up and unfortunately, I made the decision to buy a bottle of Schnapps' to "calm my nerves". I've honestly been trying to keep from using alcohol to calm me down, but sometimes I just cave in.

While he was in the office, I called Janet with the news and once again, she is so wonderful to me that I can't believe it. She has really been behind me since the beginning of this thing and she keeps telling me that I am doing the right thing. I expressed my fears to her again about him getting arrested and what his reaction might be. One possibility is that Lesser could commit suicide in which case we would be denied justice once again. Janet doesn't think he would commit suicide, as she believes that he loves himself too much! I'd have to agree with that!

This is going to be such a shock to him and such a life-altering event, that in some ways I feel badly for him. But then again, I think about how he changed my entire life and future, and I figure he has it coming to see how it feels to have your world turned upside-down, never to be the same.

Needless to say, I ended up taking what Danny calls "The Champaign Flight" up north, which means, I drank too much. As usual, I ended up throwing up before going out for dinner and then again the next morning, but at least it wasn't too bad. I did quit drinking before the night was over, but I am still ashamed that I succumbed to the bottle to alleviate my anxiety. In some ways, I feel that I am falling back into some of my destructive behaviors, but then again, these recent drinking jags aren't a common occurrence. I really didn't drink the rest of the weekend.

We ended up getting a lot of work done in the cabin and it was actually pretty good therapy for me. All I did was what they told me to do as well as doing some extra things that weren't asked of me. I was kept busy and it was a good way to get rid of my nervous energy. They still don't know what is going on in my life, but Charlie did notice that I am awfully thin right now.

It is now Tuesday and I have a light week of work, which is actually really good. I was also able to sleep until 7:30 this morning, which is a long time for me. I feel a bit more rested and am not as anxious as I was, so having this down time is proving to be good for my mental health. Not so good for my finances, but I know that God will take care of me so that I can pay my bills. It's going to be difficult to work while this thing is going on, but I will have to find a way to do it.

I'm not sure if I'll write in this journal again before the news comes down, but the next sentence I might write will be the one that I've been waiting to hear and say for a long time.

June 29, 2008 (Sunday)

It is currently Sunday and I didn't hear anything last week. In fact I called DA Koss on Wednesday, just to ask some questions, and the secretary wouldn't let me through. She said, nicely, that that is why they have the victim advocates - to talk to the victims as the attorneys rarely do. That sucks!

July 5, 2008 (Saturday)

Well, another week without a phone call, but according to my parents, DA Koss is involved in a couple of big trials, so that could explain the delay. On one hand, I feel good that nothing has happened as I think that once he is arrested, my life as I know it will never be the same again. I'm not sure how I mean that, but I just know that something will change.

July 9, 2008 (Wednesday)

No news yet from DA Koss! Yesterday was the annual Lake Geneva girls' day with friends from high school. We usually go out in the boat, eat, drink and laugh but this one ended up being fairly emotional for my friend Martha H. and I. Her parents are the Mr. and Mrs. H. in the beginning of the book and there was some discussion about this case during the day. I felt that it was important that Martha and her parents finally know why my mother cut her parents out of her life and it was because of Lesser. It was so difficult as Martha just dissolved into tears, but she said that she would tell her parents the reason why my mother never talked to her mother again.

I'm exhausted and just want the DA to call me. I am fervently praying that today is the day, but I won't or actually can't hold my breath any longer. This is just unbearable to say the least.

CHAPTER 18

It's Getting Hotter

July 12, 2008 (Saturday)

Once again, Friday was here without hearing any news, so in the morning, I called Evelyn to see if there had been any changes in the case. As I was talking with her, she said that she would check the status on the computer. She said that the warrant WAS in the system and that there were only a couple more things that needed to be done at this point!! Needless to say, I was excited that a warrant had been issued and there are three charges:

1. Indecent behavior with a child – Felony with a maximum sentence of 10 years;
2. Sexual intercourse with a child age 15 (or something like that) – Felony with maximum of 15 years;
3. Sexual intercourse with a child age 16 – Felony with maximum of 5 years.

There are also fines involved with this, but they are insignificant as the prison time is what I want for him.

The warrant is now waiting for a judge to sign it, then it will get assigned a case number and then it will go back to Detective Sharp to follow up with the arrest. Evelyn wasn't sure exactly how it worked from that point and she suggested that I call Detective Sharp. Little did she know that that was already my plan. I thanked Evelyn profusely for finding out this information, as she will be on vacation next week when all of this should happen. Evelyn said that she would call me back later this afternoon to tell me whether or not it was signed and sealed, but not yet delivered!!

As soon as we hung up, I called Detective Sharp and he said that he had been off on Thursday, but Captain N. had told him that she had signed the criminal complaint. He went onto the computer and saw that it was at the judges desk, therefore, he would begin his side of the paperwork. When I asked if Lesser could be arrested today, he said that that could possibly happen. I once again thanked him profusely and this time, I couldn't keep the tears out of my voice.

Of course my parents, Richard and David were the next calls and then Janet. She is such a wonderful soul and is as nervous and anxious as I am about this whole thing.

I made another call yesterday and that was to Martha. I needed to find out if she had talked to her mother and how it went. Martha was fortunately home and she had talked with Mrs. H. to tell her why my mother had cut her out of her life. Martha said that Mrs. H. was really happy to finally know the reason why my mother wasn't a friend with her anymore. The reason was that Mr. H. had voted for keeping Lesser around even after my mother had explained her concerns to him. In all fairness to Mr. H., had he have known what was happening, he would have done anything to help me. Once again, if I had just told, all of these relationships wouldn't have been shattered.

I understand that Mrs. H. was also gracious and said that she now totally understands why my mother terminated their friendship and isn't upset with my mom any longer. Mrs. H. understands how a mother should react when one of her children is in danger as she is a mother and grandmother herself. Martha said that Mrs. H. has been thanking her every day for finally giving Mrs. H. the answer that she has really needed and deserved for the past 35 years. I am thankful that Mrs. H. now has some type of peace and closure as I've always liked Mrs. H. and again, I'm praying that this process heals at least her wounds.

The rest of the day was spent trying to keep my mind off what was happening and praying that he would be arrested today. Unlike earlier this week, I now had some movement and some encouragement that the case had now proceeded to the next steps that comprise our judicial system.

At 3:30 pm I called Detective Sharp, as I knew that he left at 4:00 for the day, but his voice mail came on. Actually I was thankful for that as I feel badly calling him about this stuff.

Evelyn called right at 4:00 with the news that the judge had signed the warrant and that it had been assigned a case number!! FINALLY!! She seemed as thrilled as I was and informed me that she had the packet of information that victims receive all ready to go and that it will be mailed out on Monday. She will be gone for vacation, but wished me the best of luck on his arrest.

Detective Sharp called right after that and he also informed me that he had received the signed warrant and case number, but unfortunately, he wasn't able to work on the paperwork today, so there will be no arrest today. I once again should have known that it wouldn't have happened so quickly. Detective Sharp said that he would do the paperwork on Monday to which I asked if Lesser might then get arrested on Monday and this time he was more cautious and said possibly. Since I will be up north on vacation on Monday, I asked if it would be ok if I called him to see what had happened and he said I could.

Even though I'm disappointed that the arrest didn't happen today, I am thrilled that it has made it this far today. All in one day we found out the charges, the judge signed it and it was assigned a case number. The final touches!! Like I told Evelyn, I am just finding it so hard to wait until Lesser knows. The moment he is arrested, his hell will begin and that's what I need to have happen more than anything. I just hope I don't die before seeing this happen.

CHAPTER 19

Patience Isn't My Best Virtue

July 16, 2008 (Wednesday)

I decided to go up north on vacation with Danny's family for a couple of days, hoping that it would keep my mind off of what was happening. I had called Detective Sharp on Monday the 14th to leave a telephone number where I could be reached for the next couple of days in case he was arrested. Unfortunately he didn't call while I was up north and now I'm home and he still hasn't called.

Even though I was up north, there was no way that I could escape the dysregulation that I'm feeling. I'm finding it hard to concentrate, to make decisions, to make small talk with the others on vacation, to be pleasant to others and let's not even talk about my patience level. I also can't really focus; I forgot to even put my dinner in the oven; drove miles in what I thought was the wrong direction only to turn around and drive back to discover that I had been going the right way in the first place. Nothing had looked familiar to me and that scared me. I am terrified to drive because my mind is wandering so much, I'm afraid that I'm going to have an accident. The thought of dying scares me because I CAN'T die before I know that Lesser has at least been arrested.

I'm also finding it extremely difficult to even hold conversations with people, to go to the grocery store, to the post office or anywhere else. I just want to hole up in my house and not talk to anyone…even my dog.

I tried to be social while up north and I think that I did a fairly good job, but my insides were just in knots.

Saturday night while on vacation I ended up drinking too much and I was disappointed in myself on Sunday. The last thing that I want to do is to fall into old patterns and behaviors, but I found myself doing just that not only to try and reduce my level of anxiety, but also to be more fun with the others.

I had called Detective Sharp on Tuesday morning, the 15th, to find out if he had heard anything as of yet. He said that he had teletyped the warrant down to the North Carolina police and that they had teletyped him back asking for further verification of two signatures that were on the arrest warrant. I asked Detective Sharp if that was rare and he said that it was unusual for them to ask for that. Once again, I am concerned about how friendly Lesser might be with the police down there. Remember that it took months for them to send the form to Detective Sharp that verified that they had gone out to Lesser's house to verify that he is indeed the Lesser that we want.

When I asked what he thinks is taking so long as far as the actual arrest, Detective Sharp said that Lesser might be out of town working. I have no idea what he does for a living except that he owns a vacation resort but Detective Sharp told me that he sells pharmaceutical drugs too. I think that is ironic because to me, being a pharmaceutical salesman means that that person should be an honest individual and that is something that he most certainly is not.

So here I am again, waiting for the final "blow" so to speak and even that has glitches in it! I am sure that the police have given him the heads up as to the fact that there is a warrant for his arrest and are allowing him to maybe get his affairs in order. He could actually be out of town traveling, but even so, the police would most likely have to go out to his house to serve the warrant and as a result, the news would reach him wherever he is. That is why I think something is up down there.

I'm also trying to imagine things in a positive way. For instance, while driving home from up north, I tried to envision this sinister cloud that is coming into North Carolina and that this dark mass is searching specifically for him. It's like the sinister black mist that is in the television show "Lost" and it is slowly going to encircle him. I must say that I enjoyed that visual.

I also called Richard to tell him that the warrant is allegedly down there, but no word as of yet. He then came up with this brilliant idea about what Lesser may plan to do. Richard isn't sure, but he is thinking that if he is arrested in North Carolina, he won't be able to bond out, as most likely he has to come to the place where the charges have been leveled in order to do that. Therefore, it would be in his best interest to actually come to WI with an attorney by his side and turn himself in. If he did that, then he wouldn't spend as much time in jail as he would if he was arrested in NC. Also, if he were arrested down there, he would most likely have to stay in jail there until he was extradited and transported to WI. only to sit here until his bond hearing. Therefore, it would make perfect sense for him to come up here and turn himself in, but who knows at this point. Nothing has really gone as I planned from the beginning in regards to how smoothly and quickly this would go, so I wouldn't be surprised by anything that might happen.

Another thing that has been upsetting is getting the victim's packet of information from the district attorney's office. Included in the packet is the criminal complaint, information on restitution from the state and other forms. What I find a little upsetting is that some of the information that they have in the criminal complaint is wrong. Some of the wrong information includes dates and some other things, but I'm sure they will be corrected before the trial…if there ever is one!

Today is another agonizing day of waiting and there is no way in hell that I can go to work. I've already called one of my clients and explained what is going on, but the other one is actually a police officer and I don't feel comfortable telling him the real reason why I can't meet with his adopted sons. I just told him that I had decided to extend my vacation for the whole week. My other client for today has gotten into trouble over the weekend for pulling a knife on someone and now his mother wants him out of the home again. I don't even know what to say to them at this point, but I have to at least call and see what is going on. I feel badly that I can't be there for my clients right now, but I also recognize that as a therapist, I wouldn't be of any help to them. This is all so difficult!

Later in the day:

I have talked with numerous people this morning and Janet was one of them. She called to see how I was doing and to ask some personal questions...mostly about my views and attitudes towards sex. It appears that she has the same types of beliefs and feelings.

We also talked more about what we are both feeling in regards to waiting for the arrest to occur. I told her I am a total wreck, can't concentrate on anything and I have about 10 different projects going and not getting anything accomplished on any of them. I can't sit down for long and keep pacing the house. She feels the same exact way and states that she has a "nervous" feeling inside of her. She is thankful that she doesn't have to work today and is going to keep herself busy taking her mother on errands.

We both talked about calling either Lesser or the police in order to speed up the process, but I know better than to do that. Still...

I then called Detective Sharp and he hasn't heard anything, although the NC police teletyped that they have gone by his house a couple of times. I asked Detective Sharp about what was taking so long and that I feel that the police have tipped Lesser off which is giving him time to get his ducks in a row. Detective Sharp was surprisingly informative during this conversation and agreed with my concerns about the familiarity that seems to be between the police and Lesser. He said that it took them 3 months to send a single paragraph statement saying they had been out to his house to verify it was the Lesser we wanted.

He also said that another detective in his squad room had suggested that maybe the NC police were getting the extradition papers to Wisconsin ready for when he is arrested. Whatever the reason, I feel that they are dragging their feet on this arrest and asked if the police can do that. Detective Sharp said that the police "covering" for Lesser is not out of the realm of possibility and the long delay in arresting him seems to confirm that to me.

I also asked Detective Sharp if the police had mentioned whether or not his wife was at home when they "drove by" and Detective Sharp said that they didn't say anything else. Funny in that later when I called Janet just to update her on what Detective Sharp and I had talked about, she confessed that she had called the lodge and a lady named Mary had answered. It was at that point that Janet said that she was sorry, but had the wrong number and hung up.

I think that if the police ONLY drove by and didn't actually get their asses out of the car to go up to the door to find out if he was there, then Lesser doesn't know. But since it is my belief that the police would actually have to go and ask where someone is if they have a warrant, then Lesser knows what is happening and is preparing for… whatever. We also know from Janet's anonymous call to his resort that his wife is in the immediate vicinity. Therefore my question is, why don't the police just go and ask her where he is? Just when you think it can't get any crazier or "weird", it does.

It is now almost 3:00 p.m. and since Detective Sharp is off in another hour, it is most likely that another day has passed without an arrest.

It's now 4:05 p.m. and no arrest! I am physically and emotionally drained, but at least I can let it go until the next day. I'm finding these last 4 or 5 nights, I've been able to go to sleep fairly quickly and that's most likely because I'm just exhausted from waiting every day. The problem is that when I wake up early in the morning, I can't go back to sleep because my first thought is "Maybe this will be the day" and the fear as well as the excitement, makes it impossible to go back to sleep.

My total attention is then waiting for 8:00 a.m. as that is when Detective Sharp begins his workday and if Lesser had been arrested during the evening, then he would know right away. I am then anxious from 8:00 to 8:30, praying for a call from him, but if I haven't heard by 8:30, the wait is on. Then for the rest of the day, I am just a bundle of nerves and my body and mind are on high alert until I hit that unyielding 4:00 deadline.

Dear Journal, I'm calling it a day.

July 17, 2008 (Thursday)

It is already 1:30 p.m. and again, no word on an arrest. I finally called Detective Sharp at 11:00 a.m. to ask some questions and though he wasn't there, he called me back fairly quickly.

I once again expressed my frustration and exasperation with how long this is taking. I inquired as to how a warrant is served and he said that the police go up to the house to see if the person is there. I then told him that Janet had called the resort yesterday and that a woman by the name of Mary had answered which we both know is his wife.

This is just so unfair that they seem to be "protecting" him. Detective Sharp said that he had called down there earlier to find out what was going on and has yet to receive a call back. I then asked about the possibility of having either a sheriff's deputy or the state police go out there. Detective Sharp said that he had already discussed that possibility with a couple of the other detectives in his squad. Honestly, I'm hoping that he will do that.

I also talked with Richard and he had another thought which was interesting and that was that the police might be terrified to arrest him. If Lesser is a pillar of the community, like we think he might be, then the police might figure they better have everything right about this before they do something drastic like arresting him. Richard said that they are probably scared shitless to arrest him and are just dragging their feet. This has a ring of truth to it, but it still isn't fair at all.

During this time, I have also been working on putting together the Victim Impact Statement that I must submit to the court. Thankfully much of it is done as I have already listed my issues back when Danny, of all people, asked me how the abuse had affected me. That list is what I decided I would send them.

It is now 4:30 and once again, a day has passed and Lesser is still somewhere out there. I can't put words on how upsetting this whole thing is.

July 18, 2008 (Friday)

I left a message for Captain N. to ask if she could possibly call me if there is an arrest today as Detective Sharp is off for the day since he is working security for the Jimmy Buffet concert at Alpine Valley on Saturday.

At any rate, it is now 1:15 and there is still no word. I am so hurt and frustrated right now about the whole situation and I just can't stop crying today. I am pissed at the police for not going to arrest him as I KNOW they know where to find him. It just isn't fair what they are doing and I don't know what to do. Actually, I do know what to do which is to call the police department and ask them myself why they haven't arrested him yet. They probably think this is some rinky-dink crime and that I'm just stupid, or maybe as my brother suggested, they are scared shitless to arrest him if he is a "pillar of the community". I don't care what the hell he is, but he is a criminal and there is an arrest warrant, so they should just do their job and arrest him. Right now I'm tempted to file some kind of charges against the police for "dragging their feet" or whatever that would be in legal terms!

I can just feel that he knows about the warrant and has known since either the first day, Monday or at the latest Tuesday. I think that he is holed up somewhere plotting what to do and that is the worst thing that can happen. I can't believe that he might have been given the "time" to figure things out! Who the hell knows where he is and the possibility of the police dragging their feet is so upsetting because it's just another invalidation. Like, so what this happened, they don't believe it or couldn't care less that it happened and that is just another type of victimization and it kills me.

This type of indifference is probably what scared me away from doing something in the first place and it is shocking to me that in this day and age of sexual abuse scandals all over the place, that the police are still indifferent to it. I noticed when I went on their website it was all men, except for one woman who is most likely the dispatcher. It's probably "The Good Ole Boys" mentality down there and that is invalidating, unprofessional and downright unfair. I know that I'm blasting the police but so what, at this point all I know is that they refused to send Detective Sharp the information he needed for 3 months. Now it seems like they are refusing to arrest Lesser...even with a signed warrant from a judge. Their ass is grass if anything happens.

For all I know, Lesser could be on his way up here to confront me or find me or something. They NEVER should have given him a heads up and even though I don't know that for a fact right now, I know in my wise mind (DBT) that they did.

It is now almost 5:00 p.m. and ANOTHER day has passed. Right now I am so angry that I can barely see straight. It is absolute BULLSHIT that they have had a warrant for 5 days and not arrested him as of yet. It is definitely the "good old boys" and Lesser is still in control at this point. Tomorrow when I talk with Detective Sharp, I hope I don't get too angry and outspoken with him, but I do think this is absolute bullshit and I want the State Police to arrest him. They don't give a shit who he is or what he does...or at least they shouldn't.

I KNOW that Lesser is holed up somewhere planning what to do and the fact that he got this "leeway" just absolutely burns me up. Someone down there might be looking at a lawsuit claiming dereliction of duty!!!!!!

I have to try and let this go for the day but at least I am now really pissed off instead of just sad. Anyone who knows me knows that you better not piss me off or someone is in big trouble. I am getting to that point.

Tomorrow's my birthday and I really don't feel like even acknowledging it. I don't think that I will even open any gifts or cards, because I don't feel like celebrating ANYTHING. I guess that I will celebrate my birthday this year when I feel like it.

I'm also not sure if Danny is coming home from vacation tonight and in some ways I hope he doesn't. I really don't want to have to talk to anyone, do anything for anyone or even have anyone's presence around. I really just want to be left alone. Now having said that, it would be nice to have another warm body in the house in case Lesser does show up or something. I guess I wouldn't mind if he came home as long as he didn't talk or even breathe for that matter. Isn't that mean? I really can't tolerate ANYTHING and that's why it's just better if I'm left alone.

I also can't promise that I won't call the police department, but I will certainly do my best not to.

It is getting harder and harder every day that goes by. I can't concentrate to drive and because the pharmacist couldn't fill one of my prescriptions, I almost burst into tears. It was for "butt cream" for God's sake! It was harder than hell to take Uva (Danny's mom) for her hair and errands and even she and Denise (my friend) could tell that I was way off today. I am just so pissed off and again, it just reinforces to me that the world is a shitty place and I really don't care about being in it anymore after this whole thing is done. Of course I have to wait until my parents pass, but after that…I'm done…and I mean it.

July 19, 2008 (Saturday)

It's my birthday today, but I don't feel like celebrating and in fact, I'm not going to…unless I hear that Lesser has been arrested. I truly can't think about anything or concentrate on anything. I really think that I am going to call the police department. It is within my right to call and ask what is happening and as long as it doesn't piss off Detective Sharp, there is no reason why I can't. I'll think about it some more. Detective Sharp is working today before heading off for the concert, so I am anxiously awaiting his call to hear that he has been arrested.

My heart is pounding out of my chest and there is nothing that I can do to stop my body from being high-strung. To say this is agonizing doesn't even begin to describe all of the emotions that are running through me, as each day arrives with yet no word.

I am now really worried that he has taken off and if that has happened, I am concerned on a whole new level. I wouldn't doubt that he might go to Canada or something to evade arrest and if that happens, I'm afraid that we will never catch him. He has so much to lose that it would only seem reasonable to run.

I am even beginning to question why God is allowing this wait to happen. God has brought us this far and maybe He is testing my faith, but to be honest, God is relying on Man to do His bidding and humans can't always be trusted. I must believe that there is a reason why this is taking so long, but for the life of me I don't know why. If God wants to bring me down to my knees for some reason, well that's already happened 3 days ago!

I'm also starting to entertain the idea that he really might try and hurt me. He might think that if he gets rid of me, then he gets rid of the problem; or he might be thinking that he's in deep shit already, so he might as well really get into trouble; or he might be so angry with me for ruining his life that he is going to get revenge. The last scenario makes the most sense to me.

The longer the time goes on today, the more totally dysregulated I am getting. I can't sit still and I feel like I'm going to throw up, so now I'm going to go clean the toilet.

Later:

Now I'm really pissed and Danny is sorry that he ever came home. I told him not to come home, as I don't want anyone around me or the hassle of dealing with someone else. Just him breathing is annoying me at this point and Mike (Danny's son-in-law) is now here. I am so pissed off!! Danny's other friend has already called as well and I can't stand anyone being here!!!! Danny told me that I could at least say hi to Mike which I refused to do and Mike left within a minute. Danny is now pissed off at me and all of this is just BULLSHIT. Now I have to apologize and I don't want to because I can't help what I am doing, thinking or feeling and that's why I don't want to be around anyone.

Later:

Well, now I've begun packing to go to NC myself, as at least I would feel like I'm doing SOMETHING and advocating for myself. Again, my fear is that we are too late and he is gone. Danny wouldn't have "let me" leave anyhow, but it felt good to at least pack.

It is all I can do to keep myself from calling the police department to find out what is happening. Maybe if they can put a voice to the person in the criminal complaint that might make them more sympathetic. I've got their phone number right here at my side and I am just shaking. I even have their names from off their website, so I could even personalize it further. This is absolutely KILLING ME!!

I just had a "light bulb" moment in that I think what is so upsetting to me is that I have no idea what is going on down there or what is going on with Detective Sharp. I have no CONTROL over what is happening and that is driving me to the point of insanity. I have had to leave my well-being and destiny in the hands of others, and so far that isn't turning out so well. It is 11:15 now and I am so upset that I truly am afraid that I am going to have a stroke or something. I need to go for a walk, but now Danny is gone (in a huff I might add) and I don't want to leave the phone in case Detective Sharp might call. On the other hand, I really feel like I'm going to have a heart attack or something. I drank another Ensure protein drink as it seems like that is all I can really manage to get down.

I also just had this thought which is I maybe need to simply let all of this go and trust in God. Even as I think that, I do feel a little bit of peace coming over me and it makes me also realize that I have NEVER had control over this whole process in the first place. God has had the control and I just need to trust that He is going to make everything ok. Maybe that is what it means to finally get down on my knees and give in. I swear, this is a constant battle within myself.

Just had a birthday call from David and I don't think that it went very well. He was rather surprised, I think, that I am as upset about this whole thing as I am. His words of what he thought were comfort were actually like blades of a knife stabbing into me. He told me to just forget about it and move on. To go out and celebrate my birthday and that there was nothing to gain by hanging out by the phone waiting for a phone call. I recognize that there is nothing to gain, but it is what it is and I can't help it. I felt that he was really invalidating and insensitive to the situation and that hurts. Again, I recognize that he just wants to point out the futility of what I am doing, but he also has to accept that this is just what I have to do.

July 20, 2008 (Sunday)

What a day it was yesterday! I was an absolute mess and was only able to pull it together after intense praying and going out to mow. Finally the lawnmower was working as Danny put the belt back on, and since mowing is calming to me, I went for it.

Of course in the meantime, Detective Sharp had called and left a message that he hadn't been arrested as of yet and that he wished he had happier news for me. What he didn't say in his message was that I couldn't call NC myself, and after thinking about the pros and cons of calling them directly I decided to do just that.

I screwed up my courage and called. The dispatcher told me that the warrants go to the sheriff's department and gave me their number. I then called there and talked to another dispatcher who said that he hadn't been arrested as of yet as his name wasn't on "the board". She also said that she would track down the warrant and have the police officer in charge of it give me a call. I really didn't expect a call back from them yesterday, so I was able to let that part go and enjoy watching the Disney movie "Freaky Friday". I actually laughed out loud for the first time since Mom had said that even if Lesser killed himself, he would still roast in hell, but just get there a little quicker!

This morning we watched our church program the "Hour Of Power" and then I made another call down to the sheriff's department. The woman I talked to yesterday was still there and she said that she had tracked down the warrant and she had been planning on calling me back today on what she found out, so she was glad that I called. That surprised me as I thought they would just blow me off.

She informed me that arrest warrants first go to their circuit court or clerk of courts or something and then they are forwarded on to the Sheriff's department. It has been sitting at the clerk of courts for all of last week!!! She said that she is having it transferred to the Sheriff's department on Monday or Tuesday at which time they would serve the warrant.

I shared with her that I was worried about a couple of things and one is that I am scared of the man. My other concern is that he is going to run due to the seriousness of the charges. She said that she didn't think he would run as he is a business owner and I told her I was praying that he wouldn't make that choice. She also made the comment that he is probably cocky and thinks that he can beat the charges. I told her that I was praying for that as well. She was very very nice and I take back all of the mean things that I said about them in the past...but we'll see what happens next week.

I really feel much better about things since calling down there as I feel like I have a little more control or at least a better understanding of what is going on. If what she said is true, then I don't think that he knows what is going on, which would be terrific to say the least. Not knowing what was going on down there was absolutely killing me so it was comforting to have been able to talk with someone from there who seemed like she was sincere and hopefully a kindred spirit.

So once again, it's wait. I did call Detective Sharp and left a message confessing that I had called down there and allegedly the warrant is still at the clerk's office. I do wonder however why the police told him that they had driven by his house when in actuality they allegedly didn't have the warrant in the first place?

Just got off the phone with Janet to tell her where everything is at and she is relieved as well. She also has been having all sorts of thoughts about what is going on. It's also funny because yesterday while mowing, I saw a car go by that I have never seen on this road before. In fact, it was a very jazzed up vehicle that might have been some type of Hummer, but I've never ever seen a vehicle like this. Of course I thought it might be Lesser because at that point, I didn't know that the police didn't even have the warrant. Janet said that she also had to look twice at some man as she thought that it might be him. It is so comforting to know that someone else is going through all of the same exact emotions and thoughts that I am. It also means that I'm not going crazy!!

HOPEFULLY the next time I write in this journal, it will be to report that they've got him in custody. I know I've said that before and it hasn't happened, but now I truly believe that we are getting closer and closer.

July 21, 2008 (Monday)

What a day it has been so far!! This morning Detective Sharp called me and after I apologized for calling down there, he informed me that they had totally lied to me. He said that last week he had been in contact with this particular detective and that they had been teletyping to each other all last week, so what that woman had told me wasn't true at all!

Detective Sharp sounded angry on the phone at them for lying to me and of course I burst into tears. I can't believe that of all people, the police, would flat out lie to me. However, after thinking about it for a while and receiving some input from others, it may be that the woman I talked with actually didn't know anything and had been kept out of the loop herself. At any rate, Detective Sharp has called the NC State Police and they will go right away and serve the warrant. Unbelievable!!

Then came another phone call from Detective Sharp telling me that he had found out some more information and that actually, Lesser is currently considered a fugitive! Can this get any wilder? It is my understanding that the sheriff had called Lesser while he was on the road for work and told him about the arrest warrant. As a result, Lesser had decided to stay away from home although he did say that he would turn himself in on Thursday. Thursday came and Lesser called and said that he had to go to Georgia on business and therefore wouldn't be there to turn himself in, but he would now on Saturday. Saturday morning came and Lesser's wife Mary called and said that Lesser had decided to actually come to Wisconsin to turn himself in. He allegedly wanted to do this because all the arrests down there are published in the paper and if that happened, their business, which is a family friendly vacation resort, would be ruined. (Oh well!)

Well, here it is Monday and so far he hasn't turned himself in. Detective Sharp informed me that he is now considered a fugitive and that has "upped the ante" so to speak. No one knows where he is at this point and Detective Sharp said that he would call the sheriff's department in my area to inform them to keep an eye on me. I also told Detective Sharp that we already had a loaded gun in the house and although I don't know how to use it, my boyfriend is an excellent shot!

Of course I called Mom and Dad, Richard, David and Janet to tell the news at various points.

Later:

Now, I just got a call from Evelyn stating that the court had received an e-mail from Lesser's attorney and that tomorrow, Tuesday, at 1:00 p.m. he will turn himself in. I am invited to come to court for this initial appearance and I am seriously thinking about it. Of course Mom and Dad as well as Richard are totally opposed to the idea, but my wise mind tells me that I have to go.

I have to see his face, see him in handcuffs and have him see me. This is between no one but him and me, and I need to be able to face him. I have to show him that he isn't going to intimidate me anymore in life and that I am a strong and capable woman.

I think that it would also be important for DA Koss, the judge and Detective Sharp to finally meet me and put a face to the name that has been bugging them forever! I also want them to know that I appreciate everything that they have done for me and to know that I am going to fight as hard for myself as they did.

To say that tomorrow is going to be difficult doesn't even begin to describe it. In fact, I just threw up now due to the anxiety about tomorrow.

The next thing I did was to call my parents to inform them of my decision to go. Previously when I had mentioned going they about had a cow, but after I explained what I wanted/needed to do, they were all for it. They have been supportive of anything I've wanted/needed to do with this case and they expressed that they were only upset because of what it might do to me. Again, after explaining it, they totally understand and are behind me 110%!!!

Maybe I better finish that Victim Impact Statement today so as I have it tomorrow. Ugh!!

CHAPTER 20

The Day of Deliverance

July 22, 2008 (Tuesday)

Today is finally the day that hopefully I am going to face Lesser once again, although this time, it will be on MY terms. Surprisingly, I'm not a complete nervous wreck, or at least not yet.

What is interesting about this case is that the charges have been filed in juvenile/youth court, so I am treated as if I am a juvenile. The court proceeding for today is called an initial appearance. Of course I had to look it up on the Internet to see what happens at this hearing. An initial appearance is where he has to appear in court and he is told what the charges are.

This morning I finished my Victim Impact Statement and actually read it to Danny. This was the first time that I have EVER shared with ANYONE all the ways that this has disrupted and screwed up my life. I am thankful that he didn't critique it or have any major reaction to it as some of it, especially the part about my sexual hang-ups, must have been hard to listen to.

I wanted to know what he thought and he couldn't really articulate his feelings except that it was helpful to him in understanding more about what's in my head. That is what I'm afraid of, that people will finally know how screwed up I really am in the end. Then their next question would be, "And she's a therapist?!"

I think that one of the reasons that I'm not as upset as maybe as I should be is that I'm trying to look at this as a therapist and with reasonable mind (DBT). Reasonable mind is looking at it from a factual basis only, without the emotions attached. Another reason I'm not too upset is that Lesser has finally been pulled into this "game", something I thought would never happen. His first move was smart in that he decided to keep it all up here, just like Richard said.

My next move is to go to court to show all of them that I am committed to this process. I want to put my best foot forward and make a good impression on the judge and DA and all, so I've been thinking about all aspects of this. I am even thinking about what to wear. I would like to wear these black and white crop pants, but the top that I have to go with it tends to drape down too far and I definitely don't want anything revealing. I have decided to wear my Kathy Lee Gifford dress, the animal print one. It is a shapeless shift so to speak that covers me from head to toe, an outfit that is pretty and one that I feel comfortable and confident in.

I'm not sure what is going to happen today, but the more I write in this journal, the more anxious I'm becoming, so I am going to close for now. Pray for me journal!

I am currently ready to leave and had a few minutes, so I thought I would put some more thoughts into the journal. I am wondering what it will be like to see him and quite honestly, to see if I do have some type of feelings for him. Some people have been asking me if I was in love with him or did I care about him, and I don't think I was either. Seeing him should answer those questions. I am so conflicted as to what I will feel, what my thoughts will be or if I feel pity for him. I also wonder if he is as charming, handsome and witty as he was back then, but then again, that was all a façade and a means to get what he wanted.

I am shaky, but determined to pull this off today with the least amount of dysregulation. I might even throw in a load of laundry just for normalcy and to work off some of my nervous energy that I have. Yesterday I channeled that into cleaning the house.

Just saw the state patrol go by the house and it is comforting to know that they are keeping an eye on me. Of course if could just be one of the state police officers that live on my road going home, but I never see him going in the direction that he was.

I think that I am emotionally, mentally and physically ready for this…but I'm bringing a barf bag just in case!

Later:

I'm home!!!!!!!

It really couldn't have gone any better than in did in many ways. I of course was early to the courthouse, as is my nature, and I pulled into a parking spot to finish my cigarette. While sitting there, I saw two men walking towards the parking lot from the courthouse and beginning to walk in front of me. I knew right away that one of them was Lesser and I just watched him walk to the car. I can't really describe my feelings or thoughts, except that I thought immediately that he looked old and like shit. My stomach did "drop" like when you're on a roller coaster, but I was surprisingly calm on the outside. I just kept watching him, as he wasn't aware of me yet.

I didn't feel any "love" towards him, nor hate just a sick stomach. It was so weird to be looking at this "boogey man" who I haven't seen in over 33+ years, that it was kind of surreal.

I could tell that he was scanning the parking lot and his eyes rested on me for a moment while I was still sitting in my car. He scanned back to me later as I think he

111

finally knew that it was I in the car. There was another guy with him who didn't look like his attorney and then they both got in the car and began to pull out. That is when I got out of my car so that at least Lesser could see me once in case he decided to take off. I even raised my hand in acknowledgment to him when they drove past me. I couldn't believe I did that, as I didn't want him to think that I was "waving" at him, but rather my intent was for him to KNOW that I was here and he did.

I then went into the courthouse, went to the DA's office and told them who I was. I then left the office to find the courtroom but remembered that I hadn't included something on the Victim Impact Statement, so I went back down to the district attorney's office. The secretary said that DA Koss wanted to speak with me and would I wait for him. I met him and we went into a room to talk. It was great to finally meet him and we talked about what will happen today and then the next step, which is the preliminary hearing. DA Koss and I talked some more and I explained how I found Janet and the process that I went through to find other possible victims. I asked about when Janet should come and he said that she should come for the trial.

He then asked me some more personal questions, probably to get to know me better and did say that I've had quite a life. I also wanted to bring up to him a couple of issues, with one being that some of the things in the criminal complaint weren't correct. The other thing I had to tell him was that the attorney who is representing Lesser was the attorney who represented someone that Danny and I knew and as a result, Danny knew his attorney!!! I wasn't sure if that might pose a problem in the future and I wanted to get it out on the table right away.

I didn't tell DA Koss who the client was that Lesser's attorney had previously represented until he asked. At that point I said that I was afraid to tell him as he might think that I'm nasty myself for knowing such a "criminal" and one that has been a pain in the ass for DA Koss and Walworth County. I then broke down and told him Pete B. and that I didn't KNOW him, but that he had worked for Danny. DA Koss then asked for my boyfriend's name and when I told him, he knew it immediately. Thankfully, all he did was laugh and say that it is certainly a small world. I tried to explain that I really don't know Pete, but that we do write letters. DA Koss then told me that Pete writes him letters as well and that he actually enjoys getting the letters from him.

It was then time to go up to the courtroom and he said that he would escort me up, although I didn't feel the need for him to do that. He did it anyway and actually, I'm glad that he did. I then went into the courtroom by myself and Lesser was sitting there looking scared to death. He has the biggest bags under his eyes, like he hasn't slept in forever, but then again, maybe he hasn't since he's been "on the run" for a week. His eyes were red and they kept darting around the courtroom. He looked absolutely petrified, where I was calm, cool and collected. Of course that could have been a result of the Lorazepam that I had taken, but I actually enjoy courtrooms as I find the cases fascinating and interesting to watch. There were others in the courtroom for their appearances, so there were quite a few "normal" people in there as well.

DA Koss then came into the courtroom and pulled me out, as he wanted to introduce me to Detective Sharp. Detective Sharp put out his hand, but I asked if I could give him a hug, and that's what I did! It wasn't long after meeting Detective Sharp that DA Koss said to him, "can you guess who she knows" to which he replied that he couldn't.

Meanwhile I'm freaking out and said that now everyone is going to know and that they are going to hate me because I know this person. I said Pete B. to which DA Koss said, AKA Larry P.? Detective Sharp's eyes just about bugged out of his head and again, I felt the need to explain that I didn't really KNOW him, but that he had worked for Danny. Detective Sharp also knew Danny's name right away and again, we all had to laugh. This was all weird to say the least!

While we were waiting for our case to be called, we all sat around outside the court talking amongst ourselves, them talking about other cases and the like. I felt a sense of camaraderie with DA Koss and Detective Sharp not only professionally, but personally as well.

While were in the hall talking, an officer came out of the courtroom and said that it was Lesser's turn and when we went in, he was already in fact in the defense chair. I didn't hear his plea, if he even entered one at this point, but they talked about a no-contact clause with me, the cost of his bail, which was $25,000 and the preliminary trial was set up. I think it was neat in that when we went into the courtroom, Detective Sharp sat on the bench in front of me while DA Koss sat on one side of me and Evelyn on the other. It was like they were my protection and from now on, I'm calling them my 'WINGMEN".

The charges were read in open court, so all the "normal" people could hear what Lesser was there for, and he looked miserable sitting at the table. I felt justice on one hand, but also felt a little compassion for Lesser as well. He looks so rough and I really am not the type of person to destroy someone else, so I have mixed feelings. A date for a preliminary hearing was set for August 27, 2009.

Lesser then had to leave to get booked and fingerprinted as well as to post a bond! FINALLY!!! DA Koss and Detective Sharp made me wait until he was out of the courtroom before they were going to let me go. Lesser however stopped outside of the courtroom to ask his attorney something and DA Koss and Detective Sharp made me wait again until he had gone down the hall. I really felt protected by both of them and the fact that I felt such a sense of comfort and compassion from their side means more to me than anything.

The court proceedings were over fairly quickly, I talked briefly with DA Koss again and then I went out to my car to call my parents, Richard, David and Janet.

They are all elated that this part is over and Janet hit it right on the nail when she said that she is personally torn over seeing him burn in hell, and then patting him on the back and assuring him it will be ok. That is exactly the way that I am feeling at this point. I want him to suffer and the fact that he is is bringing me comfort, but at the same time, I know how much it hurts to be terrified and not in control and it doesn't feel very good. That is another perfect example of a "dialectic".

What I find most interesting about seeing him again after all of these years is that it feels like the "boogey" has now been taken out of the "boogey man". He seemed like a tired, old, beaten down man, not the man who I remember at all. That alone is a huge comfort to me.

I'll bet he beats a fast retreat out of Wisconsin! My mom and dad ran him out of Wisconsin years ago and now I ran him out of Wisconsin. I bet he rues the day that he ever moved to our state.

This has been quite a day and I decided to buy steaks and celebrate. I'm not celebrating his demise so to speak, but I am celebrating the fact that I'm finally seeing justice done by letting him know that what he did isn't ok!

July 23, 2008 (Wednesday)

Needless to say, I'm exhausted today and woke up only to puke. Par for the course as that is usually the way that I work. I am still feeling anxious for some reason; my heart is pounding, I have a nervous energy, my stomach is upset and it seems like nothing has changed.

Yesterday and all last night, I couldn't help but to keep replaying in my head all of the things that happened yesterday. I couldn't stop thinking about everything and even this morning upon waking, I began thinking about everything again.

I am feeling very depressed today because in all honesty, I feel badly for what is going to happen to Lesser's life now. It is just a shame that now at least three lives have been destroyed by his actions; mine, Janet's and his. I keep seeing his face and how terrified he was and while I do gain some satisfaction from that, I can't help but also feel physically sick about bringing such misery onto another human being. My "wise mind" tells me that what he did was inexcusable and that he deserves whatever is going to happen to him. Wise mind says that whatever happens to him is "justice" considering what Janet and I have gone through for most of our lives. But again, I'm fighting my "emotional mind" that feels very badly for what is going to happen in his life.

I'm crying off and on this morning and feel really sad for everyone and everything. I have to pull it together however as I HAVE to get some paperwork done and I have to attend a "Hat Party" for a friend of mine who is battling cancer. It's a neat idea, but I really don't feel up to being upbeat and positive. But then I think about what she is going through and that she is possibly facing the end of her life, comparatively, my issues just don't seem that important.

I did however go on the Internet to find out what happens in a "preliminary hearing" and it is where the judge will listen to the evidence already collected and decide if there is enough evidence against Lesser to then have a trial. I am sure that I will have to testify and though that is scary, I have to prove to the judge that something did happen and that we need to keep this case going. As scary as testifying might be, this is part of the "game" and I am ready for the next "move". I have been waiting for a long time to get him in a courtroom and I am more than ready to continue entangling him in my web!! Ha Ha.

CHAPTER 21

System Overload

July 25, 2008 (Friday)

Finally went back to work today and I wish I hadn't. I still don't want to work as I just don't have the emotional and intellectual energy, but I had to as I hadn't seen many of my clients in a long time and they needed to be seen.

What I didn't expect was that my first appointment was going to turn out the way it did.

I was checking my messages right before my 10:00 and on my voice mail was my 10:00 appointment's mother in tears and obviously in crisis. Her son had been accused of molesting another boy. I am sick about this whole thing as I adore the boy as well as his entire family and it's not in his character to do that. He did say that another boy had done the same thing to him a long time ago, but still, it's wrong.

That awful news set the tone for the day and the rest of the clients weren't any easier. I have a client who is fairly new to me and she is currently suicidal. I don't know her that well yet, so I'm not sure how much I can "push her", but she is the type of person that will do "it" if she decides to. Therefore I ended up in a fairly long conversation with her case worker to not only express my concern, but also to let her know that she will have to keep an extra eye on her while I'm busy with my "own stuff".

By the time I got home, I was glad to be there. I did however "blast" Danny and his friend Craig, who was over working on the Blazer, about men, their dicks and why can't they just keep them to themselves.

I've also been thinking about Lesser quite a bit and what might happen with the case. Due to the way that he looked on Tuesday, I think that he might just plead guilty and plea-bargain the whole thing. He looked so scared, that I think he might simply want this to be over with, but I guess we'll see in 4 weeks. He might come back all "refreshed" and ready for a fight, or he might come back with his tail between his legs. Either way, I am curious to see what his next move is going to be.

Janet then called last night to see how I was doing and that was so thoughtful and nice of her. She is such a wonderful person and it really pisses me off how badly he hurt her. We both talked about wanting him to fry, but then again, our compassionate and merciful side doesn't want that to happen. It is so weird how we are mirroring each other on this whole thing, which tells me that we are a lot alike in many ways. She was also fairly upset herself thinking about this whole thing and how the molestation has ruined much of her life. She talked about wanting to send him a letter about the ways that he had hurt her, and I encouraged her to do that. I also told her that I had one of my L.A. Cards that I wrote specifically for Lesser that says, "Why did you do what you did to me?" I will send that to her so that she can do what she wants with it.

We also talked about her coming up for the preliminary hearing as she really needs to "see" him and if they decide to plea bargain, she is afraid that she won't ever have the chance. I do know that it was helpful for me to see him, as he was so pathetic looking that I really felt like I was in control now. I keep seeing his face in my mind and how terrified and shattered he seemed to be, and that is definitely a new picture for me. The only picture I've had for the past 33+ years is the image of him in my rear view mirror as I drove away from him for the last time.

It was now time to write a letter to be sent to all of my friends and Danny's family explaining what is currently going on. I did so and with some apprehension of how people were going to take this news, I sent if off. Fortunately everyone that has e-mailed me back has been supportive, concerned, loving and offering their assistance in any way that I need.

July 28, 2008 (Monday)

It's Monday and back to work for me. The weekend was rather rough in a number of ways, but at least on Friday I got to see my parents! I finally felt like meeting them for my birthday lunch and it was so comforting for me to see them. They think that I look good, that my spirits are good and for the most part, they are.

I also went to my doctor on Friday because I've been having difficulty with breathing and I wanted a prescription for some other type of "chill pill". I don't think the Lorazepam will be helpful in keeping my nerves down during the trial. Of course I had to finally tell her what was going on in my life and I was bummed that I started to cry while telling her.

Dr. K. and I have a weird relationship in that it seems we argue about things. She is a no-nonsense type of doctor and I guess I'm not easy as a patient as I have my own beliefs about what is wrong and what she should do for treatment. I had a chest X-ray and though I don't have pneumonia, I do have some type of lung problem and she put me on antibiotics. I didn't ask what I had as that would be too overwhelming. I know that I have been smoking A LOT lately, so that isn't helping either.

The rest of the weekend was spent mowing and doing paperwork that I haven't gotten to in the past couple of weeks. I also had to prepare to go to court today for my kid client who offended on another boy. They did pull my client from the home and he is currently in JRC or kiddie jail as we call it. I'm still just sick about the whole thing and ended up talking with his mother a couple of times this weekend as well as with a detective from the Dane County Sheriff's Department. When that detective called, I had to stop and think for a minute about whether this was my case, or his case. This is awful to say the least.

It does feel good to be somewhat back to normal in that I'm going to work and not thinking every minute about whether or not Lesser will be arrested. At least that part is over and that was a huge part. It's still difficult as my body and mind are anxious, but I HAVE to get back to reality not only for my own mental health, but for my clients who have suffered as well.

I also received more supportive e-mails over the weekend, but probably the most important one was from Hans, my old co-worker. I had talked with him about this dialectic of feeling sorry in a way for Lesser, but wanting him to fry as well. Hans's response back was to tell me that the phrase is "justice tempered with mercy, not the other way around". He knows what a bleeding heart I am and that it is not in my nature to hurt anyone, so it was good to have him tell me that mercy is ok, but justice should come first. He is so wise and I forwarded that e-mail on to Janet, as she seems to feel the same way that I do. That phrase might be a good name for this book as I have to remember that justice needs to be met FIRST and then we'll see about the mercy part. Mercy will depend on how he "behaves" through this whole thing.

July 30, 2008 (Wednesday)

Thankfully I was home from work today because the story finally hit the newspaper. It is fairly graphic in nature and tells the number of times we had sex and the different places that it happened. To say that I am ashamed doesn't even begin to describe what I'm feeling. What is worse, is that in the article it mentions that "the woman told her mother after the family moved to Iran in 1976". Well, there are only two families in the whole entire community that went to Iran and one is the Vold's and the other is my family. Therefore either people are going to believe that it's Sarah, Kirsten or me, so I have put in a call to warn them that people might think it was one of them.

I also faxed the article to Janet as I wanted her to see his mug shot, but she didn't get a good copy. She said that she called the newspaper to find out how to get it online and it won't be up until tomorrow.

Before getting the article from Dad, he read it to me over the phone. It's hard for me to write about my father having to read this nasty and descriptive article to me and I know that it just broke his heart to read that stuff. I felt so ashamed to have my father read about my sexual relations with Lesser and his voice did crack a couple of times while reading.

Mom is having lunch with her childhood friend Mary, so Dad and I talked about how to present it to her. She is going to be extremely upset about the article and we talked about whether we should wait until she got home to read it, or bring it to her when he picks her up. I said bring it with, along with her bottle of Lorazepam, but I am really scared about how she is going to take it. I'm waiting now for them to call and although I've broken down in tears numerous times already today, I HAVE to keep it together for when my mother calls. If she thinks that I am upset, then she WILL get upset and I can't have that happen. If anything happens to her or dad or the rest of my family including Danny through this process, I will be really pissed off. I'm so nervous waiting for them to call and all I want to do is go outside to my "spot" on top of the hill and cry and cry. I am so embarrassed for my family.

I called Richard and told him about the article and then faxed the copy that Dad had made and faxed me. He is leaving tomorrow for the annual trip to Ely, which I would love to be going on. My biggest worry is that now my brother's and my parent's friends and acquaintances are going to know it was our family and therefore I am going to embarrass and humiliate my family. Richard assured me that he didn't care what people thought about him or our family and not to worry about him being embarrassed. That was so nice of him and meant a lot to me.

I also called and left David a message.

Right now, this is awful. Publicity like this is one reason that victims don't want to step forward. It is absolutely humiliating and maybe even more so because so many people are now going to know that it was me and in such a small town, that is going to spread like wildfire. I am so embarrassed that my family name has to be dragged into this.

All I can do right now is pray that God will comfort my parents and the rest of my family as this isn't going to get any easier.

Just got off the phone with Mom and she is doing very well in fact! She is THRILLED that she gets to look at his mug shot from now until she doesn't want to anymore. I told her that this was her "Christmas present, birthday present, Mother's Day present and all of the presents wrapped into one! She is certainly being a trooper. I'm just sorry that it hit my dad so badly.

I'm done for the day.

July 31, 2008 (Thursday)

I haven't talked much about how this whole thing is affecting Danny, but last night ended up not being very good. When he finally read the article, I don't think that he was too happy and whether or not he realized it, he basically invalidated everything. His comment was something along the lines of "I didn't know that you had sex that many times and you must of liked it because you kept going back". That statement was a dagger to my heart but it just shows me once again that people will think that, but to have my boyfriend say it was just plain hurtful. I was absolutely crushed and of course first I blew up at him and after that, I burst into tears.

His stupid ass comment did start me thinking however, just like when he asked the stupid question of how this experience had affected my life. That stupid question led to me writing down everything and then turning that in for the Victim Impact Statement. A very powerful Victim's Impact Statement I might add, so he was helpful to me in a weird way.

As I began thinking about his comment and why it did keep happening, all of the reasons began filling my head. His question also made me begin thinking about how the defense is going to ask the same thing as well as a lot of other questions. All I can say is that if someone hasn't experienced sexual abuse, they really can't understand the control that the other person has over you. It's not as easy as people think to get away and tell someone what is happening.

I'm also wondering whether his attorney might hire a private investigator to begin investigating my past and present. They might say if I was so unhappy from being abused, why did I look happy in school photos and was successful in high school. I was prom queen, voted for Harvard Milk Day queen and was the female athlete of the year. The defense could say that I must not have been too upset because of all of my high school achievements. The reality is, I didn't have a hand in any of that. It was the students who voted for all of those things, except for the athletic award, so I had no control over those things.

As a result of all this obsessive thinking, I thought it would be important to write down ALL of the questions that I think DA Koss will ask me and include my answers to all of those questions. I also thought of ALL of the questions that Lesser's attorney will ask and I wrote up answers to all of those as well. I thought I did a good job writing all of this up and I have to thank Danny for that, as he was the impetus to get me thinking about the next moves in this "game".

I'm afraid that this whole thing is going to tear apart Danny's and my relationship because when I went to bed last night, it was pretty much decided that we were going to break up after this is over. Now, we have said that before to each other and regardless of whether we do or don't break up, I really do have to stay at least another 6 months or until this is over before I can move.

Hopefully, this too shall pass. Since being together for 24 years, we have decided to split quite a few times, but then stronger heads prevail and we stick together. I hope that that continues to be the path this time. I do however feel that this whole experience is going to drastically change my life and I don't know what will happen to our relationship as a result of these changes.

I already want to quit being a therapist, because I don't want to deal with all of this stress anymore. I've got a full day today and I'm just regretting that I have to go to work, but I have to keep money coming in. This is just so difficult on so many levels right now and I find it difficult to do anything at this point.

Pray that I make it through the day and am able to provide my clients with the emotional support and direction that they need.

Once again, today I feel like I just want to finish up with this world.

August 1, 2008 (Friday)

It's been a difficult week and probably the most upsetting thing this week was the newspaper article and the fact that it completely "outed" me. I continue to feel embarrassed and ashamed because so many people know "my business". I think about my friend's parents knowing about this, the people at the bank, people from church, teachers, my dentist, professors and everyone else who knows me. I can't begin to describe how painful this part of the process is.

I am such a private person in regards to sex and my sexuality (or lack of) and to suddenly have the whole community know about my past sexual abuse and activity is just too much to bear.

After thinking about this for a couple of days, I decided to call Dan at the Lake Geneva Regional Times, as he was the reporter. I did this for a couple of reasons. One is that I wanted to make him aware that the one piece about the family moving to Iran was huge in that it identified to the readers who I was. To move to Iran in the 70's was so foreign to Americans at that time, that it was big news in the community when we went.

I told him that my parents have been getting calls about this and I am getting e-mails from people asking me how to get the article. I also wanted to make him aware for future articles about other victims, to be cautious about what he writes as something that seems innocuous, might reveal a person's identity.

Dan felt badly that the information about Iran gave me up to people, so I am thankful that he could understand how this might affect me. I wasn't angry with him or anything, just concerned for "the next person".

We also talked about the publicity piece and that he had covered the McGuire case extensively. He asked me if I was I going to use my name and I told him that at this point I wasn't sure. I was however a psychotherapist and if I decide that revealing my name is helpful in some way to others, then maybe I'll do it. He also talked about the fact that this is going to be a long process and that with the McGuire case there were numerous other newspapers involved. I told him that that might happen with this case, as Youth For Christ/Campus Life is an international organization with a good reputation.

After talking with Dan, I finally had the emotional meltdown that had been building inside since that article came out. I just sobbed and sobbed due to my feelings of embarrassment, being ashamed, humiliated and extremely vulnerable to people right now. I am just crushed as a person that this has come out and that people know that I had sex and how many times and where. It was finally just too overwhelming.

I also broke down with Danny, as he doesn't show any emotion whatsoever or say kind supportive words. But in all fairness, I really don't think he knows what to say to me. He is a very private person and to have this type of "business" spread around about his girlfriend has to be embarrassing to him as well.

After our big blow-up the other day, this is just another possible "cut" to our relationship as I feel that he is ashamed and disgusted by me now. He says no, but there isn't a tone of warmth in his voice and that is of huge concern to me. I truly hope this case doesn't tear us apart, but if it does, then that was meant to happen.

I also for the first time since this started, went to Danny and wanted a hug. This whole time I have been trying to deal with this in private and not let anyone see how dysregulated I get. Showing people that I am upset embarrasses me, as I don't feel that others don't need to be exposed to "my drama" so to speak.

So for me to just hug Danny and sob, was a big step in letting him know how upset I am today and that I truly feel sorry for how this is emotionally and mentally affecting his life. Having said that, it is still me that has to deal with the brunt of it all and I ended up just sitting alone up in my bedroom sobbing.

I have to work out this pain, humiliation, shame and guilt. I knew that I would be affected somehow when others who aren't close to me find out but it seems the worst part is knowing that everyone else knows that it is me. I worry about the good name that I have always had in the community. Are people now going to think that I am a slut, or I must have liked it and why didn't I kick him to the curb? I realize that I can't control what people think, but knowing that there are some out there, who are thinking this way, just cuts me even deeper. Even a co-worker at my clinic actually said to me "that I must have enjoyed it or liked him or something because I kept going back to him"! And she's a therapist!

As far as possible future publicity, once I get over the trauma of this newspaper article, I don't think other newspaper articles will be anywhere near as devastating or have such a great impact on me. I don't care about people who have no idea who I am knowing what happened because I don't care about them. It's the people that do know me from childhood to adulthood that I was worried about and now they know. I'm sure I'll get over this, but it is rather painful and it's a deep, deep cut to my core. Those kinds of cuts don't ever heal.

OK, here comes my Pollyanna and that is that at least it is now out there so that's one less thing that I have to worry about as it already has happened. Now it's just dealing with it.

It is also another move in this "game" and that is understanding the media and what the possibilities are in regards to what they are going to print in the future. I want the reporters to take a kinder and softer approach, as it is so embarrassing to have all of this in print.

It's been an emotionally exhausting week, but I need to prepare myself, as that will most likely be the norm for the rest of this whole ordeal. I honestly thought that it would get easier in regards to my emotional and mental state once he was arrested, but that isn't turning out to be happening.

CHAPTER 22

It Doesn't Get Any Easier

August 7, 2008 (Thursday)

Today I called the DA's office as required to set up a date to talk with DA Koss before the preliminary hearing. I found out that not only is he on vacation for the next 2 weeks, Detective Sharp is on vacation next week as is Evelyn! I feel abandoned!! I just hope that DA Koss is ready as he gets back on Monday and the preliminary hearing is on Wednesday.

I talked with Evelyn for quite a while asking her the many questions that I had. Some of them included could I keep talking with Janet; could Lesser hire a private investigator (which he can); the newspaper article; why I am appearing in court alone; and how I adored DA Koss and Detective Sharp

I also told her that I have been putting together a packet of information for DA Koss that includes how he got so involved in my life; why I didn't tell; how I finally got rid of him; things like that and at the end, she complimented me on my courage in this whole process. This process is difficult to say the least, but to have her say that was extremely validating.

Janet also called last night as she had received the newspaper that my dad had sent to her. She decided that she isn't going to come for the preliminary hearing because what she had wanted/needed was to "see him" and that was accomplished with his mug shot in the newspaper. She is getting scared about everything and wondering if she was at fault because she stayed with him all those years. I think she also feels guilty because she was in love with him and did consider it to be a relationship. What she has to know, is that he cultivated that "love" and "sense of relationship" to continue to molest her.

I suggested that she begin putting together her timeline so that when she is in court, she will know dates and the like. I told her to just write down everything that she remembered and to even put it on a calendar. I think it is important that she do that not only to prepare herself for her testimony, but also to see how involved he was in her life.

It was while I was putting together a calendar of all the activities and events that occurred during the time he was here, that it really hit home about how much he had insinuated himself into my life and that I was no match for this guy whatsoever. He so invaded my entire life, that I had no chance from the beginning. This realization not only really pisses me off, but also makes me that much more sad. I was just a kid for God's sake and no match for this sexual predator that came into my world. Janet needs to see that she also had no chance; no matter how long she stayed with him nor what she felt for him. He was a lowdown jerk and that's all there is to it.

Another emotional day to say the least and now its just hurry up and wait to see what happens on the 27th. I am prepared however.

August 19, 2008 (Tuesday)

One week and one day until the "next move" and I am so not sure what is going to happen.

Emotionally I continue to be on a roller coaster with some days better than others. Now I have to have another root canal, so on Monday instead of talking with DA Koss on the phone, I'm going to go see him and then have the root canal.

I am so tired right now and it is SO DIFFICULT to give anyone anything. Working is just anguish as I don't have the emotional energy necessary for them. Maybe it is more patience that I don't have right now and that normally doesn't bode well for my clients or anyone else. It is then that I usually will challenge my clients to do better in life and to suck it up so to speak. I am also going to be taking next week off, so I have to make sure that they will be ok after pushing them.

It's all I can do right now to emotionally take care of my parents, Danny, Janet and my clients, let alone myself. This past weekend I had to go to Danny's 40th class reunion and it was difficult to "be up" for the event. The next day we went over to the Mississippi boating, which was calming thank goodness. The river seems to be a little cleaner after all the flooding and crap that had gone into it this spring with all our rain, so I finally went swimming in it. I love to swim and for me, that is calming. Again, utilizing distress tolerance skills so that I can be refreshed for the next week!

August 21, 2008 (Thursday)

My patience level has been nil lately and I ended up yelling at my last teenage client as he was just being obnoxious and annoying…in other words…a teenager! Yes, therapists, or at least this one, have on occasion yelled at my clients. I did apologize however! It's funny in that he and I have "fired" each other a couple of times, but we have been together for 3 years and we actually have a great bond.

When I got home, Danny told me that Janet had called, so I called her back. She was just checking up on me and to tell me about a great "Christian" book that she had read. The book is called "The Shack" and it's by William Young. She was really excited about what was in it but she didn't want to tell me too much about it. She encouraged me to read it at some point and I told her that I might, but that right now, I didn't feel like reading something like that. I promised her I would look for it after this situation with Lesser has been resolved. The next day however when I was at Wal-Mart, there was the book right in front of me! I actually laughed out loud as that was obviously a sign from God that I should get the book and I did.

I just finished it last night and it really is a terrific book. I am going to get it for some of my clients. It's hard to describe what the book is about, but it is a conversation with God, Jesus and the Holy Spirit where they explain their intentions for the human race and it's not for people to hurt each other! It is really uplifting and deep to say the least. I will have to reread it at some point.

August 24, 2008 (Sunday)

It's a beautiful morning in Wisconsin with cool air and the sun shining. It feels more like September than August and that is fine with me. It hasn't been really hot this summer; in fact we haven't even had a day when it hit 90 degrees. The cool mornings and evenings are fine with me and since September and October are two of my favorite months, I'm looking forward to the weather.

It's been a long emotional week, but then again, what's new. Danny has been out of town since Wednesday helping Charlie with his cabin up north. It's actually been nice that he has been gone because I continue to be annoyed by everyone and everything and he bears the brunt of that frustration. Even driving is anxiety producing, as it seems like every idiot is out on the road when I am.

Once again I have to utilize distress tolerance skills in order to regulate my emotional and mental state, so I put that nervous energy to work in my house. I decided to finally clean out the closet that holds all of the cleaning stuff as well as other things. I then used Murphy's Oil on all of the wood furniture upstairs as well as started getting clothes around for St. Vincent De Paul. After that, I went out and mowed, which was another 3½ hours, but at least the belt didn't come off this time. Even after all of that, I still had all of this energy but at least emotionally I was a bit calmer.

Saturday I spent running errands and doing laundry but when I got home there was a message from my best friend Lisa and she was crying. I quickly called her back, but she wasn't answering. She didn't call me back until about 2-3 hours after I left numerous messages and her news wasn't good. It turns out she has lung cancer! I am just sick about this, as it seems that Lisa has had every bad break in life that you can get and that just isn't fair. She always has tried to do the right thing in life and she has a good soul, so I don't understand why everything happens to her.

We talked for quite a while and cried together. I can't imagine this world without Lisa in it. We've always promised each other we would retire to Jamaica when we're old and feeble. We'll live on the beach and sit in the slated beach chairs and since we'll probably be incontinent, we'll just pee through the slats and keep moving the chairs down the beach. What terribly sad news today.

Danny should be home early this afternoon and though I'm looking forward to having him here, I'm also such a raw bundle of emotions, especially with this news about Lisa; I hope that I can tolerate him. Nothing against him, I just am having difficulty tolerating anyone right now.

Tomorrow is the day that I meet with DA Koss and then go for a root canal. I thought I might as well get two nasty things done with all in one day. I have also been working on "his defense" for this case. I am such a nerd, that I literally wrote up every point that could be covered by either side as well as a rebuttal against what the defense might say. Since DA Koss has been on vacation for the last two weeks, he might like the help. I have worked hard to provide DA Koss with every strategy for the case that I can think of. I have to finish that information and I would like to do it before Danny comes home so I don't have the distraction or annoyance!

If I don't get back to you today, I will most certainly write what happens tomorrow.

August 25, 2008 (Monday)

The meeting with DA Koss went well as I had already pulled together so much information all I had to do was give it to him. The bummer part is that he said the trial probably wouldn't happen until February 2009! He has to try another case that involves a baby who was shaken to death and that is in December. He wants to have the time and attention to devote to my case, so he is going to have my trial wait. I am so depressed about that and can't quite process my disappointment yet. I so want this to be over with but it seems to keep going on forever. Then of course I feel guilty for thinking of myself instead of for the family of this dead baby. The legal process is sure turning out to be an emotional tug-of-war.

The other worry I have is that I have to stay safe until the trial. I again expressed my concern to DA Koss about Lesser trying to do "something" to me, because as DA Koss and Detective Sharp and I talked about, if I'm "not around", then this whole thing goes away. DA Koss believes that the time to worry about him possibly doing "something" to me is after he is convicted. I believe if he did something it would be before the trial, as then he wouldn't have all of his dirty laundry aired.

I just don't know what to do right now. I am scared that he might have me killed or something and all these ideas of what to do are flying around in my head. I'm thinking about going somewhere and just hiding out for the next 6 months, but that won't pay the bills.

I don't know what to do and I just feel totally overwhelmed by everything that is on my plate. I don't want to keep being a therapist as I just can't pull together not only the emotional piece of myself, but I also just don't care about their problems right now. I feel that my heart is hardening and that is not a good sign. I have no idea what else to do, except to pray.

Another thing that Lesser has pulled is that his attorney asked for a continuance of this preliminary hearing on Wednesday as he said he couldn't financially afford to come up here. Fortunately, it didn't work and the preliminary hearing will go on as planned. Lesser really might be a jerk throughout this whole thing and I will have to be ready for anything. Even having it take forever for the trial to begin. Remember, the goal here is "To Outwit; Outplay and Outlast" this jerk. I just hope I'm alive to see it happen.

CHAPTER 23

Setting The Hook

August 28, 2008 (Thursday)

Thank goodness yesterday is over, but the preliminary hearing went well. I got to the courthouse and sat with Detective Sharp, Evelyn and DA Koss for a while before the preliminary hearing. He told me some of the questions that he would ask, such as my age and stuff and then it would be the defense attorney's turn to ask me some questions.

We then went up and Mr. F. was sitting in the court. I'm not sure why he was there and I actually thought he was our old family attorney Mr. S. until he introduced himself to Evelyn as Mr. F. I hadn't seen him in over 30 years and didn't recognize him. I apologized for thinking he was Mr. S., but honestly, I don't think he had heard what I called him anyhow. He said that he was hard of hearing. It was nice of him to come in support of me although it kind of "threw me".

We waited for a couple of other cases to appear and then it was our turn. I went up to testify and I have to say that I had to laugh when I saw the waste paper basket sitting by the witness chair. I had asked for one in case I throw-up, which seems to be all of the time nowadays. I then panicked a little, as I didn't want anyone to think that my "laugh" meant that I thought this procedure was funny. I always smile and/or laugh at the wrong times.

At any rate, DA Koss asked the standard questions of my name; age; how I met Lesser; when I met Lesser; how many times had we had sexual intercourse and where. He then finished and it was Mr. K.'s turn. He asked quite a few questions and DA Koss objected to about 4 or 5 of them. One of them the judge thought for a long time before sustaining it…meaning I didn't have to answer.

He asked questions like did I remember the first time we had sex to which I replied no, but I remembered it was cold. He asked what I did for a living and if I worked with sexually abused people. DA Koss knew where he was trying to go with this line of questioning, objected to it and that was stopped. He asked about the Campus Life organization and what was its purpose. I responded that it's a Christian organization that has youth groups for young people. He then asked some question, or something leading towards the idea that it was for young people who were "naughty". DA Koss also objected to this line of questioning and that was stopped.

It was over fairly quickly, about 10 minutes, and I felt good about how I had handled things. Evelyn had written me a note that said I had done "fabulous". That was very nice.

The judge decided that there was enough evidence for the case to be bound over and then set an "arraignment hearing" for 1:00 in the afternoon due to the fact that Lesser has to travel so far for all of this stuff. Detective Sharp, DA Koss, Evelyn and I then went downstairs and talked about how it had gone. All of them said that I did a very good job and was pleased with how everything had gone. We sat around for quite a while decompressing I guess you could say and we talked more about the case.

I asked what an arraignment hearing was about and they explained that was where he will enter a plea of guilty or not guilty. Another question I had for Detective Sharp was if he had any more ideas about how I could keep myself safe. It would be so easy for someone to drive by while I'm mowing, put a bullet in my head and keep going. He said that he is having the Green County Sheriff's Department continue to drive past my house on a frequent basis, which is of some comfort. Again, I think that he would do something before the case ever made it to court instead of after his possible conviction as DA Koss believes. Why would he wait and not only have all of his dirty laundry aired, but to be convicted in the first place? He would simply make it all go away before anything got started.

I must say that I am so thankful to have DA Koss, Detective Sharp and Evelyn with me on this as I think we make a good team. Not only that, but I feel comfortable and safe with them. DA Koss also made the comment that he was going to contact the man who filed charges against Father McGuire and tell him about me. When I asked why, DA Koss replied that it was to tell this man that his coming forward to prosecute McGuire, gave me the information and impetus to come forward myself. That's very nice.

I must say that while talking with the three of them, I did lose my composure on a number of occasions and teared up. I also told them that there was no way in hell that I could have done this years ago when I was younger as it is just too overwhelming on so many levels and DA Koss agreed with me. I am so grateful that they are with me on this that I just don't know how to thank them, except to do the best job I can to help win the case.

I just remembered that I also reminded them during our "decompressing" that I had gotten jewelry from Lesser, but had thrown it off of my pier when I had "kicked him to the curb". They asked how far I had thrown it and then they talked about having the Walworth County Sheriff's dive team go out and look for it. I was amazed at this suggestion and told them that they will never find it as the mail boat has been coming into the pier for over 35 years and that boat always churns up the water so much. I explained there is a big hole off the pier where the mail boat begins to reverse its engines after dropping off the mail runner.

DA Koss said that it would be good practice for the dive team and that they needed some type of exercise, so Detective Sharp is supposed to call them. I would be amazed if they ever found either the necklace or ring, as I believe he gave me a ring too. I am also embarrassed as now the people who bought our house are going to see divers out there and wonder why. I don't want to say that diving for this stuff is stupid, but it's probably not necessary as I feel we have a great case. I also feel badly about spending the taxpayer's dollars on something like this. Whatever.

After decompressing with "the team" I then went out to my car when the reporter from Janesville came running up to ask me some more questions. I told him I wasn't sure if I should be talking with him, but gave him some basics about Campus Life. He thought it might be some type of camp or something, or that we met like once a week for an hour. So I told him that no, it was an organization where we did a lot of activities together and that we were together all of the time. That's all I felt comfortable sharing with him as I don't want to "screw up the case" in any way. I then called Mom and Dad and we decided to meet for lunch as I was going back to the arraignment at 1:00.

Finally I called Janet and told her how things went. He still looks absolutely terrible with his saggy facial skin. He looks nothing like the person that he was before. It also seems like his cockiness is gone; but then again, he had claimed he couldn't afford to come to the preliminary hearing, which is bullshit. He really looks pitiful and in a way, I do feel sorry for what he is going through. There is that mercy again, so I have to remind myself…justice before mercy!!

It was good to see Mom and Dad and I think that they needed to see me. Dad had said that Mom had been "shaking" all-day and ended up taking a Lorazepam to calm her nerves. We of course went to Popeye's and had a piña colada as they make the best ones in the area and a nice Greek lunch. We talked about what happened in court as well as the Democratic Convention…Mom's favorite topic! We talked about what a great job Hillary did in her speech and once again, I lamented that I wished she were the presidential candidate, although Barak would most likely be a good president as well.

After lunch I went back to court and a bunch of people were waiting to go into the courtroom. I sat fairly far away from Lesser, who was standing there alone staring out the window looking really pathetic. Then it seemed like everyone went into the courtroom all at once and it ended up being just him and me in the hallway! I didn't know what to do, but I felt like I should say something to him. Instead I quickly made a beeline for the door, which was right past him and went in. In all honesty, I felt very sorry for him and felt that I should comfort him and tell him it would be ok. Conversely, I also wanted to tell him sarcastically that Janet said "hi", but I chose not to say anything and just went on in. It "felt" like he wanted to say something to me as well, but nothing happened. It was a "weird" moment for both of us I think.

His case was eventually called and I'm not quite sure what happened, except that there is to be a "status hearing" October 15th at 1:00. They also said something about cameras and I'm not sure what that was about except maybe instead of him coming back to WI all of the time, they will do a video feed from NC. If that is the case, then I wonder if "his community" knows about his situation.

As soon as the hearing was over, I left and once again, had to walk right past him. I kept my head down, but again, my inclination was to say something comforting…as I'm nailing him to the cross. My emotions are so conflicted and it's not that I feel like he did nothing wrong to me, it's just that I can't tolerate seeing another human being or creature for that matter, in pain. I want to fix it.

On the way home, I called Richard to tell him what happened and then I decided to call Lisa and see how she was doing even though I didn't think I could handle another emotional event for the day. Unfortunately, she was just sobbing when I called. It was a difficult call to say the least and I barely had enough emotional energy left to give to her, but I feel I have to, as she really needs it right now. She had an appointment with a thoracic surgeon, but he doesn't quite know what is going on with her lungs. It might be an abscess or it might be cancer, but she will meet with a pulmonologist either today or tomorrow (hopefully) and find out exactly what is in her lung. She also got fired from her new job today, so she was crying about that too. It's one thing after another for her. Needless to say, I ended up with a sick headache for the day but again, that seems to be par for the course.

CHAPTER 24

Just Let Me Off This Ride

August 30, 2008 (Saturday)

It's Labor Day Weekend and thankfully the week has ended, although the drama continues.

Lisa FINALLY called me back last night after I have tried numerous times to reach her and she is really sick. She was going to go to the ER to get admitted as she just can't breathe and felt terrible. I am so worried about her and she gave me some numbers to her older brother and sister to get in touch with them to tell them what is going on.

The other thing that happened yesterday is that Detective Sharp had called wondering if I could meet him and someone from the dive team to go out on their boat and mark the area where I threw the jewelry. I have to laugh, as I don't think that they will find it due to the mail boat churning everything up for the last 34 years, but I will do whatever they ask me to do.

I called back and what we are going to do is go to my old pier and drop a GPS thing into the water. Then in September when the dive team does their practices, they will practice by looking for my jewelry. This just seems surreal at times. I really thought that my involvement in the case would fall off after the preliminary hearing, but maybe not.

Right now I feel like I am in a war where you go out and fight the enemy and then withdraw after a ferocious battle to regroup. It's a time to bandage wounds, get some rest, eat some food and prepare for the next onslaught. I feel that I should be "regrouping" right now, but it's difficult to do because of the type of job I have as well as what is going on with Lisa.

Despite all that I have on my plate, I still have to get ready for the next battle. I can now physically feel all of the things that are wrong with me and I feel that I have to attend to them during this "break". I have a crown that has a big piece out of it and it hurts. The tooth that I had the root canal in this week is still sore and it now needs a crown. My neck hurts and I feel like I'm getting a sinus infection, but fortunately I got some antibiotics as a result of my root canal, so hopefully that will catch whatever else might be wrong. My hands, wrists and elbow hurt as well, but they have for years. I finally did follow through however on my orthopedic surgeon's recommendation to finally get my hands tested. I feel that I have to be as physically healthy as possible to continue this fight with Lesser because if I'm not physically feeling well, then my mind doesn't work well either.

I have to remember that my motto is once again: "To Outwit, Outlast and Outplay" and I'm getting ready to do that.

As a result of having to go out on the lake next Thursday with Detective Sharp, I had to call clients yesterday to change their appointments for Tuesday and Wednesday.

August 31, 2008 (Sunday)

Yesterday Danny and I went out on the boat to "chill out" but to be honest, the only thing I thought about was Lesser and the case. I am so exhausted by this whole thing and physically I'm shot, but my mind just keeps running over everything that was said and done on Wednesday. I don't think that I said more than 20 words to Danny the entire day, but I just didn't feel like talking. Fortunately he was fine with me not talking and in all honesty was probably happy that I for once didn't chatter away!

Then Pete called and I did talk with him a little about the case. He was very nice on the phone and we talked about DA Koss and Detective Sharp and how much I admire and like them. Pete likes DA Koss too, but isn't too happy with Detective Sharp, but of course that's because Detective Sharp was the investigator on HIS case. I still can't get over the fact that DA Koss isn't holding it against me for not only knowing Pete, but for staying in touch with him as well. I have to laugh because DA Koss is probably scared to death that if he loses my case, Pete will haunt him until his dying day! Ha Ha.

I can only think that DA Koss is a devoted civil servant, hell bent on bringing justice to those that deserve it. I also have the feeling that he, as well as Detective Sharp is out for blood with Lesser. I get the sense from them that they are bound and determined to "get Lesser" and because of that, I feel that I can just "sit back" so to speak and let them do their jobs. I feel comfortable knowing that they know what they are doing and that maybe they are going all out to get Lesser because they like me as a person as well.

I also called Lisa this morning and she doesn't want visitors. I don't blame her, as when I'm sick, I don't want people to come see me. I just want to be left alone and so it is with her. I will call her tonight and see how she is feeling.

September 4, 2008 (Thursday)

I was supposed to go to the lake today to meet with Detective Sharp and go out on the police boat, but he called last night and cancelled. He has to investigate a sexual assault that occurred and then he is going on vacation next week musky fishing. It is also supposed to rain, and it currently is raining, so he postponed it. No problem for me as I can do it anytime and interestingly enough, I am VERY relieved that I don't have to go over. I'm not sure why all of a sudden looking for the jewelry is such an upsetting event for me, but for some reason, I'm just so happy I don't have to go.

September 8, 2008 (Monday)

It's Monday and back to work for me. At least I'm not so upset about Lisa as I had a chance to see her this past weekend. She not only needed my help in getting her house in order, but she also needed someone to help her figure out what she is going to do about her illness and her life. We talked about quite a bit and hopefully she now has some sort of plan in place. As a result of seeing her I am able to let go of my worry about her for a little while so hopefully I'll be able to focus my energy again on work.

I also find that I am not thinking much about Lesser at this point as Detective Sharp is up fishing in Minocqua and there is nothing on the schedule until the status hearing on October 15th. That is helpful for calming down as well.

September 14, 2008 (Sunday)

Last week was a really rough week with a lot of ups and downs and I'm still finding it difficult to replenish my emotional energy.

First is that on Tuesday, Lisa found out that the mass in her lungs is in fact an abscess and that she will have to be on antibiotics for 4 weeks to hopefully clear up the infection. She will then have another CT scan to find out if there is anything else going on in there. That was a huge relief to say the least.

That relief was short lived as within 1 hour of hearing the good news with Lisa, I was concerned about the welfare of one of my newer clients. It seemed like she was saying goodbye to me and the world, and as a result of that and her unwillingness to go to the hospital, I had to call 911 to have a safety check done.

I hate doing that for a number of reasons. One is that I don't want to embarrass the client in front of their neighbors by having a police officer show up. Another reason is that I don't want them to be angry with me for calling, but as I've learned, that's my issue and one that my supervisor has cautioned me about in the past. Regardless, I feel awful that I had to call the police.

Then on Wednesday I just couldn't stop crying and just seemed overwhelmed with life. Danny had gone out of town until Friday night and I was alone with my thoughts and emotions. In one way that was good, as I didn't have to worry about taking care of his needs, but could just try and relax.

Unfortunately, I just wasn't able to re-regulate and Thursday was another tough day. I would find myself tearing up for no reason at all and finding it difficult not to cry. There was no rhyme or reason, I simply felt like crying all day. What I am coming to realize however is that I can't keep doing therapy. It is so difficult to deal with all of the problems that my clients present with on a good day, but lately, I just can't provide them with the immense emotional strength that they need from me. I dread going to work these days and even the drive to work is anxiety producing for me. I really feel like I'm falling apart emotionally and that is not a good thing.

Saturday I spent the morning doing errands, laundry and shopping for pants. That is something that I absolutely HATE to do, but there was a big sale at a store in town and I don't fit into any of my pants right now. There are only 2 pairs of pants that I have that remotely fit as I continue to lose weight. I didn't know how much weight I had lost until trying on the pants. I normally wear a 12/13 but am now in a size 9/10. I can't even remember the last time that I wore that size, but suffice it to say, I was a teenager for sure.

After doing errands, I had some nervous energy so Danny and I went to the Fayette Bar to have some lunch. It's a bar we go to when snowmobiling and they always pour a good shot of Schnapps and have good food, so I felt like going there. The shot didn't end up tasting too good and I could only eat ½ of my ham and cheese sandwich, but it was fun to get out. Danny then drove through Yellowstone Lake State Park as I usually love to do that and it was calming to me. Calming until we happened upon a big turtle crossing the road and he stopped right in the middle. I immediately had Danny stop, as I wanted to get him out of the road so he wouldn't get accidentally run over, but he wouldn't move. Since Danny had said he was a snapping turtle, I didn't want to get too close. I had to leave him in the middle of the road and of course, then the tears started again.

I think what is happening to me is that when I am presented with any situation that could possibly indicate some pain or hurt to anything, I freak out. For example, here were some dogs that I saw on our road trip that were in little crappy houses on this farm, and that set me off on a crying jag. The inability of these dogs to have a better situation in life was just so upsetting to me and once again, it is Man that is hurting these animals.

I think what is happening to me is that I am extremely vulnerable right now. The protective layers that I have bandaged onto my soul, have been ripped off due to the case and as a result, I'm susceptible to intense emotions any time that I encounter a situation that I feel is an injustice. I feel the victimization all over again not only for myself, but for whatever person or creature this injustice is against.

I ended up having to take a Lorazepam to try and once again calm myself down. I don't like that I am taking so many of those pills, but I just can't "physically feel" right now as it is too emotionally upsetting for me.

Here it is Sunday and I'm finding myself tearing up and crying again over the littlest things. I cried because of the devastation that Hurricane Ike did to people's property, watching the evacuation of some of the people and even cried because Danny keeps insisting on giving Tucker so much "people food". He is going to kill him with all of the crap that he feeds him and it makes me really angry that he doesn't listen to me about this. I listened to him when he told me that he thought giving Tucker marrow bones to chew on, was hurting his teeth. From that comment on, I haven't given him another marrow bone, but he won't give me the same respect and that pisses me off.

I don't know what this next week holds for me, but to say that I dread it doesn't even cover it. I am anxious already for next week and actually, I'm down clients, so I really don't have to see many people.

Then the fact that I don't have many clients worries me as that means that I won't be making much money, and that is of concern. It's always something and I feel like a hamster on their little wheel in their cage. No matter what I try and do, it seems like I just can't get off "this wheel" and this wheel keeps going faster and faster. That is exactly why I need a vacation of some sort.

The Packers are playing at noon today, but even that sucks as Bret isn't the quarterback anymore, and their success or failure really doesn't matter to me right now. I wish that Brett could have stayed with the Packers. As Todd our friend would say, "It ain't right" that he's playing for the Jets.

Enough whining, but I feel better writing this all down as at least it's one way that I can get rid of some of the angst without bothering others.

CHAPTER 25

Just A Little Humor

September 22, 2008 (Monday)

Today is the day that I met with Detective Sharp and two officers from the Walworth County Sheriff's Dive team. We met in Williams Bay, but there was no one there to operate the police boat, so we sat around and talked about what to do for a while. While discussing what to do, I found out that the dive officer had gone to Williams Bay High School and I asked him if he knew Peter S. as he was involved in this case and he did!! After talking for a while, they decided to instead drive over to my old house and do it that way instead of going by boat. We were all kind of bummed as it was a beautiful day at the lake and the water was like glass. Of course, all the turkeys (tourists) are gone for the summer, so that's probably why the lake is so calm.

I rode with Detective Sharp in his car and we talked about our jobs and some of the wild people that we have to deal with in our professions. He told me about this stripper who had hit him while he was sitting in his car, which was pulled over to the side of the road. I guess it had been snowing like crazy, and she was driving like a bat out of hell when she just plowed right into his squad car. It was fortunate that he happened to be in the car, or he would have been killed. He also talked about a time when he was bouncing at Chuck's and was trying to throw this female out, when she pulled a knife on him. How stupid is that chick as he said that he was in uniform too!

We got to my old house and it felt so comforting to be walking down the lawn to the pier and just being "home" again. Danny had made me this metal thing that was maybe the approximate weight of the ring and necklace to throw into the lake so we could see how far I might have thrown it. Well, I was nervous and when I threw it, it only went two feet and straight down. I was so embarrassed!!

As we were all on the pier gauging about where I might have thrown the jewelry, there happened to be some fishermen not too far off so one of the police officers called to him to come into the pier. The look on the driver's face was funny because he looked scared. He even asked what he had done wrong. The officer asked them to do him a favor and take him out in the boat so he could do something, but when the guy asked what we were looking for, I thought it was interesting that the officer didn't tell him. At any rate, we were all joking around on the pier with each other as well as the one fisherman they let off the boat so the officer could get on.

They went out to the approximate spot and he put it into his GPS coordinates and then they came back in. I told the fishermen to come to Chuck's, which is my hometown bar and where I was headed next and we all kind of laughed and they took off.

We left too after the one officer asked me some questions about how the mail boat comes into the pier and things like that. As Detective Sharp drove me back to my car we briefly talked about the case and Detective Sharp thinks that Lesser might take some kind of deal. Detective Sharp thinks that would probably be the smartest thing for Lesser to do, but who knows what he will do.

I then met Mom and Dad at Chuck's for lunch and I told them about the fishermen and we all laughed again as they will have some story to tell and it wouldn't entail fish!! Later I was coming out of the bathroom and going back to our table when I saw who was sitting behind us…it was the fishermen! We all laughed again and they asked me what they were looking for so I told them some jewelry that I had thrown into the lake. My mom then made a comment to the fishermen about how nice they were to come in to the pier to help us and their response was that when there are three men with guns asking you to do something, you do it!

I am not upset about looking for the jewelry today and I think it's because we did a lot of laughing and joking around. It was also nice to be at my old house for even a little while.

CHAPTER 26

Back Into Battle

October 14, 2008 (Tuesday)

It's been a while since I've written, which is fine with me. These past couple of weeks I have been able to emotionally, physically and mentally re-regulate to get ready for the next fight.

Danny and I were able to take off for a couple of days so that I could try and relax and we decided to head north along Lake Michigan and go to Mackinaw Island. We had lunch at a really cool restaurant that was on Lake Michigan. We were right near Door County and we thought about taking a drive through there, but there were still too many tourists in the area and that made me nervous for some reason. That's when we decided to just head over to Escanaba Michigan.

For the most part, I was able to relax, although I did think about the case a lot. I also thought that I saw Lesser driving in a car and there were in reality police all over the place, so then I started imagining that maybe Lesser was going to plan a hit and the cops knew about it and were following us. It took quite a while for me to let go of that imagery, but there really were a lot of cops on our entire trip and I thought that was weird. Oh where the mind can take people!

The next day we headed to St. Ignace MI and stayed right on Lake Huron. The water was about 30 feet away and the seagulls were plenty. We had some smoked fish that we began to feed one lone seagull and before we knew it, it looked like a scene right out of the Hitchcock movie "The Birds". All of a sudden tons of seagulls showed up and began fighting for the pieces of fish. I retreated back into the room as the vast number of them scared me!

The next day we took a hydro-jet ferry over to Mackinaw Island and spent about 4 hours touring part of the island.

Of course there are no cars allowed on the island except for a police car, a fire truck and an ambulance. Horses do the rest of the work and it was cool to see those big beautiful animals.

We did go up to The Grand Hotel and had to pay $10 apiece just to walk on the property! It was worth it as I have seen The Grand Hotel in the movie "Somewhere In Time" with Christopher Reeves. Walked back down to town and took a tour by horse and wagon and that was fun as well.

We ended up leaving there about 4 p.m. and driving to St. Saunt Marie, which is on the Canadian border, but I didn't like the looks of the town as it looked "scary" to me, so we decided against going into Canada. Besides, Danny didn't have his passport with him so it would have been a hassle to try and get across. We decided to drive to Marquette MI and spent the night there. The next morning however Danny found out that one of his clients had died, so we made the decision to head home early. I was disappointed and dismayed as it had not been the vacation we had anticipated, but at least we got away and got to see some great colors in the trees!

It was a good thing that we came home because on Thursday, Uva (Danny's mother) got sick and Danny has been dealing with it ever since. We think she got a cold and the flu at the same time, but the biggest problem is that she is so dizzy all of the time, so later this week I will take her for some "dizzy tests". It always seems like something is going wrong and therefore someone needs my help.

Tomorrow is the status hearing with Lesser and I'm starting to get dysregulated again. I find that I am having terrible dreams and that I am once again clenching and grinding my teeth so badly at night, that my whole jaw and neck hurt in the morning. Of course I lost my mouth guard and to get another one is another $200, so I have decided to just suffer for a while.

October 15, 2008 (Wednesday)

Today is the day of the status hearing and I'm nervous of course. I decided to go onto Google to see if Lesser still comes up under Youth for Christ/Campus Life and he does. I also found a site called "Youth Pastor Watch", which must be an organization that keeps an eye out for wayward pastors. They listed part of the article on the case and then had some people respond to it. A couple of people made comments about my case and while one comment was nice the other wasn't the nicest, but whatever.

It is interesting, as well as scary, to me how people are talking about my case on the Internet. People I don't even know are making comments and some are suggesting that I'm doing this for the money. I would have written my own comment, but I didn't find it until today. I will have to keep a closer eye on the Internet about this situation, but at the same time, reading these blogs upsets me.

My stomach is churning, my heart is racing and my body is tense anticipating what is going to happen today. I of course Googled "status hearing" to see what happens during this part. A status hearing is an informal discussion between all the parties about what evidence has been collected. Lesser can also change his plea or ask questions if he doesn't understand something. As usual, I will bring my stuffed teddy bear Budweiser with me for this hearing. Most importantly however, God please be with me and comfort my fears.

It's taken me until this morning to pull it together enough to write in here. Wednesday turned out to be awful for a couple of reasons.

First is that when it was time for our case, his attorney claimed that he hadn't had the chance to conduct his "discovery" yet and therefore we would have to reschedule the status hearing. He claimed that he wasn't able to find all of the information in the DA files and that was why he couldn't do his investigation.

There was a different DA there handling all of the cases for the day and I think she was pissed about his answer to the court. I guess the DA's office is transcribing interviews and other things onto CD's, DVD's and such and that some of the information is scattered at the moment. The DA has however sent out letters to the defense attorney's about this new process and informed them all that they can find the information at the respective police departments. Of course Lesser's attorney played dumb, so the judge rescheduled the status hearing for November 19th!

I was disappointed and angry about the whole thing, as I believe this time Lesser won. Now we have to wait another 6 weeks for this stupid hearing and this waiting is really beginning to take a toll on me!

On the way home, I decided to do my own "investigation" and stop at this bar in Beloit where a friend of mine goes. It's not in the best area and looks really scary on the outside, but Jeremy had said that it's fine inside. I wasn't ready to go home yet as I was still mad at Danny for staying at his friends having a couple of drinks the night before, when he promised me he wouldn't.

I didn't stay long not only because their shots were good sized, but I also hadn't eaten all day and had taken a Lorazepam so I thought I better head towards home. I then called and met Danny at another bar and suffice it to say that I ended up puking all night. I remember laying on the bathroom floor saying how sorry I was to God that I had allowed myself to fall back onto old and dysfunctional coping mechanisms. I feel that He has entrusted me with doing all of this so that I can help others heal and I felt like I had let Him down.

Needless to say, yesterday I didn't feel very well. It was a good thing though that I didn't end up at the hospital as I thought for a while that Danny might have to take me. I really don't do liquor very well anymore and that's fine with me. Lying there on the floor so dizzy and nauseous, reminded me once again why I don't like to drink to excess anymore.

Yesterday, October 16th is also not a good day for a number of reasons. One reason is that 25 years ago today, Bill (my husband) got killed in a car accident. Another is that October 12th or so, about eight years ago is when Riley, my beloved Chesapeake Bay retriever, died. The good news about the 16th however is that is

Uva's birthday and she turned 89!! Unfortunately she still isn't feeling that well so that sucks.

I also had to call my voice mail yesterday and once again, there was nothing but bad news. A client who I knew was anxious and depressed ended up in the psychiatric hospital. For her to do that meant that she really was losing it, so I had to talk with the hospital staff for a while. Then I finally got in contact with another client from the past that had called me and it turns out that he has been arrested for rape.

I am so exhausted today and it is an exhaustion that reaches down to my bones. I am tired of this emotional roller coaster that just won't stop and I'm tired of having to deal with everyone else's problems on top of my own. The problem is that I really do care about my clients and that makes it all that more emotionally draining for me.

Unfortunately, I'll have to give this round to Lesser as far as winning and that pisses me off. I should have known that they were going to play dirty and use every tactic in the book. Now I wouldn't put anything past them. I have to be ready for this battle with him and maybe this was a wake-up call on many levels in regards to the longevity of this process. The fact is that they are going to play dirty and that I can't revert back to old coping mechanisms.

CHAPTER 27

The Big Scare

October 20, 2008 (Monday)

It's been quite a couple of days since I last wrote and a lot has happened.

What happened is that Friday I got a call from my family's good friend, Mrs. Vold who informed me not to freak out, but Dad was currently in the hospital due to a dizzy spell. I guess he had woken up to go to the bathroom and then got very dizzy and had to crawl back to his room. He thought it might pass, so he just laid down again, but a little later, he ended up crawling to where Mom was sleeping and told her to call 911. She called the Vold's instead and fortunately they came over as quickly as they could. Mrs. Vold who is/was a nurse assessed the situation and called 911.

Mrs. Vold said that Dad was currently in the emergency room and that they were going to release him after tests showed nothing, but then he had another dizzy spell and collapsed! They once again hooked him up to stuff and that is where the situation was at that time.

I immediately called Richard, jumped in the shower and took off. Mrs. Vold called again when I was on my way over to the hospital and said that they were once again going to release Dad. They offered to drive him home, but since I was about 5 minutes away, I came and got Mom and Dad as Mom had gone with them. It was so very nice of the Vold's to attend to my parents that way and we are all very fortunate to have them in our lives.

Dad was still extremely dizzy, but all of his tests had come back negative for anything, so that was a good thing. Richard immediately drove up and came to the house to see what was going on and I was so thankful that he was there so I didn't have to assess it myself. It was scary to say the least as Dad never gets sick.

It was decided without question that I would spend the night with them and see how it went as Dad was still dizzy. I went to McCullough's to get his medicine as well as Pino's to get some pizza. None of us really felt like eating, but we had to have something, so this was the easiest. Richard stayed until after 5 and then took off for home. He has to go to MI tomorrow for a wedding and had to take off early. I was just so happy to have his support and Mom and Dad were grateful as well.

We then had a nice night watching all of their political shows as well as the DVD "The Count of Monte Cristo", which was an excellent movie. They of course stay up until after "Nightline", so it was after 11 when we finally turned in. I was afraid to take my Excedrin PM as I wanted to be able to hear Dad if he needed my help during the night.

The next morning he felt a little better so of course he did too much and had another bout of vertigo. I think he then realized that he HAD to take it easy or he wasn't going to get better.

We decided that I would go to the grocery store and stock up on food as well as go to the post office to mail off a thank you card and a little present for the Vold's. It was actually fun running the errands around the area as I ran into Lee O. in the post office and saw other people I knew in the Sentry.

The love that I felt from my friends in the area was so comforting and it was certainly a pleasure to be home. I stayed until Saturday afternoon at which point it was decided that since Dad was feeling better that I should go to a wedding Danny and I had been invited to. I missed the wedding but while at the reception my thoughts were on my parents and hoping Dad was feeling well enough to be on his own. I did end up calling them before leaving the reception to see if they wanted me to come back. Dad said he felt good enough to go it alone, so I went home.

This has certainly been a wake-up call as far as what we need to think about in the future in regards to Mom and Dad. If something happens to Dad, Mom wouldn't be able to live on her own and that is something that we need to begin to assess. They have nursing home insurance, but I don't want Mom in a nursing home. I think if she was in a nursing home, she would be absolutely miserable and that scenario isn't going to happen if I'm alive. I have already talked with my brothers and Danny about me moving home to live with Mom if something happened to Dad and that is still what I'm planning to do.

She is comfortable in her house, she has everything she needs, she has her patterns and habits that are comfortable to her and she isn't going to go anywhere. The same is true for Dad, as he isn't going into a nursing home either.

This situation with my Dad is what I'm most afraid about in life…the reality that someday I am going to lose my parents. I don't know what I'm going to do without them and having to deal with this crisis, only reminds me that they are getting old on me. Right now I honestly feel if they aren't alive, I don't want to be around. They are the only people I trust 100% in this world. Isn't that a shame?!

October 28, 2008 (Tuesday)

Time is slowly creeping towards the 19th and I look forward to it with anticipation and with dread, which is another dialectic. This whole process is such an emotional seesaw!

This past weekend I spent reading this journal and discovered that it stunk! I'm beginning to doubt that anyone will ever want to read this and that thought is depressing me. I've put so much time and energy into this journal with the hope that it might be of help to others in some way. It seems like once the depressive thoughts begin, it's easy to feel hopeless about a lot of things.

CHAPTER 28

Yes We Can

November 9, 2008 (Sunday)

It's been a while since I've written and a lot has happened in the past couple of weeks. Most importantly, the presidential election is over and Barak Obama has won!! I honestly didn't know how anxious I was about the election until the night he won! I think there was a collective sigh of relief from around the world and I was one of them!!

I am so proud of America right now and especially proud of the white race. I don't think Obama could have won solely on the African-American and Latino votes and really needed "us" to put him over the top. I am proud to think that the white race was able to put race aside and vote for the man who would be best for the job…and everyone did! Finally this "oppressive cloud" that has been hanging over America for the past 8 years is lifting! There is finally light at the end of the tunnel in regards to humanity and hope and that feels good. It is surprising to me how his election has lifted a "heavy weight" from my shoulders. I feel more optimistic about the future of not only America, but my future as well.

On the flip side however I am finding it impossible to "relax" and find myself doing house related projects all of the time. So far I have rearranged the living room 4 times, washed all of the windows as well as the blinds. I've reorganized the storage area upstairs, switched the summer clothes to winter clothes and organized all of my greeting cards. Next up is to put plastic on some of the windows and winterize the house as well as I can. I feel like I HAVE to get "my house" in order and this intense need to get it done is driving me crazy. It's like I have to have everything around me in "order" so that I can focus on fighting Lesser.

I also feel like I have to have some type of "change" in my life, although exactly what I need changed, I'm not sure. I did however get my hair cut differently this last time, which is something that I haven't done in at least 20 years. It's nothing drastic, nor is the furniture that I've rearranged for a "change", but it's like I have to "shake things up a bit". Having said that however, I don't want too many changes or too drastic of change as that would be dysregulating. Honestly, I don't know what I want anymore.

147

Later:

I just looked at my e-mails and I had received a response from Dr. O'Beirne (a past professor of mine) in regards to an e-mail I had sent her about this journal. I had recently run into her at a conference and when I saw her, it popped into my head that I should share this journey and ask her whether she thought a journal like this could be of help to others. I didn't ask her that day as I needed to think about it, but I finally got the courage to ask her through an e-mail.

To be honest, I was afraid of what her response would be as I admire her in so many ways. Dr. O'Beirne is one of the most intelligent people I know in regards to psychological matters while at the same time has a caring spirit for others. Her answer was that she thought it COULD be of help to others and has offered to meet with me to discuss this whole thing!

What is now interesting to me is that since reading that she thought a journal like this might be of help to others, I have been an emotional wreck and I don't really know why. I am currently having a mini-meltdown and just can't stop crying.

I wonder if my response has to do with Dr. O'Beirne validating not only my experience, but also my hopes that maybe this story could be of help to others. To be validated by Dr. O'Beirne is huge in that I respect and admire her so much and from her response, I know that I am doing the right thing. At least I think that is what she thinks?!

Now doubt about that statement is entering into my mind. See how crazy this is as one minute I think that she is supporting me and the next minute I doubt that. I don't know anything about anything lately and just want this mental tug-of-war to stop.

November 10, 2008 (Monday)

I'm still a bit dysregulated from yesterday, but I did set up a time to meet with Dr. O'Beirne before the status hearing. I am nervous about our meeting, as I don't really want to mix "business" with "personal stuff". I hate it when people ask me for my opinion on something they've written so I'm hesitant to ask Dr. O'Beirne to do that for me. But at the same time, I really really want to ask her to read it, as I need to know if it is any good.

CHAPTER 29

Back To Health

November 11, 2008 (Tuesday)

Today was my annual physical and to check the spots on my lung and liver. Fortunately they haven't changed in the past 6 months, which was a huge relief because I continue to smoke like a smokestack.

We then talked about my anxiety level and after talking about her recommendation that I begin taking the anti-anxiety medication Lexipro, I decided to do it. It just seems like the stress is building up and all the Lorazepam is doing is dealing with the symptoms after they arise. The Lexipro should keep me from being so up and down and though I don't like the idea of taking this, I think that I need it. Now I understand how my clients dislike taking psychotropic medication, as it is scary to me for some reason. I feel like it will change my "personality" or something.

Then she did a breast exam and lo and behold, she found a hard lump. I now have an ultrasound this afternoon and then will have to meet with crazy (fondly said) Dr. M., the "butt" surgeon on Thursday. Now I have to have him deal with another one of my private parts! Doesn't this shit ever end.

I called Danny to tell him and of course I started to cry. He was leaving for Rockford and I had to go to Wal-Mart, so we decided we might meet later, after the ultrasound. However, while I was shopping at Wal-Mart, I looked up and there he was. He had come to see how I was and to give me money for my medication. He really is a wonderful guy and though he pisses me off at times, he really does care about me.

I'm now home and wasting time until the ultrasound. My next fear is that some guy is going to do this and I just can't handle that right now. I asked the appointment ladies if there was a female technician and there is, so I think that I will insist that she do it.

The good thing…Obama is president!!!!!!

November 13, 2008 (Thursday)

Got home from work today and there was a message from Detective Sharp. It was "shocking" to hear his voice, as I haven't talked with him in a while. Just hearing his voice reminds me of the seriousness of what is happening in my life.

Detective Sharp had wanted to inform me that they had dove for my jewelry, but didn't find it. He said that there was a huge trough there from the mail boat coming in and out and that if it was there, it was buried under many feet of silt.

That didn't surprise me as I had told them in the beginning that there wasn't any way that they were going to find it. In all honesty, I am thankful that they didn't find it. My intent while throwing it off the pier was that I would never have to see it again and I don't want to now. Let it stay buried forever for all I care. I also don't think we need the jewelry to further our case as we have plenty of other ammunition. Besides, David was with me when I threw it off the pier so at least I have a witness to swear that it happened.

November 16, 2008 (Sunday)

Finally got some good news last week and the lump that was found, is really nothing. I had to go for about 5 more mammogram X-rays and spent 2 hours at the clinic, but Dr. M. says that I have nothing to worry about. I wasn't THAT worried about it for some reason, so I went off to work.

This week is the status hearing, AGAIN, and we'll see what will happen this time. I am anxious about it, but I think that this Lexipro is working already. The doctor said it would take 4 weeks to get into my system, but I think that I'm chilling out already! I even followed a truck pulling a load of cows for a really long way and I didn't totally freak out!! I was too scared to pass it however!

I am also hoping that the trial will be scheduled for sooner than February, but I won't count on it. The only solace that I can take from this wait is that Lesser must be more anxious and worried than I am. On one hand that makes me feel good, but on the other hand, I'm sorry that someone is suffering so much. It's this constant "tug-of-war" or "dialectic" in my mind as I'm just not comfortable with "destroying" anyone.

November 17, 2008 (Monday)

I wasn't able to sleep very well last night and I feel too overwhelmed today to go to work. I also am now obsessing about this journal, as I want to leave a copy with Dr. O'Beirne to see what she thinks about it.

Again, my hope is that this journal could be of help to others who dream about doing what I am doing. It's not as easy as one would think and honestly, there are times when I wonder if this was all worth it. My health has definitely faltered during this process; my relationship with Danny fluctuates; my emotions are so raw that I'm sensitive to EVERYTHING; and worst of all, there are gray hairs emerging more and more on my head! A little attempt at humor.

CHAPTER 30

The Next Round

It's the night before the status hearing and I just got home from work. Danny is being a nerd so I am currently watching MY television program in the other room and bitching to you dear journal. Danny seems to get really "pissy" right around the time that something is happening for court. I guess this isn't easy for him either, but I feel he could be a little more compassionate. He has been supportive but not empathetic.

In trying to get him to understand how badly I was hurt and how much this is affecting me, I asked him if he has ever been hurt really, really, bad or totally betrayed in the past by someone. Fortunately for him, he never has, so then how can I expect him to understand what it feels like to have your soul irrevocably destroyed?

Another thing that I was thinking about was that Lesser has never denied that he did this to me. A person would think that if he were innocent, he would be enraged that he would have been dragged into this, but he hasn't peeped. Therefore in my mind, that is an admission of guilt right there. He's never said a word to me and if I was lying about this, you would think that he would accuse me of being a liar. Just one thought of many that was rumbling around in my head on the drive home.

I am SO THANKFUL that I don't have to see clients for about 1 week. That doesn't mean that I don't work, but rather I don't have to see anyone and that is so helpful to me. I am so tired and my friend Julie told me that besides being too thin, I was also getting dark circles under my eyes. That doesn't surprise me as I feel like I SHOULD have dark circles under my eyes. This is so stressful!!

I thought about covering up my dark circles for court so that Lesser doesn't think that he is "getting to me", but I can't do that. First of all I don't have the make-up because secondly, I don't wear make-up, so it would be weird to wear concealer. Finally, I do want the other people involved in this to know that this is taking a toll on me. This isn't easy for me either and there is no reason to hide that fact from anyone. I guess what I am saying is that I am proud of my "scars" as I have earned every single one of them.

I am also a little apprehensive about meeting with Dr. O'Beirne tomorrow only because I want to ask her to read this journal. I really want/need her opinion about whether it would help others or not. But honestly, I am afraid that she won't like it or feels that it won't be of help to others, and I don't want to hear that. Maybe she won't even want to read it and then I don't have to worry about it.

I know that I spent 3 days straight on this journal trying to "clean it up" for her to read. I felt like I had to turn in an "A+ paper" to her and was obsessed with it until it was printed out for the second time late yesterday afternoon. Right now I am proud of it, but lately I've been changing my mind about things all the time. For example, I now HATE my haircut and I think that I will go back and have him chop off the rest of it. I wanted change, and then once I got it, I didn't like it.

November 19, 2008 (Wednesday)

I'm home from the status hearing and it sure didn't go the way that I had expected it to, but then again, I'm not sure of anything anymore.

Lesser wasn't there once again and I had a chance to quick mention to DA Koss that I wasn't thrilled about that as I feel part of his punishment is having to come up for these hearings. DA Koss didn't say anything about that, but did say that he had heard that there might be a plea.

The other court cases took FOREVER and then it was our turn. I heard his attorney say that he was filing some motions and one was for dismissal. I just about fell off the bench, and when I looked at Evelyn, her mouth was wide open as well.

Then there was some banter about the statute of limitations and about some case waiting to go to the Wisconsin Supreme Court regarding the statute of limitations in WI. The case is called MacArthur and I will have to look it up.

Finally there was some discussion about an "in camera" thing regarding any counseling records that I may have out there. Like Richard says, they're just going to keep throwing shit at me, but that's ok! I've already had poop literally thrown at me (and hit me) by a client, so bring it on!

When I left the courtroom I was of course angry as I didn't understand what just happened, but I thought we might be in "trouble". DA Koss couldn't talk with me after court but did tell me to "shoot him an e-mail". I did have a chance however to ask Evelyn about this MacArthur case and though she wasn't sure, she said that if the Wisconsin Supreme Court hears this MacArthur case and decides in favor of this case, then we might lose due to the statute of limitations. Evelyn thought that if the Wisconsin Supreme Court refuses to hear that case, then she THINKS that I am ok, but told me to check with DA Koss, as he will know for sure. To me this was another curve ball and I don't think that DA Koss was expecting this as well. I don't know why I think that except it didn't seem like he said too much in court.

The next hearing will be December 17th when they argue about whether the statute of limitations can be applied in my case as well as some other things. What those things are I'm not quite sure about yet. The judge also insisted that Lesser be present at the next hearing and I agree!

What I am discovering is that there is a lot of shit that they can throw against the wall. They can do things to not only delay this process, but to try and destroy my reputation and air my dirty laundry. I say go ahead and do it because I'm already a step ahead of them, just like I planned. I have already spread my "dirty laundry" around myself by providing all of the information that I could think of to DA Koss and therefore the defense team. This was just one of my "many moves" in this game so far and one I learned when I was a door-to-door insurance sales person. I had to learn how to answer people's questions and concerns with honest answers in order to get them to buy the insurance. I am employing that same strategy to this case, and hopefully it will work!

I also met with Dr. O'Beirne and she is certainly one special person. She was so validating and helpful as I told her about what has been transpiring these past couple of years. I also left my "book/journal" with her to get her opinion on whether or not it is something that I could publish down the road. She is gracious enough to do that for me and it's interesting how I am able to let go of the worry about whether it stinks or not, at least for a day or two. I am so afraid that she won't like it and if that's the case, then I'm not sure I want to hear what she says; but of course I do!!

I am so very tired tonight and another realization today is that this is going to take FOREVER. I just hope that I can "Outplay, Outlast and ?. I can't even think of the other one and "Survivor" is my FAVORITE SHOW. Oh, I just remembered; to Outwit. See how my brain isn't working very well. That's why I'm shutting down for the day.

Thank you God though for Dr. O'Beirne and for DA Koss, although I'm afraid that after what happened today, he is going to be outwitted. I had previously told DA Koss that I thought the defense would be formidable players and though I'm sure that he has things under control, I still get scared. I have to keep reminding myself that DA Koss took down Father McGuire and therefore the Catholic Church and that he knows what he is doing, but it is difficult to trust him. Trust is a huge factor for victims of abuse and I find it so difficult to literally put my life into his hands.

November 20, 2008 (Thursday)

This morning I immediately looked at the MacArthur case that Lesser's attorney brought up yesterday and to be honest, it doesn't look good for the good guys. I'm not sure exactly what "happened" with this MacArthur case or if it is applicable to me, but I am scared to death that this is the end of the road.

The next hearing for my case has been listed on the Wisconsin Circuit Court website as a "motion hearing". What I think they are going to discuss is all of the motions that his attorney presented at the status hearing. I think they will argue about whether to dismiss the case; they will argue about the statute of limitations and they will argue about introducing my counseling records.

I also called DA Koss right away this morning to find out what happened yesterday, but he was on his way up to court and once again told me to send him an e-mail. I did so asking what happened yesterday and is this case in jeopardy. It is almost noon right now and I just checked my e-mails and he hasn't responded yet. I hope and pray that this isn't the end of this journey.

I am so nervous and anxious today and am trying to stay busy doing all sorts of things. I've carved my last pumpkin as I find carving them relaxing and comforting; probably because I have to concentrate on the pattern that I am cutting out. I just don't know what to think, but I am so scared that he has won.

FINALLY heard back from DA Koss and what happened is that Lesser's attorney filed two motions. One is in regards to the statute of limitations and the other is for my counseling records. He said that he has already argued the statute of limitations motion in the McGuire case, so he is pretty confident of winning that one. He said that he thinks he is just "fishing" for stuff as far as the counseling records and to call him tomorrow. He didn't seem at all concerned about either of the motions or anything and hearing that in his voice was very comforting. I had been so afraid that they were pulling something out of their hat that had stumped DA Koss. I should have known and TRUSTED that he has everything under control. What a day it was waiting for him to get back with me, but what a huge relief!!! I didn't know that I hadn't been breathing all day until I got the great news from DA Koss!

November 22, 2008 (Saturday)

I talked further with DA Koss yesterday afternoon and we talked about the two motions that Lesser's attorney filed. He isn't concerned about the statute of limitations because even though the MacArthur case happened after he successfully prosecuted Father McGuire, it ruled in our favor.

We then talked about the other motion, which was about my counseling records. I shared with him that I had already found out that there really aren't any counseling records available from Dr. Hadley, the psychiatrist that I saw for approximately a year about 25 years ago. I told DA Koss that I had already found her and talked with her when the investigation started heating up and she had told me that she hadn't kept her records. I also told DA Koss that Detective Sharp had already interviewed her so he should have that information.

There was also a psychiatrist my parents took me to back when Lesser was still around, but I only saw him a couple of times as I refused to talk with him. I have no idea who he was or where he was.

The only other therapist I saw was when I was working as a therapist at Jane Addams and refused to do crisis because it is too traumatizing for me. Due to my refusal to handle crisis calls, the director of the mental health center, sent me for counseling to "fix" my PTSD. I know that I talked with this therapist about Lesser, but I also didn't see her too often and didn't know if she still had her records.

I told DA Koss that I have no problem with them getting my records, but he said that he didn't feel that Mr. K. had done a good enough "showing" and that most likely that motion for my counseling records would be denied as well. He said that if the judge did agree to my counseling records, then it would be "in camera" which means that only the judge can look at them and he will decide if there is anything exculpatory. I asked what that meant and he said that it would be something that would hurt my defense. When I asked what would be considered exculpatory, he said that if it was in the counseling records that I had said that I lied a lot, or that I just hated Lesser and he didn't molest me but I wanted to ruin his life by claiming that anyway. Since that isn't true, again, I have no issue with my records.

DA Koss also asked if I was going to be there on December 17th and of course I said yes. I could tell however by the tone of his voice that that didn't sit to well with him so I asked him if me attending was a problem. He said that the only thing that he was worried about was that if Mr. K.'s motion was denied, but I was sitting there, Mr. K. would have me testify about my records right then and there. I told DA Koss that I didn't have a problem with that and that my concern about me not showing up would present to the court as if I had something to hide. I don't feel that I have anything to hide, so he agreed that I could come.

Finally we talked about Lesser not having to show up for court and how that was upsetting to me because I feel that that should be part of the "punishment". The fact that he has to show his ugly face to everyone and have them know what he did. DA Koss couldn't have been nicer on that one and said that he has to pick his battles with the defense carefully and that isn't one he wants to fight. He said that he understands that I want/need him to come, but that his job is to convict Lesser, not to punish him. Ha Ha.

That of course calmed me down and I made sure that at the end of the conversation, he knew how much I appreciated what he is doing for me. I wanted him to know that he is important to many people, as he is the one who has to bring justice to victims. I also told him that not only did he have a brain, but he had a heart as well. I am so thankful to have him on this team and I find that he is as calming to me as Detective Sharp.

Since talking with DA Koss, I thought I better begin remembering how I ended up with Dr. Hadley and basically what happened. Therefore I called Mom this morning as I remember it was her that originally found Dr. Hadley and really liked her. The problem was that I couldn't remember how she got to Dr. Hadley, so we talked about that this morning.

It all started in January of 1984 or maybe I should say before that. I had been married to Bill but at that time I had filed for a divorce from him. Bill had become upset during the process and had actually gone into my parent's home when no one was there and took all of our wedding presents and personal possessions that we had been storing there. Not only that, but he had also turned all of the pictures of me in the house face down. Needless to say this had scared my mother so she was already upset about me being "safe" from Bill while going through the divorce.

Then there was an incident at the school where Mom taught when one of her students had missed school. Another little girl had asked Mom if it would be ok if she brought this girl's homework to her and Mom said yes and gave her the other girl's homework. Then the little girl shared with my mother that the house she was delivering this little girl's homework to, was a "bad house". What really upset Mom is that Mom LET this little girl go to this house, knowing that she was going to a "bad house". The tremendous guilt she felt about that triggered something within Mom about safety and me and that night she had a terrible nightmare about me. She dreamt that I was in this big black hole of boiling hot oil and that I couldn't get out of this hole. She dreamt that she kept trying to get me out of the burning pit of ail, but that she couldn't do it.

I had been staying at my parent's house since I filed for divorce and the morning she woke up from this dream, there was something "off" with her. She kept saying that she "was in deep, deep trouble" and just kept saying that over and over. She kept asking where Dad was and I had to keep repeating to her that he was on errands. Mom wasn't able to remember anything that happened that morning and when she forgot that she had just hung up the phone after talking with someone, I knew something was really wrong. I somehow got a hold of my dad and told him that something was wrong with Mom and that he needed to come home right away.

Mom had to go to Lakeland Hospital as there was something obviously wrong with her but we had no idea what it was. We all thought it might be a stroke and I remember waiting in the emergency room as they tried to figure out what was wrong with her. Later that night, she finally "came around" and was able to talk and remember things, but the whole experience was weird and terrifying to say the least.

They had her spend the night and through follow-up with our family doctor, Dr. Kolar, he diagnosed that she had had an episode called "Transient Global Amnesia". Dr. Kolar and Mom had discussed what happened and determined that Mom had "lost it" due to her being "triggered" by sending that little girl to a "bad house".

Mom was so upset that she didn't tell that little girl not to go to the "bad house" and then that translated into her believing that she had "sent me" into an unsafe situation in regards to Lesser.

Her whole breakdown had been a result of what had happened with Lesser so long ago and all of the bad things that had happened recently, threw her into this state of mind. The whole thing was so scary and even today, we have to make sure that if Mom gets really upset about something, she won't go into that "state of mind" again.

Dr. Kolar suggested that Mom seek therapy and recommended Dr. Hadley. Mom had gone to see her and it was then that Dr. Hadley said that she needed to talk with me, so that's how I ended up on her couch.

There are a couple of things that I remember about Dr. Hadley and my sessions with her and they include good memories. First is that she had a private practice in this two story cottage that was set off from her main residence which was on a lake. I remember it to be a beautiful, calming place and that if I was ever a therapist; this is the type of place that I would like to have for my practice.

I also remember that she would knit or crochet and eat popcorn while we talked. For some reason, her knitting needles moving in such a pattern was mesmerizing and I found her very easy to talk with. I also felt very comfortable in my surroundings and because of all that, she is the first mental health professional that I told about the abuse.

The main thing that I remember from seeing Dr. Hadley is that she finally validated that what Lesser did was wrong and that she had a name for people like him and that was "snake oil salesmen". She also called him a pedophile and reassured me that I had no chance against this guy.

I thought it was important to provide my counseling information to DA Koss, so I spent some time writing down whom I saw, when I saw them and what I learned as a result of therapy. I recognize that all the information I have provided to DA Koss is available to the defense team, but I have no problem with telling them what happened in treatment, as I believe it only strengthens our case. Another psychological ploy in "this game" that hopefully will work!

I have always been cognizant of the fact that ANYTHING I have given DA Koss is available to the defense and being aware of that is part of my "game". I feel that I have been able to take away a lot of the defense's "ammunition" by admitting to things in the first place, as well as offering a list of rebuttals to questions that I feel they will ask me. I feel that I have already made the case against him by providing DA Koss with all of the incriminating information I could, while at the same time, I have tried to "squash" any points that the defense might make. I hope it works!!

I am also finding that I am in a much better mood because I know we aren't in jeopardy with the case…as of yet! I have learned another lesson this past week and that is to not let whatever they throw at us, get me too upset.

November 23, 2008 (Sunday)

I love the "Hour Of Power" as the messages are always uplifting and filled with possibility thinking and I wanted to shared today's message with you journal as it seems to apply so well to fears and questions that I have about life right now.

John Maxwell was the guest speaker and the message was from a book he wrote called "Running with Giants". His sermon was about taking certain people out of the bible and pretending that you were running a lap in life with them. The message was "what would these people say to you for encouragement if they had that one lap to run with you in life"?

First up was Noah and if Noah was running a lap with you, what he might want you to know is that "One person can make a difference". I needed to hear that due to the thoughts, doubts and feelings I've been having about being a therapist. It was important for me to know that I have had a positive impact in people's lives and that I should consider still doing that.

The next was Rebecca and that she would tell you while you were running the lap with her to "Serve others with a generous spirit" because when you look at the life of Rebecca, it was a life of serving others with no strings attached. That is something else that I try to do as a therapist, so I felt like this was another message from God that I should continue to help people in some capacity.

Finally was David who would encourage you with the words "You can overcome limitations that other's place on you". No one thought that David could defeat Goliath, but yet he did. This spoke to me in regards to this journal and that no matter what anyone else might think about its prospects, if I have the faith, then that is all that matters.

This sermon seemed to speak to my fears and doubts about my future and what God has in store for me.

Loved it!!

November 26, 2008 (Wednesday)

Came home yesterday and in the mail, there was a subpoena from DA Koss!! That is rather surprising as just Friday he wasn't sure that he even wanted me there, and on Tuesday I receive a subpoena?!

I can't believe how receiving that subpoena has upset me. I know that this case is in the courts, but still to receive this in the mail is disturbing. It is also such a turnaround for DA Koss that I wonder what he is thinking. I will e-mail him later to ask why he subpoenaed me. I think the reason is that once he read the information I sent him on my counseling, he thought that it was powerful and WANTS me to tell it. Now I think I will have to testify for sure on December 17th and of course I'm already going over it in my mind and I just can't seem to stop.

I know that I am going to obsess for the next three weeks about having to testify, like I did before the preliminary hearing. I just want to make sure that I have my story straight so that they can't confuse me or twist my words. I also think of all the things that the defense could ask me in order to try and trip me up somehow and it's already driving me crazy. I've only had the subpoena for 10 hours!! I really feel like I'm just going to crumble. I am so tired and feel so overwhelmed by all of this "badness" that at times it's difficult just putting one foot in front of the other.

Just talked with my parents about everything and now I'm feeling better! We discussed how interesting it is to see how the threads from the past are now beginning to make sense in the future. For example, Mom's breakdown led us to Dr. Hadley, who can now testify for us that I did talk with her about Lesser molesting me. If Mom hadn't have had that breakdown, we wouldn't have that proof.

It's like we were building our own "web" over all these years and that web is now hopefully going to snare Lesser. Of course we didn't know that this web was being spun by us, but now it is coming into focus and it is really cool to see. He spun his web around Janet and I years ago and we are now spinning a web around him. I love it!!

Checked my e-mail and the reason DA Koss subpoenaed me was so I can claim mileage! All that worrying for nothing!! This whole court process can certainly be traumatizing!! I e-mailed back that I haven't been claiming anything monetarily from the county and that I don't plan on it. They are doing enough for me and the last thing I want is to take their money. What an idiot I am for allowing my thinking to get "carried away" about the reason behind the subpoena. Will I never learn?!

CHAPTER 31

Reason To Hope

November 30, 2008 (Sunday)

Thank goodness Thanksgiving is over! It's not that I didn't want to see everyone, but it was going to be "different" without Kay. As usual, the Schmidt family was wonderful and though some (except me) cried at one time or another, we still were able to have a good time.

I think this Lexipro is "working" as I'm nowhere near as emotional about things and seem to be more "consistent" with my mood. There are side effects that I don't like however and so as soon as this nightmare is over, I'm quitting the Lexipro.

December 2, 2008 (Tuesday)

I had sent an e-mail to Dr. O'Beirne asking her about my journal, as I hadn't heard from her about it since briefly talking with her at the advisory council meeting a couple of weeks ago. I mentioned that if she thought my journal stunk, that she should just tell me as I have the strength to hear it. At least I hope I do.

I was thrilled with her response to my e-mail, as she does indeed like the journal so far!! She said that she thought it could be an "incredible resource"!! A resource for what I'm not quite sure yet, but it was a huge relief to have her say that she thinks it would be of help to others!! FINALLY some good news for a change! I have a smile on my face today, a new attitude towards continuing this journal and hope for a bright future.

I just can't thank Dr. O'Beirne enough for helping and I know that God sent her to me for this part of my journey. The Lord does work in mysterious and wonderful ways. Dr. O'Beirne is another piece of "moss" that is collecting on that stone that is crashing down the mountain!!

December 3, 2008 (Wednesday)

Yesterday I thought all day about Dr. O'Beirne' words about my journal being "incredible" and I can't believe that she thinks that! I know that I have been working hard on this journal for a long time, but to have someone else think that it might be of help to others has created hope that this might work.

I wanted to see what Dr. O'Beirne found "incredible" about this journal so I decided to read the whole thing. However after reading it, I'm still not sure what is so good about it. I do think that this is an interesting story, but I also found that I sure do whine a lot about being tired and overwhelmed. What a baby I am and my grandfather, Pop, would tell me to "suck it up" and do this without complaining, so I will make an attempt to do that. Having said that, this is the one "thing" that I can whine to on a continuous basis without it getting tired of me, so maybe I'll keep "whining."

I am thankful that today I don't have to go to work. There is supposed to be a snowstorm and I REALLY can't drive in bad weather. I am so anxious doing ANY driving lately that contemplating driving in a snowstorm is too emotionally overwhelming. It is amazing to me the effect that this case is having on almost all aspects of my life. It's like I'm in constant PTSD mode and it's getting worse!!

I was thinking quite a bit on the way home from work last night about how I feel like I am decompensating. My weight continues to plunge, I have dark circles forming under my eyes, I have no energy and just want to stay away from people. I don't know how I can hold on for another two-three months. It's been 4 months since his arrest and if DA Koss didn't have those other big trials, mine most likely would have been over by now. I certainly wasn't expecting to wait 6 months for the trial and who knows if it will even happen then. Prisoner Pete told me that Lesser's attorney was most likely going to keep "milking" Lesser for money by using postponements and other things to keep delaying this process.

The only comfort I can find is that when this whole thing is over, I want to go to a beach and just lay there for about 1 month!! I also have to remember that I have to "Outwit, Outlast and Outplay" these jerks and I WILL do it, no matter what happens to me.

The next court date is two weeks away and it's all that I am thinking about. I do continue to use my arsenal of distress tolerance skills to help me feel better when I'm overwhelmed. Some more ideas that I implement is rereading client's thank you notes to me, watch movies and even decorate trees with tinsel on the way to work. Then when I drive by those trees either on the way to work, or on the way home, I see them and smile. There is a special tree that I always decorate year round about 3 miles from our house. It's a beautiful wooded area that you drive through and it's just neat to see the tree decorated amongst all of the other ones.

Other things I'm going to do today is work on paperwork and fix the Christmas tree that fell down AGAIN last night while we were watching television. It had fallen the other night and I had accused Danny of knocking it over. Of course he hadn't and we set it back up. I do have all my ornaments on ½ of the tree as the rest of it is in a corner. Probably all of my ornaments were too heavy and the stand was broken as it was, so that is why it fell over! I have such beautiful ornaments and every one of them has a special meaning to me. It took me 4 hours to put up the tree this year and it looked beautiful. It is now TIED to the antelope head that is hanging on the wall. All the ornaments are askew as are the lights and tinsel, so I will have to fix that at some point, but for now, I feel extremely tired and hopefully will just rest for the day. (See, already whining in the next paragraph!)

To leave it on a good note, when I got home last night, all of our outdoor Christmas lights were on and I must say that it brought a smile to my face. Danny really does up the house and I tease him that it looks like the Griswald house in the movie "Christmas Vacation." It is beautiful and it is rare that I find things to smile about.

CHAPTER 32

The Art of Decompensation

December 4, 2008 (Thursday)

Yesterday was a tough day in that I felt emotionally exhausted. A couple of my clients called and I didn't even have the energy to call one of them back. I did call her this morning though and explained to her about my inability to "emotionally be there" for her right now and maybe I should refer her to someone else. Fortunately she understood where I was coming from and will try to do better as she refuses to go see someone else right now.

While talking with her, I realized that I am really beginning to decompensate as far as being able to be "in this world". I have to go to work today and the thought of even going outside is really upsetting to me. I will also have to take Tucker for his late morning walk and I'm panicking at that idea. It's like I'm becoming agoraphobic on top of everything else. Another sign and symptom of PTSD?!

One of the problems with this process is that there is no road map for how I am "supposed" to respond to what is going on in my life. Therefore I have no clue about what is going to happen to me emotionally, mentally or physically. I am finding out however that as the time drags on, I get more and more emotionally dysregulated…almost to the point of incapacitation. I just want to stay in my warm house and not think about anything but this case. I can't seem to get my mind off of my journal, the upcoming court date, when the trial might be and wondering what other crap will they throw at me. It's difficult to make plans for going up north, as I don't know when the next court date will be until the next court date on the 17th. It's getting to the point where I can't and don't want to make any decisions and even thinking about what to make for dinner can reduce me to tears.

I am not eating, not drinking anything and smoking like a chimney and I know that I need to take better care of myself, but I just can't. The only time I feel like eating is if I've been in my house for a couple of days straight. Then I seem calm enough to be able to get a couple of bites of food down. But when I work, I don't eat in the morning and don't eat all day and even though I'm starving by the time I get home, nothing tastes good. The only way I'm keeping on weight is my nightly candy and ice cream mixed with chocolate sauce and chocolate brownies. I guess you could call it "comfort food".

I just worry about how much further I'm going to go down into this hole I'm sinking into. The good thing is that this time, I'm not drinking myself into the hole. I am rather experiencing all of the emotions and working through them, vs. drowning them in drugs and alcohol like in the past. Of course I've had my moments with alcohol, as I still tend to gravitate towards that when there is too much going on in my head and I need a break.

Having to process all of these emotions and "feel" them is the most difficult part of this process. All I can do is analyze to the best of my ability what is happening to me and then take the necessary steps to make sure that I don't go insane through this whole thing.

I find that I am making stupid mistakes all of the time as I'm not really "thinking" about what I'm doing. I have broken 2 coffee pots, backed into a steel pole in my new car, made terrible dinners, re-broke the X-mas tree stand. It seems like anything I touch lately either breaks or isn't done "right" so then I have to redo it and of course that is frustrating to no end.

I've forgotten to order new checks and therefore have no checks to pay the bills. I've "lost" bills only to discover them right before they're due and then have to pay over the Internet, which costs more.

This morning I shared with Danny how anxious and upset I've been feeling lately about doing anything, and his statement back was, " To Grow-up"! Needless to say my primary emotion was hurt and then the secondary emotion, anger kicked in and I exploded at him. I can't help the way I am feeling and there is no magic pill that is going to help me get through this whole process, so he has to understand that it is what it is. I'm not sure if he understands that I really CAN'T help what is happening to me physically, emotionally and mentally. I am really sorry to put him through this, but it's something that just HAS to be done, as I'm certainly not quitting now!

In order to get out of the house today, I will have to tell myself all of the positives about why it will be ok to go outside. One is that the sun is shining and the newly fallen snow looks beautiful. Another is that the drive to Mt. Horeb is a gorgeous ride, so that should be aesthetically pleasing. I also have to go to Wal-Mart and pick up my medicine as well as some presents, so that will hopefully be enjoyable as well. These are the tricks of the trade that I use to get myself out of the house. I am thankful however that I can order a lot of my X-mas presents over the Internet, as then I don't have to deal with the crowds. SEE I am becoming more and more agoraphobic! This is insane!

CHAPTER 33

Parents From Heaven

December 9, 2008 (Tuesday)

It's been a rough couple of days, only because I ended up getting the stomach flu from my client on Friday! It was all that I could do to make it to a team meeting where I ended up telling them that I was having a rough time of it lately. This "team" has been together for over three years, so I felt comfortable sharing this personal information. Another reason I felt comfortable sharing is because my client's own mother had been molested by her father, so if anyone knows what I am going through, she does. This mother had told a teacher at school when she was a teenager and as a result, had to go to court to testify against him and he did end up spending time in prison.

After the meeting she came up to me and said that she understood exactly how I am feeling. She also said to me that if it was this upsetting for me as an adult, think how she felt going through the process as a child. I have always praised her on her courage to go through that whole process, but now that I'm going through it, I am in awe of how she could do something so difficult at such a young age. She said that by far, going through the criminal process was the most difficult and traumatizing event in her life. Going through it myself right now, I would have to agree with her.

Saturday night I woke up puking and it continued throughout Sunday and Sunday night. I just laid on the couch all day Sunday and most of yesterday, although I did get some X-mas presents bought over the Internet and some X-mas presents wrapped. I think that it was actually good that I got this stomach flu as it forced me to slow down. I didn't feel like doing ANYTHING and therefore didn't, so I got some much needed "down time".

I also spent a couple of hours talking with my parents on Saturday and that was helpful in calming me down. I told them all of the stressors that I am under and that I feel I am really decompensating. They have helped me so much in the past not only financially, but also emotionally and mentally as well. They have really been my "therapists" through this thing and though I know that isn't probably a "correct" thing to do, it really helps a lot.

They are the only ones that know EVERYTHING about me and I'm not afraid to share what is happening with me. I also feel very guilty in that Dad has had to finance me for so long. He pays much of my medical expenses and all of my dental expenses. My dental bill for one year alone was over $10,000. I had 4 root canals and 4 crowns in one year! I don't know what I would do without them.

I also shared with them my thoughts about being concerned about working when I am so upset and if it is ethically correct to do so. I shared with them my idea about borrowing some money to get me through January and February, as I'm sure that I will only get more dysregulated as this trial comes closer. It's important to me that they don't think that I am a "slacker" in the way that I am emotionally responding to this whole ordeal. I have continued to work long past "wanting to" and it's getting harder and harder to deal with clients.

Not only do I have my clients to worry about, but many other things as well. I have to keep the relationship with Danny going as best I can; I help a lot with his mother; Lisa is still on my mind; I worry about Janet and her family; I worry about my parents and their health and sanity through this process; I worry about what the defense will throw at us next and feel that I have to "pre-plan" everything. There are other people I emotionally support as well and they include my friend Julie, my older lady friend from the Laundromat, Jan, and Prisoner Pete just to name a few. I constantly send cards to people who are sick, or done a good job or who need support. There is so much on my plate that people don't see and I don't want my parents to think that they are helping to support my ass while it sits on the couch. The reality is that I am constantly working on paperwork or this journal when I'm home and if I'm not doing "work stuff" I have to do stuff around the house.

It was so important to me that they understand that there is so much more going on with me and what I am dealing with and of course as they always do, they understood. Dad also understands how humiliating and embarrassing it is to ask for financial help at times.

Talking with my parents about this whole thing is so helpful and as long as they understand what I am doing, thinking, planning and everything else, that is all I care about. I can't even put into words how much they mean to me, or how much I appreciate EVERYTHING they do for me. They say that this is what parents do, but they are far and beyond "normal" parents and I am so thankful to have them.

I have mostly decided that I will quit being a therapist because the reality is that I have never made much money working with the clients that I do. Most of them are medical assistance clients and I work with them for a couple of reasons. One is that no one really wants to work with people on medical assistance, as it doesn't pay worth a dime. The clients usually have chronic and overwhelming issues and to get paid so little for so much time and effort isn't appealing to other professionals. The other reason I work with them is because they are the population most at need as well as the fact that you will always have clients to see.

I can't handle many clients on my caseload, as the ones I do have are "difficult" with many issues. I work with abused/neglected children and borderline individuals and I consider those two categories some of the most difficult to help. It is emotionally draining for me to be a therapist because I put "myself" into the case. I literally will "join" with a family or with a person to get the emotional connection needed to help this client make the changes that they need to make in their lives. As a result, I emotionally invest in all of my clients and right now, that is proving to be too much.

Another thing that happened is that David and I have been in communication the past couple of days and I shared with him how much I was decompensating. He has told me to see a therapist and then said something that sticks with me, and that is "don't win the war only to lose the battle". He is exactly correct and I will have to keep that in mind.

A lot is going on, but for now, it's a snow day as we are expecting 6-11 inches of snow. It is beautiful outside and I have "permission" to just lie on the couch as I'm still recovering from the stomach flu. I will try and enjoy my "day off" and be mindful of God's beauty and how the earth looks clean and new with the freshly falling snow!

CHAPTER 34

Comfort From Above

December 10, 2008 (Monday)

One week to go until the next "move" in this "game" and I know that I am feeling better today, as I have returned to my normal "manic" state. I'm not normally manic, but that seems to be the norm lately.

I've been up since 4:00 a.m. rereading this journal yet again; I've cleaned the house; wrapped presents; made business calls; shopped on the Internet and now I am going to begin working on my X-mas cards again. I got about 2/3 of them done yesterday before I couldn't do anymore. I also am short on cards, so I'll have to get some more.

December 14, 2008 (Sunday)

It's been quite a hectic week. After recovering from the flu, I went to work on Thursday and spent ALL of Friday cleaning the house as the girl's were coming out for our yearly X-mas party. I didn't want to have to go out to a bar (back to my agoraphobia) therefore I had to invite them to my house. That alone is rare as I don't invite anyone out here, but we had a very nice time.

Today our church program, the "Hour of Power", was one of the best services I've seen in years. It touched so many emotional and intellectual levels in me that I'm keeping it to watch again and again if I want.

First is that I'm feeling very vulnerable again and that seems to be par for the course when there is a court appearance. I always look to my church program for encouragement, support, hope and a positive attitude and it certainly didn't disappoint me today.

The "Hour Of Power" has been such a crucial piece in my transformation from an alcoholic-cokehead to a more productive and happier person. Danny and I have been watching it every week for approximately 23 years and I know that Dr. Schuller's positive messages that mix spirituality with psychology helped me to overcome my "issues" in life. He wrote a book called "Turn Your Scars Into Stars" and that is one message that drove me to go back to school to become a therapist. I am still trying to "turn my scars into stars" by writing this journal in the hopes that it might help others recognize they're not alone.

The "Hour of Power" always has a guest speaker, guest musician and lately a guest pastor. Today's guest speaker was this Australian woman by the name of Bronwen Healy who runs a charity with her husband, called "Hope Foundation". Bronwen used to be a heroin addict and prostitute yet she was able to turn her life around when she became a Christian. Bronwen and her husband now work with the people that she used to be, drug addicts and prostitutes. She feels that there aren't many who want to work with that population, but she has gotten a "whisper" from God that she needed to do this and go where God has told them to go. Bronwen is a remarkable young woman who said in regards to their ministry, "if I can use my past to help change other people's future, then her past happened for a reason"

That is EXACTLY how I feel as far as the reason why I became a therapist and why I am writing this journal. I still want to help others, but I want to help more than just the ones that I can see in my practice. I want to "grow up" and be just like Bronwen Healy! My admiration and respect for her is immense. She is a funny, intelligent, well-spoken and well-raised young woman who got waylaid by drugs. She is now using her past experiences to help others and to me, that is what God wants us to do in life. Be kind to others and help people out in whatever way you can. Listening to her gave me hope once again that this whole process that "we" are all going through is happening for a bigger reason than just me getting justice.

Next on the program was this fabulous singer and songwriter by the name of Fernando Ortega who sang his song "Jesus, King of Angels". I was so moved that I burst into tears during the song. It felt as if Jesus was comforting me RIGHT NOW and is standing with me in this fight.

This is my "new song" that I want to play while driving over to court. I usually play all of the songs that I love including religious ones, as it is a way for me to calm down before getting to the nastiness that is happening in court. This is my newest and most inspirational song. It is so simple and just a love song to God.

As if I thought the service couldn't get any better, Bill Hybels was the guest pastor. He is the pastor of Willow Creek Community Church, which is a huge church in Barrington IL. In fact, an old friend of mine, Mark H. attends this church and has tried to talk Lisa into coming. Bill Hybels is a very good speaker and a good storyteller and today was no different.

His sermon was on "God's Whisper's" and to listen to them. I totally agree with him as I have heard "God's Whispers" throughout my life and have generally followed them. I think that it was a "God Whisper" that told me to "kick Lesser to the curb so long ago"; A "God's Whisper" that it was time to kick my alcohol and drug addictions although that whole thing was more like a sledgehammer blow than a whisper. It was still God saying that it was time to stop and begin to heal.

Another "whisper" was once I got sober, the idea of going back to school and getting my Master's Degree in Counseling so that I could help others not make the same mistakes as I did.

I believe another "whisper" was starting my greeting card business, as I'm still positive that I'm not through with those yet! Another "whisper" was when David and Rene e-mailed me the story about Father McGuire. After a few days of thinking and praying what to do, I believe that "God whispered" to me that I needed to do this with Lesser whether I wanted to or not. It really seems like I had no choice in this matter, but was simply something that was going to happen.

Of course I hear "God Whisper's" all the time, whether it be that I get an urge to say something nice to a complete stranger or give someone a compliment. I have stopped and helped so many people as well as lost animals that I truly feel these are all "whispers" from God and that He wants us to take care of each other in this world.

The only troubling thing was that Bill Hybels shared a story about his father hearing a "whisper" that Bill needed to go to a Christian camp in Wisconsin and though Bill resisted going, he personally found Christ while at that camp. It literally made me sick to my stomach when he told the story about going to this Christian camp in Wisconsin no less and of course all I can think about is my camp "experience" with Lesser. I actually was dying to know which camp he went to as maybe we went to the same one? He never did say which camp, but it just brought up "icky" feelings. I was able to get past it however and enjoy the rest of the sermon.

Since it is my belief that this whole criminal process was a "God Whisper" and after hearing the words of hope and encouragement from Bronwen, the soul-touching music of Fernando and the wise words of Bill Hybels, I feel ready to face the challenge in court on Wednesday!

I do remember that this whole thing has been in God's hands in the first place, but I think today was a reminder from Him that He "has my back" and that I am most certainly not in this alone. Not only that, but I also feel that I am simply His vessel, doing the work that He wants done. I hope that belief of mine doesn't sound conceited as that isn't how I mean that, but rather He chose me to do this epic and difficult journey. Actually, I am proud and honored that He has given me the opportunity to hopefully help many others.

Tomorrow it's back to work but for today, I will be mindful of God's message to me; that it was His "whisper" that started this whole thing and therefore, He will help me through it. I also feel that God understands how difficult this process is for me and that Fernando's music was meant to soothe and comfort me. It is something that I can play over and over to help me remain mindful that through Christ, all things are possible.

Later:

I couldn't help but send Fernando Ortega a "fan e-mail" telling him how much his song meant to me this morning. I hope he gets it and knows that he helped at least one person this morning and that he helped me more than he will ever know. Danny is sick of me rewinding the tape and playing the song, so I guess I'll have to stop for now.

CHAPTER 35

Finally An End In Sight

December 17, 2008 (Thursday)

Finally this day is here. It seems like it takes FOREVER for each court date to arrive and today is no different.

It is currently 5:00 a.m. and since I couldn't sleep anymore, I decided to get up and "bang away" as Danny calls it, on my journal. There are so many thoughts, fears and anxieties going through my head that I thought it best to simply get up and put them all down in my journal.

There was a snowstorm yesterday and so it looks beautiful as I can see freshly fallen snow out the window and the neighbor's lit up manger scene looks so peaceful. Danny is up north working so it is quiet in the house, I have the Christmas wreath lit up in this room, a cup of coffee with Irish Cream (the breakfast of champions!) and I'm set to put some thoughts down.

Actually, I don't know where to begin, but that seems to be the norm for me lately. I find it very difficult to make any decisions about anything while at the same time, there are a thousand different thoughts flitting through my brain. Having to "think" about Christmas and get all the things done that I do at this time of year as well as the usual chores has really been stressing me out. As a result, I made the executive decision to stay home from work yesterday not only because of the snowstorm, but also because I was too nervous to leave. I actually got a lot accomplished with all of this nervous energy I have.

Now I'm trying to think of things to do while I WAIT for this hearing this afternoon. It was moved to 4:00 p.m. instead of 3:00 as I guess the judge has a funeral. I'm just glad that it isn't the judge's funeral as that might cause further delays!! I still have more presents to wrap, so I'll do that as well as prepare for possibly testifying today. They argue the two motions that Lesser's attorney put forth last time and they deal with the statute of limitations and my counseling records.

I will of course do my normal "rituals" before going to court, or anywhere important for that matter, and that is to "s#*@, shower and shave". (We used to say that as teenagers when were planning on going out.) I feel that I have to look my best as that brings me confidence when I'm facing difficult situations. My outfit has to be comfortable not only physically, but mentally as well. My hair has to be clean, shiny and full of body, not to mention highlighted and cut. My eyebrows, as well as my chin nowadays, are plucked, my legs are shaved and I feel clean all over. Maybe that is what it is…I need to feel clean, as this is such a "dirty experience". Just like after being raped, you want to take a shower to get the nastiness off of you.

I usually drive straight to the courthouse with minimal stops in between. I am so nervous driving over and I really don't want to talk with anyone, so I usually have my car full of gas and I don't drink too much of anything so I don't have to stop. I will listen to all of my favorite music on the way over and while waiting in the parking lot if I'm early. I did go and buy that Fernando Ortega CD on Monday, so I will definitely listen to that today. I have figured out that it is like a prayer to God and it is just beautiful, peaceful and calming to me and that's what I try to accomplish on the way over; a sense of peace, calm, determination and preparedness.

Finally, I bring my stuffed teddy bear, Budweiser, with me for the ride. Deanna bought him for me to comfort me when Bill got killed. I named him Budweiser because that was his horses' name when he, my friend Holli R. and I went horseback riding and camping overnight on the Continental Divide. We had gone to visit her in Colorado while on our honeymoon out west and this was one fun event she had planned for us.

Sometimes I will bring my "client book" with me, which is all of the thank you cards I have gotten from clients over the years. ANYTHING that I can do to give myself confidence and peace, I do.

I don't think that I've talked about going to court alone and though people have offered to go with me, I don't want them to. Richard asked me the other day if I wanted him to go and I said no. One reason I want to go alone is that I don't want others exposed to this "nastiness". It is so upsetting to even be there, that I don't want to put anyone through it.

Another reason is that I want to show Lesser that I don't need an "army" to help me with this. I am strong enough to do it myself. Having said that, I wonder if the judge is wondering why I come alone. I hope he doesn't think that no one is supporting me or believing me in this.

I'm done rambling for a while and am now going to prepare for court this morning. I don't know if I'll get back to this journal before I leave, so wish me luck!

December 18, 2008 (Thursday)

We FINALLY have a date for the trial…April 20th, 2009!! While I am thrilled that we finally have a date, I'm definitely disappointed that it's not for another 4 months. This is another example of a dialectic where I'm feeling happy, but at the same time very dismayed. Feelings that are at opposite ends of a seesaw and that is

173

what is so hard about dialectics. The intensity of the two "battling" sides causes intense dysregulation in a person.

I first went to the DA's office before the hearing and DA Koss, Detective Sharp and I talked about a number of things. I told them that hopefully the trial was going to happen soon as I feel that I am beginning to decompensate. I think they could tell that I have lost quite a bit of weight, but neither of them said anything about it.

DA Koss also said that Lesser's attorney has been making "rumblings" about possibly agreeing to a plea bargain, so I asked how much time he might get if he plea bargains. DA Koss said maybe 15 years and then asked me what I would like to see happen to him. I told them about my internal dilemma about wanting him to fry, but then my "other side" saying I don't want to TOTALLY destroy him. I thought maybe a couple of years of actually sitting IN prison, but did say that I will of course defer to whatever DA Koss thinks is enough. I think that both of them were a little shocked at my suggestion of so little time for him. I'm sure they wonder why I don't simply want him to fry and show him no mercy, but that's who I am, good or bad. From our discussion, it seems like DA Koss and Detective Sharp both want him to be in prison for quite a long time.

Detective Sharp also told me about going on the Janesville Gazette "Blog" site and that he had found a blog from this person who knows Lesser. I guess people were blogging about this motion hearing today and someone posted that her mother knew Lesser and that he was a jerk or something along those lines. Detective Sharp e-mailed this person to see if she would talk with him about her statement and she e-mailed back that her mother had been and still is friends with Jeannie, Lesser's ex-wife. This "blogger" had heard that he was a womanizer and basically "a dog" (sorry to dogs!) while she was growing up. Detective Sharp might try and talk further with this person. It still freaks me out that people are blogging about me on the Internet and I did share with DA Koss and Detective Sharp that I have wanted to respond to some of the blogs, but haven't because I knew better. Detective Sharp confirmed that I shouldn't respond to anyone right now.

I finally shared with DA Koss and Detective Sharp the fact that I am writing this journal and that it was an "Oprah" book. DA Koss laughed and said he wondered who would play him in the movie...Johnny Depp?! DA Koss also made the comment that he wished there was a class or something available to victims and their families that will explain what happens during a criminal trial. Maybe my journal could do that as well!!

We then went up to the courtroom and Lesser was there! He was dressed a little bit better than in the past, but he still looks a little rough. Maybe he just normally has huge sacks under his eyes all of the time. What is really weird is that I had no feelings whatsoever today. I wasn't nervous while in court nor was I upset at all. Maybe it's the Lexipro as well as the Lorazepam I had taken an hour earlier, but I really felt nothing. It's like he is a "non-entity" anymore. I don't know what to think about the lack of any emotion whatsoever.

His attorney argued the motion about the statute of limitations knowing he was going to lose, according to DA Koss. I guess his attorney wanted to make it known that if this MacArthur case goes back to the Wisconsin Supreme Court, or even the Federal Supreme Court, Lesser would be able to appeal whatever happens with this case. The judge denied his motion to dismiss the case based on the statute of limitations! Another win for the good side!

The next motion was about my counseling records and this is where is got nasty. I had given DA Koss my Autobiography and Life Experiences papers, one of which is in the front of this journal. His attorney was using my written statements and saying that I was mentally ill and obviously unstable as a child and an adult. He argued that my parents had even said that I was a disciplinary problem; was rebellious and sullen as a teenager. I looked at Evelyn who was sitting next to me with a look of disgust at their tactics, and she whispered to me "all teenagers are like that"! I almost laughed out loud. Mr. K further added that I had major AODA issues and that I had even been hospitalized for them.

He then talked about me being a counselor for sexually abused people and that maybe this was a counter-transference thing and suggested that this might even be some recovered memory stuff or whatever. Mr. K. was upset that my counseling records were like a "black box" and he wasn't allowed to look into it. That led to a discussion about Dr. Hadley and the fact that she was not only still in the area, but that Detective Sharp had already interviewed her.

I was surprised that DA Koss didn't say anything while Lesser's attorney was ranting on and of course in the gallery, I was sometimes smiling at what he said, sometimes shaking my head or having some other what I hope was appropriate, reaction to what he was saying. I knew the judge was looking at me and I don't think any of my visceral emotions were out of line or obvious, but it was difficult to hear all of these lies being said about me and I couldn't refute them!

At any rate, I don't think they won that one although I don't care about my counseling records. DA Koss confirmed later that we won this one too!

Lesser's attorney also talked about bringing a couple more motions before the court and one of them was to suppress Janet's testimony. If she can't testify that might "hurt", but I would like to think that we could win this without her. She hasn't been in touch with me lately although she has forwarded on some good e-mails. I'm not sure how she is feeling about this whole thing now, but I will be sending an e-mail to everyone about this, so hopefully she'll respond. I could easily call her too which I might do.

Finally they all talked about this going to trial and it took a while to find a date, as DA Koss is rather busy the next couple of months. It was finally decided that the trial would begin April 20th and go through the 23rd. They then talked about a jury trial and how to proceed with that. They mentioned something about having jury members. It is difficult to comprehend what is happening in court as the attorneys not only talk so fast, but they throw around all of this legal jargon that I don't understand.

DA Koss, Evelyn and Detective Sharp, and I then went downstairs to talk. He is going to send out subpoena's to people I had on my list that I had sent him. I'm not really sure how it proceeds from here, so I'll have to find out some more information about what happens next, but for now, I have to process and figure out what just happened.

We didn't stay long afterwards and as we were walking out, I said thank you to DA Koss again and went to put out my hand to shake his, but he put up his arms for a hug!! I wished him a Merry Christmas and hugged Evelyn and Detective Sharp as well! I then asked Detective Sharp to walk me out to my car as it was dark and I was scared. Of course he was wonderful so he did and then I went home. I did stop at Applebee's on the way home to celebrate this round with my favorite meal, which are their baby back ribs!! That and a piña colada! At least this time I celebrated appropriately!!

Today I am exhausted to the bone and just want to rest. It seems like the day after a court appearance I am more exhausted than usual, but that is understandable. The anxiety and nervousness that I feel leading up to it, is exhausting, so I allow myself to have a day or two afterwards to lay low and process things.

I also forgot to mention that Fernando Ortega responded to that e-mail I had sent to his fan club!! He said that song also had a lot of meaning to he and his wife and she even helped him write it. I will have to e-mail back and ask permission for writing the words to his song in this journal. His compassionate response, to someone he doesn't even know, meant the world to me.

The other day I talked with Richard about this journal and Dr. O'Beirne's positive comments as well as my budding belief that this really might be of help to others, so we discussed what the next step should be in getting this published. The next step towards getting this published is to write a query letter and a proposal letter. Those are then sent to different publishers in the hopes that someone might like it. Therefore I need to write the proposal letter and get my journal in the shape that I want it so that I can send it out.

I figure if I can get this done and out to editors in January, I might have some answers on whether a traditional publisher will pick it up. If by some miracle that happened, then I don't have to worry about being a therapist anymore. Honestly though, that most likely won't happen, so I will have to come up with a Plan B to produce an income. Problem is that I can't come up with a Plan B right now. I still have visions of owning a tree farm, but that wouldn't be able to happen without some type of financing and I certainly don't have that!!

I have no idea what the future holds for me and I just have to trust that I will get a "God Whisper" as to what to do next with my life. I truly feel that I have helped enough people in this world and that my time is done. I am right now receiving X-mas cards from old clients who continue to tell me what a positive influence I was in their lives and that is so heartwarming to say the least.

I am going to try and not think about all of this today, but that's always easier said than done. Danny is home from up north and thankfully has to go to work today. Even though I missed him while he was up north, I was so easily annoyed these past couple of days before the hearing, that we easily would have gotten into arguments and neither of us need that.

We also have an X-mas party for the snowmobile club tonight, but a major winter storm is coming in this afternoon and evening, so hopefully it will be cancelled. I would like to go, but I am just too tired and don't feel like being social tonight.

December 19, 2008 (Friday)

I didn't have the energy to write anymore yesterday. In fact, after talking business with Richard, I was exhausted. I think that the news that there is finally an end to this beginning April 20th was something that I needed to digest and process. It has been such a long journey but it feels like we are nearing the end of it. It feels like I am in an Ironman competition where the first two legs of the race are over and you're on the last leg. At that point, a person is just "willing" their body and mind to keep going. I know that they have to "push through" the agony and exhaustion to make their goal and that is the way that I feel. My situation demands however that at the end, I am as mentally sharp as possible.

That is probably what I figured out yesterday, is that I have to make sure that I have the energy and "brains" to finish this off. Therefore, I have to figure out how I am going to handle the next 4 months in regards to work, money, time-off, this memoir, clients and all the other things that I do in life.

I also talked with Janet for about an hour in regards to what happened in court and that there is a trial date set. She was a little freaked out by that, as was I... I think. All I know is that I had a rough day yesterday and that I was exhausted.

Janet is such a kindred spirit and she insists that she wants to see him in court before he is hauled off. So I will have to e-mail DA Koss to tell him if he thinks some appearance by Lesser might be the last one, then he needs to tell Janet so that she can see him.

I also thought that I should go on the Janesville Gazette site and see if there was anything in the paper about the upcoming trial...and there was!! Quite a big article with a very good mug shot of Lesser. There are also all those blogs underneath it where people discuss me, deconstruct my age at the time and talk about it. One person even wrote that he looked terrible, as she had known him about 15 years ago. I think that is the person that Detective Sharp had been in contact with. It's made me sick to my stomach to read all of that this morning.

I know that I will only be able to think about this upcoming trial for the next 4 months and that is going to be torture. The Pollyanna side says however that the fight is almost over and I currently have the advantage. Now is not the time to "fold" so to speak, so I have to reenergize like you wouldn't believe.

Danny wants to go snowmobiling today and it is gorgeous outside, but I just don't want to go. There is so much to do and it just seems like it would take too much energy to go riding. Maybe wait until tomorrow, but I know he'll be angry if I don't go. Tucker is driving me crazy as well, so it would be good to get out of the house and go!! But then again, Danny is driving me nuts as well. Poor guy! He just can't seem to win for losing is how I think the expression goes.

December 21, 2008 (Sunday)

It's been a rough couple of days in regards to the fact that I can't stop thinking about what happened on Wednesday and the fact that there is going to be a trial. I find that I tend to ruminate and relive everything that happened in court over and over in my head.

The other day I e-mailed my friends and family as to when the trial is going to happen and that subpoena's were going to be sent out to some people and listed those people. I also said that they would most likely have to come back to Wisconsin for the trial and to begin making arrangements. What I didn't expect was some of the replies I got back from some of my friends. I was very surprised and hurt that a couple of them had stated in no uncertain terms that there was no way in hell they were coming to Wisconsin and that something else needed to be figured out.

I think their responses freaked me out in regards to the "adamancy" that they expressed in regards to not coming back if subpoenaed. I sent one of the e-mails to my family and asked them how I should respond back as I was upset by their comments. Blessed Richard called me immediately to tell me that people who lived far away could most likely do a deposition. That was a relief, so I then sent out another e-mail to everyone telling them not to panic as Richard had said that most likely everyone could do a deposition or something from where they are.

I also received back responses from Sarah and Kirsten in regards to my solicitation of ideas of where Janet could stay while she was here. I said that I wanted a place that was cozy, with a kitchenette, safe and preferably on the lake. I wasn't even thinking of their summer cottages, but they both offered their cottages so that both of us could stay. Their offer was so heartwarming and the cottages are PERFECT for this situation. I could stay in one and Janet in the other. We are right next door to each other so if she gets scared, I'm right there next to her. We would also both have our own "spaces" to retreat to, which I think is important. Finally, Chucks, my hometown bar, is right down the street!!! I'll bring it up to Janet, but she said when I talked with her earlier that she wants to stay at an Embassy Suites. She enjoys their continental breakfast in the morning and free cocktails in the afternoon. I think we could take care of both of those things even if she didn't stay there!!

I also got great responses from my good friends Marca and Julie who both said that they would do anything they could to help me. Joanne C. also sent me a very nice e-mail saying that she was glad that it had gotten to this point, as she knew in her heart that he did this to Janet and I and that he needed to be held accountable. I don't know if she thinks she will have to testify or not, but I'm sure she will as she was the one who not only gave me Janet's name, but also confronted Lesser about his relationship with Janet. I was also surprised that her message was as kind as it was as I was afraid that she would be upset about getting a subpoena. I think once people receive those, they are going to freak out, as it isn't really nice to get one in the mail.

David then called me later from LA to give me some suggestions on how to manage this situation. He had seen my flurry of e-mails about subpoenas and stuff and was concerned about my reactions to some of my friend's reactions. David felt that maybe I should "soften" what I had said to people and that they hadn't been on the "front lines" as long as I have, so there isn't really a need to "scare" them. I know that he was trying to be kind, but it backfired in regards to how his comments made me feel and think.

I have done a very good job with this whole thing and in the way that I am "managing" the situation. There is a lot of psychology behind the things that I do and I have already planned a lot of my strategy, so I feel I have a better grasp of what is going on than David thinks. I DO have to "scare" people as this is the ending of the process and they need to begin thinking about this whole thing. I started to cry on the phone to David and told him that I have been doing this whole thing on my own so that others wouldn't have to be involved. But now is the time for other's to step up and help me and yes, they need to be "scared" or stirred to action as this is going to happen whether people want it to or not. I want my family and friends to be "prepared" for what is coming and to get any questions or fears that they have answered so as to get them out of the way. I am ONLY thinking of them and it just hurts that David doesn't see all that I have been doing with this case. To be fair however, I haven't called him about every little thing that happens as I do with Mom, Dad and Richard, so he doesn't know all that I have done. I don't want to bother him with that stuff for a couple of reasons. One is that he works his butt off and is always flying somewhere in the United States. Another reason is that he doesn't like to talk about this. I know he feels terrible that he didn't protect his little sister, especially since he was right in the middle of the whole thing. I know that he feels bad when we have to talk about it, so I just don't want to expose him to any of it if at all possible.

I felt badly that the conversation didn't go so well as I love David with all of my heart. I know that I am being WAY to sensitive to all of this, but I can't help it.

December 22, 2008 (Monday)

Today it is literally freezing outside with −25 to −35-degree wind chills, so I am going to stay inside today and work on this journal.

After Wednesday, I really thought that I would be able to "put this case down" until April, but I'm finding that reality is different. So far it is all that I think about and Danny and I had another big argument the other night in regards to this as well as other issues. He was complaining that this whole thing is controlling my life as well as his and that he is tired of it. I know that he is tired of it and so am I, but it is what it is and now is when I need the most support, not him bugging me for things.

I am also upset that no one has ever sent ME a card of encouragement or anything and that bums me out. All the cards, phone calls, e-mails that I do for others, and no one returning that kindness hurts. But then again, I don't think there are many people like me who do things like that for other's without thinking or hesitating. I ALWAYS send out get well cards, encouragement cards, sympathy for people losing either other people or pets, congratulation cards, you name it. But I guess my love for sending AND RECEIVING cards is what started my business L.A. Cards.

I shouldn't complain though as I do get encouraging and supportive e-mails from people and I am truly thankful for those, but they just aren't the same and not something that you can put into a scrapbook or memory book. I know, quit bitching!

CHAPTER 36

A Brief Respite

December 24, 2008 (Wednesday)

It's been quite a few days and I made the executive decision to begin my vacation on Monday instead of going to work. It was still −25 - -30 degrees with the wind-chill, and I just didn't feel like braving it. Then Tuesday was another snowstorm, so I just decided to leave it all alone.

I can't tell you the tremendous relief I feel in that for the next two weeks, I hopefully don't have to think about or deal with clients. Since I have also made the decision for sure to quit doing therapy, I have actually told a couple of people. I'm not sure what I will do, but as the Reverend Mother says to Maria in "The Sound of Music", "whenever God closes a door, He always opens a window".

I am really beginning to get excited about my "future" and to see what window is going to open for me. I have faith that God will show me the next direction that my life is going to take, and I am anxiously waiting to see what He will reveal. There is such a calm that has come over me now that I have made those decisions and decided to leave it up to God to decide what I do next. I just hope that this time His "whisper" is something "calming"!

Christmas is tomorrow and I am looking forward to hopefully having a relaxing and calming time. Merry Christmas yet again journal!

December 26, 2008 (Friday)

Yesterday we had Christmas with my family and it was wonderful to see everyone. It's been a long time since we have all been together and it was comforting to be with my entire family. I also got my most favorite gift, which is a new pair of Ugg boots!! Tucker had chewed up my right Ugg boot last year and since the company doesn't sell just ONE boot, I had to get a whole new pair!! Ugg did at least give me a discount on this pair. I love them.

Tomorrow Danny's family is coming to our house for Christmas, so today I've been picking up around the house. I actually slept until 8:30 this morning, which is unprecedented for me. It felt good to sleep in however and the weather is conducive to it as it is dark and gloomy outside today. We're supposed to have freezing rain either today or tomorrow and that is going to create quite a mess.

I'm so thankful that I don't have to drive to Madison or anywhere else. Knowing that I am on vacation has been liberating to say the least as well as a much needed break from that stress and worry. I also went to see Brian, my ear, nose and throat PA and he put me on antibiotics, so hopefully those will help me start feeling physically better as I knew that I had a sinus infection or something going on.

January 3, 2008 (Saturday)

We JUST got back from almost a week up north snowmobiling and hanging out and we had a wonderful time!! It is so peaceful and calming to be in the north woods and I am once again mentally recharged and strategizing my next moves in not only this "game", but for my life as well.

We left on Monday and stayed at Linda and Charlie's cabin. It is a gorgeous 2-story log style cabin that is not only beautifully decorated, but feels very "homey" to me. The first night I slept until 9:00 a.m.!!! The bed was so comfortable and I just slept and slept.

To explain a little about the sport of snowmobiling, it is a sport where people ride snowmobiles on marked trails and these trails can go on for hundreds of miles. There are signs on the trails that tell you which direction certain towns or bars/restaurants are located and you simply follow those signs. There are also signs along the trail that warn of curves ahead, caution signs, intersection signs, stop signs, yield signs, signs cautioning about driveways ahead, speed limit signs and other signs as well.

The size of the trails ranges from a single lane road type to just enough room for two sleds to pass each other. The trails go through woods, wind around, and have hundreds of blind curves as well as hills and lake crossings. A person really has to be careful riding as someone could be coming around the blind curve on your side of the trail and you would easily crash head on. There are also riders who go very fast around these curves and that can be dangerous needless to say. Add alcohol to the mix and it is no wonder that snowmobiling can be a very dangerous sport, so I am thankful that we made it home safely once again.

I do have to say however that usually Danny and I have no problems riding and staying together, but this time we had a problem that has never happened to us before. I got stuck behind some slow people while we were riding through Eagle River. As a result, I didn't see that Danny had turned off the trail and he thought that I was right behind him...his mistake! I ended up going about 10 miles further down the trail trying to catch up with him before I realized that he wasn't ahead of me. I had gone through numerous major intersections and Danny wasn't at any of them. I found that suspicious, as one of the rules of snowmobiling is that you wait at every major intersection until everyone shows up.

I finally decided to turn around and go back to one of the major intersections, turn off my machine and wait for him to find me. After what I thought was plenty of time waiting and no Danny, I tried to start my sled to head back, but I couldn't start it, as I don't have the strength. Therefore I had to wait until some other riders came by and I flagged them down. I told them that I had gotten separated from my boyfriend and that he was most likely waiting for me at this bar we had intended on going to TOGETHER. The guys were surprised that he hadn't come looking for me and I agreed that he had BETTER be looking for me or he was dead! They helped me start my sled, as that is another rule of the trails - to help anyone in distress. I then headed back to town and eventually made it to the bar where we had originally planned on going to.

I thought I saw his sled outside and I was ready to be very angry with him for sitting in the bar while I'm lost on the trail, but when I went in, he wasn't there. Then I got worried and upset, as I then knew he WAS looking for me and it had been a long time since we had been separated. The bartender let me use her phone to call his cell to tell him I was at Sweetwater's and to come there. I was so upset knowing that he was probably upset and finally after about ½ hour, I finally saw Danny's blue jacket riding up to the bar and I don't think that I have ever been so happy to see him!! He was just as happy to see me, which was actually nice to see. He had also been scared to death, which was also comforting as it shows he still cares about me. It turns out that he had made the turn and didn't wait to see if I was following. He had gone up and down the trails looking for me and had even gone to the point where I had stopped to wait, but at that time I was further up the trail. Danny had seen a cop in town and said that he was almost tempted to go tell the cop that he had lost his girlfriend. He would have if he hadn't have checked his messages and heard mine. The cop probably would have said, "And the problem is?" anyhow as most guys would probably like to "lose their girlfriends". Ha Ha.

Well all's well that end's well and our little "adventure" seemed to reaffirm to both of us that we really do care about each other a lot!! Not a bad lesson!!

We came home on Saturday as an ice storm was coming in at home, but we were ready. I wanted to see Tucker anyhow!! The mission of calming down and getting rid of some anxiety was achieved up there. The dark circles under my eyes are much better and I must have put on some weight because I did eat and drink while up there. I could however feel the stress and anxiety building up the closer we got to home and all I did on the drive home was think about this journal and what to do next.

The respite is over, but I feel very energized, calmer, more focused on the future and my goals. I find that I'm able to "think" and make decisions again. I still feel agoraphobic and don't really want to go out, but at least my thoughts aren't any where near as "scrambled" as they were last week.

CHAPTER 37

A Conversation with God

There have been many things that I have been stressing about lately and one of the big questions in my life is what to do about my future. Since I don't want to be a therapist anymore, the problem then becomes, what am I going to do to generate an income that will finally be able to sustain me. Therefore, finding a job to achieve total financial independence is one of my goals for 2009. I'm having an extremely difficult time though figuring out how to do this.

I have my private hopes and dreams and I have shared them with some people, only to have them remind me not to put all of my eggs into one basket. That is something that I have done numerous times over the years and of course I end up "losing all of my eggs". Even though my wise mind knows this information, I still don't like to hear it from people, so I made the decision on the way up north not to really talk about my hopes and dreams for this journal to anyone. I say that, but then I told Linda and Charlie about this "book".

The only person I can really trust with my true hopes and dreams is God and so for about two hours on the drive up north, I just prayed to God about many things. It was more of a conversation with him about where I want to go in life and how can I get there. I've mentioned the phrase "When God closes a door, He always opens a window" and that phrase keeps going around in my head. There are so many things that I would like to do to and one is to continue helping people in life, but not the way I currently am.

I will now share with you the private hopes and dreams that I shared with God, as I know that you won't mock me journal or discourage me in anyway. You have always been supportive and what I like most...you don't talk back!! Ha Ha. You don't tell me that I'm wrong about things, or to be careful, or be prepared, because you already know everything there is to know about my thoughts and what is going on with me in every sense. So here goes.

My dream for my next phase in life is this; I hope and pray that this book will be the answer to many of my problems as well as my hopes and dreams. I envision that it will be helpful to many people. I can see sending it to Oprah and being on her show as well as other shows to discuss the ramifications of sexual abuse.

I envision professors who teach psychology courses assigning their students to read this, as it is a personal, private and honest memoir about the traumatic effects of sexual abuse. I tell things in this journal and especially in my victim's statement that I really don't want anyone to know. However if someone feels validated and liberated from me baring my soul, or if I can help professionals in the field to understand more about the effects of abuse, then it was worth sharing my most intimate thoughts and feelings.

I envision myself lecturing about it with students and others and giving workshops of some kind. I'm not sure about that part, but again, if this revealing memoir can help, then so be it. That is obviously what God would have intended for this book and I hope and pray that it is.

There, I've said it. I want to be an accomplished author; a speaker and educator and hopefully that will generate an income. I don't ask for much in life and never have. I don't buy clothes, jewelry or anything really. All I want in life is to be able to pay my bills without worry every month, have a little cabin on a lake up north, a safe car to drive and to be able to take vacations a couple of times a year. That's all that I want and I really don't think that is much to hope for.

My conversation with God revolved around all of this and to humbly ask Him to please help guide me on this next phase of my life. He always has, but I am most scared about generating an income and I'm tired of that feeling. I will be fifty-years-old this year and it is time that I am able to quit worrying about how much a meal costs, prices at the grocery store, or filling up the fuel oil tank. Danny currently isn't in debt AT ALL. EVERYTHING he has is paid for and that includes two jet boats, 4 snowmobiles, two vehicles, no credit card debt or anything. That is where I would love to be next year and my admiration for him in his ability to make and manage his money is tremendous. My parents also have no debt whatsoever and this security is what I would like to have happen in my life. Everyone would laugh at this statement, but I know that you won't my faithful journal, and so I share it with you.

My conversation with God also included my thoughts on what I should do about suing Lesser, if he is indeed convicted. I'm sure there are many people who think that I'm doing this for "the money" and some blogs have even stated that. Not only that, but people I know have said it to me as well. That really hurts me, as that isn't why I am doing this at all!! This has been the most difficult endeavor that I have ever encountered in my life and not something that I have done for money.

It has totally disrupted my life, my families lives and of course Danny's life and not in good ways. This whole thing has sent me on an emotional journey that has not only lasted for three years, but has dredged up ALL of the old feelings, beliefs and emotions.

This isn't to say that the possibility of suing Lesser as well as Campus Life/Youth For Christ hasn't crossed my mind. A long time ago I shared with DA

Koss, Detective Sharp and Evelyn, that I haven't made a decision about what I was going to do, and I was telling them the truth. I still don't know what I am going to do, but I am almost 80% sure that I will not be suing Lesser and there are some reasons for why I don't want to.

First is that I didn't do all of this in order "to make money". I filed criminal charges because what he did was wrong and he needs to be held accountable for the damage that he caused in many people's lives. My grandmother, Grammy, always had a phrase that said that "Your sins will find you out" and I think that is what is happening to Lesser. I just happen to be the vessel that God is using to punish Lesser for all of the hurts that he caused people during his lifetime.

Secondly, the truth is that I don't want his stinking money. I consider it to be "dirty money" and I don't want anything to do with it. It reminds me of when an attorney wanted me to sue the last bar that my husband Bill was at before he got killed in a car accident, as he was legally drunk. This attorney wanted me to sue for loss of society and companionship, but I considered that "dirty money" and wouldn't even consider doing it. That same feeling applies to Lesser and his money and I want nothing to do with it.

Third is that I feel if he convicted of this crime, the repercussions of that is going to be punishment enough. His life is going to be totally destroyed and couple that with the fact he will have to go to prison, is enough punishment for me.

Finally, is that if I did sue him, then all those naysayers and bloggers would say "See, she did it for the money" and I don't want them to have that satisfaction.

I have not however made a decision about suing Youth For Christ/Campus Life. It is my belief that they knew about this jerk when he was in Lake Forest and then sent him to us. Mr. F. had told me that someone had told Mr. P. that they had the "perfect guy for us, and that maybe we could straighten him out". THAT pisses me off and if anything, I want to teach this organization a lesson about providing safety to the adolescents that they serve. Unfortunately the only way some big organizations learn is to hit them where it hurts, which is their pocketbooks. Therefore, that might be a possibility, but we'll see.

It was also during this conversation with God that I planned out the future of this book. I am going to send what is already written to traditional publishers first and see if there is any interest. If there is no interest from publishing companies, then I will self-publish. Quite honestly, I am excited about the idea of sending off this book to publishers. I knew when this process started that my life was going to drastically change and I still believe that, I'm just not sure right now how. I can only hope and pray that God continues to guide me.

CHAPTER 38

It's In The Mail

January 9, 2009 (Friday)

Thank God it's Friday, as the saying goes, but it was an exciting week as this is the week that I sent this journal out to traditional publishers! It was thrilling to see it bound and ready to go!

I have been obsessing about getting this book out since I left for that snowmobiling vacation and today is the day that I got them into the mail. It is sooooo exciting while at the same time very scary. That's an example of another dialectic in how can I be feeling two extremely different emotions at the same time! I don't think that I will tell many people what I have done as I am afraid of not only "jinxing it", but also what happens if it stinks and no one wants it?

I have to tell about something funny that happened with the clerk at the post office when she asked what I was mailing off. I told her that I had written a book and was sending it to publishers in the hopes that it will get picked up. She jokingly asked if it was about sex and when I didn't say anything, she "went off" as if it WAS a sex book. Since no one else was in there, I told her what it was about and she felt awful that she had teased me. She actually had a lot of questions for me about it and my experience. It was kind-of weird to be talking about this at the postal counter, but since I have known her for years, I decided to share. I guess I better get used to people asking me my story, even if it is the postal clerk!!

January 14, 2009 (Wednesday)

Not much is happening as far as the case right now, although I did e-mail DA Koss to see if Lesser's attorney had filed a new motion or anything else. Koss reported he hadn't heard anything but he had gotten a Christmas card from Prisoner Pete!

Since this case is on the "back burner" again, life is getting back to some kind of order. I FINALLY balanced my 4 checkbooks and found out that I had of course overdrawn one of them. Fortunately it's set up so that the bank will simply take the money out of another account so the check doesn't bounce, but still. It seemed like the whole month of December was a blur for me as I was SO dysregulated by everything. I am now feeling back in control of my life and getting things done that I have been putting off. It feels good to be getting back on track so to speak.

Another thing is that I have been weaned off Lexipro, as my insurance company won't pay for it. The doctor prescribed something new, but I'm not sure I'm going to take it, as I'm feeling "much better". I'll see how "anxious" I get over the next couple of weeks or so and see if I need it again. The medication did help in that I didn't feel like there was this constant "motor" inside of me or at least the motor was in "neutral" vs. a high gear!

Since my trip up north, I have really been having a sense of "relief" for some reason. I'm not sure if it was my conversation with God that began this new state of mind or what. I know that I feel a sense of relief about this memoir being in to publishers because that piece has been taken care of. The great news is that I truly don't have any anxiety about what news I will receive back. It's not like I'm expecting an answer right away and quite honestly, even if the traditional publishers don't like it, I will most likely self publish it. I feel that it is worth a shot to at least try! As the saying goes from my old insurance company, which was owned by the great W. Clement Stone, "Where there is nothing to lose by trying, and a great deal to gain if successful, then by all means try".

Today is going to be freezing around here and even colder tomorrow. I saw most of my clients yesterday, as I knew the week was just going to get worse as far as weather. Tomorrow it's supposed to be –35 to –45 below with wind chill. Therefore, I will continue to catch up on paperwork and MAYBE take down the Christmas tree. I finally turned off the outside lights (except for the trees), but I am still finding it hard to take down the tree.

After analyzing why I just "can't" seem to take down the tree, I believe the reason is because if I do, then that means that this season is over and therefore we are moving closer to the trial date. Isn't that weird thinking, but that's what I think and feel. It's still three months away, but once the holiday season is "over" then to me that seems like a downhill slide to the court date.

As I'm writing this I'm beginning to realize that maybe the reason I am feeling less anxious and more in control is because instead of this journey being "uphill" for me anymore, it's now on the downside for me! I feel like I have already climbed the mountain and am now at the top looking down. I'm a little terrified about how to exactly "negotiate" getting down the mountain, but at least it is all down hill from this point. Of course there will be obstacles to avoid on the way down, but I am still going down and if I have to, I'll sit on my butt and slide down that mountain.

That reminds me of a time when we went rock climbing with Lesser and partially up this huge rock, I became paralyzed with fear and couldn't move up or down. Everyone left me there alone and I remember Lesser saying that I will figure it out. I eventually slide down on my butt the entire way, but that should have told me then and there what an ass he really was. In retrospect, I wonder if he didn't "enjoy" me being terrified and vulnerable and if he did that to me for "psychological" purposes such as control and fear.

I also can't help but think what Lesser is feeling right now as well as how he's going to feel in the future. I had to visit a client of mine in the county jail yesterday and of course it was horrible. I did get to meet with him in a conference room, but he was totally chained around the waist and hands as well as his feet. They even chained him to this metal ring under the table. That whole process is so horrifying and scary to me and it made me wonder how Lesser is going to handle this if it happens to him. I'm not sure that I could live in a prison environment, especially if I knew that I would most likely die in prison. Therefore, I'm wondering if he is thinking the same thing and wondering if it would be better if he killed himself. I truly hope he doesn't kill himself as that would be a shame for many reasons, but I have no idea what he is currently going through. I do hope that he is sweating bullets and it's in some way a comfort to know that he is "just beginning his climb up that mountain" and let me tell you, it's a bitch of a climb. The problem for him is that I don't think there is any "top of the mountain" for him, but rather only uphill all the way.

January 20, 2009 (Tuesday)

A lot has happened in the past week. First is that last Wednesday night, I ended up getting the stomach flu AGAIN and from the same family! There are 10 family members living in a 2-bedroom apartment, so there is usually some illness being passed around. So much for the flu shot this year, but honestly I think that all the stress I'm under is compromising my immune system. Even so, Danny and I went snowmobiling with David (my brother) and Bobby (my nephew) as well as a couple of other guys. I HAD to go, as it is a rare opportunity that I get to spend that kind of time with David and Bobby, so I went and I'm glad that I did. I was also very impressed with Bobby's riding as he hasn't been snowmobiling too long and we ride hard.

It is now Tuesday and inauguration day for President-Elect Obama!! It is an exciting day, but it is also tempered with the fact that Saturday night, Lisa made a pretty desperate suicide attempt and is currently in a hospital somewhere. Her sister Kathee called me last night to tell me about it and it sounds pretty bad. We'll just leave it that a biohazard team needed to come in and clean up her place.

It's definitely a dialectical day in that on one hand, I am thrilled and excited about our new President. But on the other side of the teeter-totter is profound sadness about Lisa. I am feeling these conflicting emotions on an alternating basis and it's not a fun ride.

To try and get my mind off of nasty things, I am now going to watch the inauguration of our NEW PRESIDENT!!! What a truly wonderful day this is in the history of the United States of America and I sincerely hope that he and his family stay safe. This is just too cool and I am so proud of our country right now. As Tiny Tim says in the "Christmas Carol" – "God bless all of us; each and everyone!"

January 23, 2009 (Friday)

TGIF!!

This has been an extremely busy week and I actually just got home from work and decided to put some things down in my journal.

First is that I am anxiously waiting to hear from DA Koss about whether or not Lesser is going to accept the plea bargain that DA Koss had offered him! I had no idea that DA Koss had even offered him a deal, so my first words were "WHAT PLEA BARGAIN are we talking about"?! Well, lo and behold, the day that DA Koss, Detective Sharp and I were sitting around before court and "talking" about what sentence we think he should get, I guess we were actually talking about a plea bargain!!!! Boy, that one went right over my head.

How I found this out is because I had sent DA Koss an e-mail asking if our trial date could possibly get "bumped" for some reason like my clients did this week. He said yes, and that he still hadn't heard back from Lesser's attorney about the "offer". I of course e-mailed back, "What Offer?!". DA Koss told me that he would drop two of the lesser counts if he pleads guilty to the most serious charge, which is count two. I believe that is having intercourse with a 15 year-old. The maximum time for that is 15 years but the attorneys would argue about the sentence. I think that's what it is, but I'm sure I'll get it straight real quick here. I felt stupid as hell that I hadn't even realized that there was an offer on the table. I know that DA Koss had mentioned the possibility of them accepting a plea a couple of times, but to be honest, it went right over my head. There are so many legal things to process during a criminal case that this just went right past me.

Therefore as soon as I walked in the door, I checked my e-mail and there is nothing there from DA Koss yet. He had told me that Lesser's attorney would have an answer for DA Koss today. I have no idea what that answer will be and I'm torn on many levels about it.

On one hand I want it to go to trial for a number of reasons, but the most important ones are these. First is that I will finally be able to tell my side of the story and let people know that it wasn't about sex or anything like that. Another reason is that he should have to "face the music" so to speak and be embarrassed, humiliated and ripped apart in front of people. He should know what it feels like to be ostracized and stripped of all of his dignity.

While I want it to go to trial, I also don't want it to go to trial. The main reason I don't want a trial is so everyone doesn't have to testify, as it is so difficult and gut wrenching to say the least. Another reason I don't want it to go to trial is the possibility that we could lose, but I don't anticipate that.

I just don't know what to think right now as today might be the day that will be "the beginning of the end" so to speak and I can begin that new chapter in my life. Now that I KNOW that I am leaving the field, I feel like such a huge burden has been taken off of my shoulders. It feels like there is a whole new world out there and that I can do anything I want to do. I know that I want the next 10-15 years of my life to be drama-free with a sense of calm and peace. I also know that I still want to help others, but just on a larger scale.

Next time I write in this journal, it may be "over". But then again, I can't assume anything about anything when it comes to the criminal justice system and the lawyers that manipulate it. Whatever the answer is, I am more determined than ever to see this through. Remember, my mantra is to "Outwit, Outlast and Outplay" the others and though I knew that I could outwit and outplay them, for a while I wasn't sure that I was going to be able to "outlast" them. But after my conversation with God and seeing how He has created me and molded me for His purpose, I know that I can do anything because He is the one who is guiding me and always has been. It is so cool to see how all of the threads and pieces of my life are now coming together into a beautiful patchwork piece of art.

Later:

It is now 5:15 p.m. and no word from DA Koss, so I must assume that Lesser's attorney didn't give him an answer today like he said he would. I really thought that he would follow through with his statement to DA Koss that he would have an answer. I guess I still haven't learned the lesson not to trust what a defense attorney says.

I will leave if for today on that note. I am disappointed that we didn't get an answer, but honestly, I didn't know until yesterday that there was even an offer on the table. As a result, I'm going to try and let it go and just think that April 20 (hopefully!) is the next day of importance.

January 24, 2009 (Saturday)

Woke up this morning and even though it was a somewhat "good" day yesterday hearing that Lesser might plead guilty, I find that I am very upset today. I don't know why, but I felt it was important to note that fact. This is too much at times as it seems like this roller coaster ride is NEVER going to end!

CHAPTER 39

Change Is In The Air

January 25, 2009 (Sunday)

What a difference a day makes and I must say that I feel like a totally different person today. There is so much that is going through my head about the possibilities of my future and I am thrilled about it.

I think what helped me figure out what to do with myself, was talking with Lisa and trying to help her identify what she was going to do to develop hope for a future and to stay alive. And that is where my light bulb moment happened because when I was talking with her about what she wants in life, I discovered what I want for the next 10 or 15 years or whatever time I have left on earth. I realized that I NEED to have a peaceful existence without drama and stress. I've come to the realization that it is now time for me to focus solely on me, Danny and the other people I love.

In looking back at my life, I realized that I had gone from being pretty mixed up and on drugs, to pulling it together to complete graduate school and become a therapist. Helping others with their tragedies is all that I have done since "pulling myself together". There is a new awareness that now it is time for me to take care of Danny and myself and to live a happy, fulfilling life.

These realizations have really changed my attitude towards most everything. I find that I'm being more appreciative with Danny as I truly am thankful for him. He has had to put up with my issues for years and I feel that now is the time for us. I find that lately I've been smiling, laughing and enjoying being with my friends. We went to the snowmobile races yesterday and then out to lunch with some friends, and it was really fun to enjoy life again. I only did three runs this time, so I didn't break 100 mph, but I did get 1-99 mph and 2- 98 mph runs, so that wasn't bad and I was in first place when we left.

I think what is also helping with this newfound zeal is that feeling of getting over the top of the mountain. It has been one hell of a climb, almost 36 years, and I have MADE IT. It continues to feel like I am going downhill and that is such a wonderful feeling. I have done all of the hard work necessary for me to hopefully have an easier and happier life and that I can at least breathe. Of course this newfound energy and positive attitude doesn't bode well for Lesser because there is no way in hell that he is going to "outlast" me on this. The "outlasting" part was really debatable at times, but I am not going to lose this one.

I feel like I have been absolutely crushed into the ground these past three years and that God has done that in order to mold me into the next chapter and phase of my life. I hope that doesn't sound conceited, but I truly see how He has brought me to my knees a couple of times these past three years, but that has only strengthened me as a person and as a person of faith. I have really suffered emotionally, physically and mentally not only these past three years since the process began, but ever since the abuse occurred. I am done suffering and ready to finally become the person that maybe I could or should have become if Lesser hadn't had taken so much out of me. But then again, I wouldn't be the person I am if Lesser hadn't have been in my life, and I do like who I am.

February 1, 2009 (Sunday)

Thank God it's February!! January always seems like such a long and cold month and when the calendar reaches February, that's when I begin to feel spring coming on.

The other big change that has recently happened that is fun in a weird way is that DA Koss and I are beginning to work more on the case together. I had sent him a long time ago my list of people who had something to do with this case and I decided to send that to Janet to see what she thought. She responded back that she knew the two big Christian leaders whose names were on the list and to me that is important as they should remember Lesser and maybe even Janet. These men might also know why Lesser left the Lake Forest area and again, I bet it was because of Janet.

I forwarded Janet's comments to DA Koss along with a few questions of my own. I have been wondering what happens now with the subpoenas and does he talk with everyone. He replied that he did and that the person who was subpoenaed is given instructions on setting up an appointment to talk with DA Koss.

I also asked him if I should basically sit back and be quiet, or should I help out if I could, and his reply was to help out all that I want! Of course I loved that response and told him that he might be sorry for saying that to me. I have played this trial out in my head so many times that I feel I am fairly well prepared for whatever they might throw at me.

CHAPTER 40

What's Next?

February 4, 2009 (Wednesday)

It's currently 5:00 a.m. and I've been up and thinking since 4:00 a.m., so I thought I might as well get up and put some of those thoughts down on paper. I want to talk to someone and since Danny is still fast asleep, I thought I would talk with you.

Some of the things that I'm thinking about this morning is the upcoming trial, this journal, my health, my financial concerns, Lisa and of course my clients. I went to see my doctor yesterday as I still haven't been feeling well and of course there are some minor things going on. My sinuses are still draining which is therefore in turn causing the dizziness as well as the gastrointestinal irritation, which is then causing me to throw up on a daily basis. I'm told that the pain in my neck and throat is actually my lymph nodes being swollen due to the sinus issue and that my dizziness and nausea are also a symptom of the fluid in my sinuses.

Another thing that I've been thinking and worrying about is this journal. I had asked my good friend and former co-worker Ruth to read it too because I wanted her opinion on whether it was any good and if she thought it might be of help to others. Ruth has now finished it and wants to meet me for lunch or drinks. I might need the drinks depending on what she has to say! I had also given it to Deanna (my sister-in-law) for her opinion, and she has also e-mailed me telling me that she is still reading, but wants to talk with me about it when I'm in the right frame of mind. Oh Oh! Last but not least, I gave it to my friend Tammi, who I consider "normal". She hasn't ever been exposed to anything like this, so I wanted to know if this could help a "regular" person. Tammi had already given me feedback saying how it had helped her to understand the ramifications that sexual abuse has on its victims and that it really is a societal problem.

Both Ruth and Deanna have now got me wondering about what they think about this journal and I hope and pray that it is good news. I'm sure they will offer constructive criticism, which is what I wanted, but knowing me, I'll take it in a defensive manner. Therefore, I've been thinking about taking the offered advice with an open mind and with humility. Easier said than done, but that is what I have to do.

I'm still worried however that they think it is terrible and that of course would crush me.

There is just so much running around my brain since I woke up this morning and I'm already feeling exhausted and it's not even 6:00 a.m. yet. Thank goodness today is one of my off days as far as being in the field, so hopefully I can try to relax today. Lisa is safe in rehab, my clients are doing ok and Danny has to work. The problem is that I can't seem to get rid of this feeling that "something" is going to happen. I can't identify what that "something" is except for it always seems like some drama is happening and I find myself wondering what will happen next!

CHAPTER 41

Biding My Time

February 7, 2009 (Saturday)

This past week has had it ups and downs and fortunately there were more ups than downs.

The first good thing is that Lisa made it to rehab safely and in one piece, so that is an accomplishment right there. It is their turn to help her and therefore I am going to let go of that for a while. That's a huge relief right there.

Another great thing that happened this week is that yesterday I met with my friend and old co-worker Ruth to discuss this journal. I had sent it to her with the hopes of getting some advice and guidance and that is what she was able to provide. Ruth is not only smart, but also kind, generous, empathetic and a lot of fun. We worked together as therapists at Jane Addams, which is a community mental health center in Freeport Illinois and we almost immediately became friends.

The best thing for me is that she liked it and feels that it could be of help to others. Ruth also suggested discussing in more detail about how he groomed me, how he was able to get us to keep secrets, the ways that he insinuated himself in my life as well as some other information that she thought was important for the story. She provided excellent advice and of course presented it to me in the perfect way.

The other thing Ruth said that was surprising and opened my eyes is that she is mad at Danny. The last thing I want to have happen is for people to think that Danny hasn't been kind to me during this process. I am a high-strung and difficult person to live with as it is, so he is being wonderful in regards to "handling" all of the emotional abuse that I throw at him. Many guys would have said "good-bye" to me many years ago, but he has stuck with me during this whole thing and that is important to me. He hasn't always been empathetic and understanding, but he is who he is. I do think however that his attitude and perception about the ramifications of sexual abuse has changed as a result of what he is learning from me. He has never been exposed to anything like this and never experienced this type of betrayal in his life, so he doesn't know how it "all works" so to speak. Unfortunately for him, he has had to learn on the job!

Another thing that Ruth said that stuck with me is she asked me if I had ever wondered if I would have been a different person had Lesser not entered my life. My answer is that I do feel my life would have taken a different trajectory had he not "totally screwed me up" and that I have in the past grieved for that loss in my life. I also feel that my Victim Impact Statement cites all of the ways that he had changed my life, so hopefully including that in this journal will answer that question for not only her, but others as well.

I must add that it was really good to see Ruth not only to reassure myself that I am on the right path, but also to laugh and be normal for a little bit.

The downside of the week was that once again I am not feeling well and I know that it isn't psychosomatic this time. I have been throwing up phlegm almost everyday for about 1 month and of course my neck hurts as usual, but now it really hurts. I had some blood tests and found that my potassium level is really high, so I'm currently on a low potassium diet and we will recheck it next week. I am also scheduled to see the Physicians Assistant, Brian at the Ear, Nose and Throat to see about my neck and that's only because I finally INSISTED that someone doing something to see what is there.

Tonight Danny's snowmobile club is having their club bonfire, so I will probably go to that as I'm feeling social enough to interact with others.

CHAPTER 42

Sick Again

February 12, 2009 (Thursday)

This has been mostly a week of taking care of medical issues and I'm getting really tired of it. Monday started with another CT scan of my neck and once again, even though I have a lot of pain, there is nothing that they can find wrong. I also had to have my potassium level checked and that was at least down, but so was my blood pressure. I normally have low blood pressure, but it was 98/58, down from last week even.

Then Tuesday I took off for work and while driving, I felt like I was going to pass out. I felt so "weird", that after my first appointment, I headed to the emergency room, which is NOT something that I do. My blood pressure was 145/?, so they hooked me up to some IV's for hydration and waited until my blood pressure went back down. The ER doctor was wonderful and encouraged me to seek out an internist that would help figure out what is wrong with me. The tests they did on me came back for the most part normal, but he said that it is abnormal for a person's potassium level to be high solely from diet, so he thinks something is wrong. I can't tell you how good it felt to have a doctor validate that he believes there IS something wrong with me and that I should indeed pursue it.

Yesterday it was off to my surgeon to review the CT scan as I insisted on him looking at it and once again, he can't find anything wrong on the CT scan either. Therefore he thinks my pain is muscular skeletal in nature and that I should possibly see a physical therapist. I asked about seeing an endocrinologist to see if he could find out what was wrong with me. He thought that was a good idea and so finally I got a referral to a great doctor who is an endocrinologist at the clinic on Monday.

One thing that has come out of this whole thing with Lesser and with my new insight and energy for the future, is that I am taking back control of my life. Part of that new commitment to myself, is knowing that I have to take charge of my own health and not wait around for doctors. I know that something is going on with me as I am physically all over the place recently. I am afraid to go to work because I still get dizzy and light-headed when I walk around. My back is absolutely killing me and I feel that I just need to stay physically calm and regulated until I feel much better.

Even though my current health woes are physical and not psychosomatic in nature, I still blame Lesser for all of it. The stress that I have been under for 3 years added to the stress of my job and everything else in life I deal with has caused my health to fail once again. It pisses me off.

We were supposed to go up north this weekend to snowmobile, but all of our snow has melted down here, so there most likely isn't too much up north. That and the fact that I'm not feeling well forced us to stay home. That sucks too!

February 15, 2009 (Sunday)

It's a beautiful day here in Wisconsin...the sun is shining, there is some fresh snow layering the ground and everything looks "clean" again. All of our snow had melted, so everything had looked brown and dingy, but this light snow covering has helped.

I'm not feeling as dizzy and lightheaded as this past week so yesterday Danny and I went to see the movie "Slumdog Millionaire" for Valentine's Day. It was an excellent movie and I can't remember the last time that Danny and I had gone to a movie, so we really had a nice time. My back is still killing me, but I took a Tylenol 3 and that helped me to get down there and sit through the movie. Last night however it hurt so bad that I didn't get much sleep. I probably should have taken another Tylenol 3, but honestly I didn't think about it.

I see the endocrinologist tomorrow and I'm a little nervous about what he might or for that matter, might not find. I feel like my "circuit board" has short-circuited in various spots and I would like to know why as I'm tired of feeling sick. Once again, I have to wonder if this latest health "episode" is stress related symptoms, or is there something really wrong.

February 16, 2009 (Monday)

Got a call right away this morning from my Ear, Nose and Throat surgeon's nurse and she informed me that after reviewing his notes about me this weekend, the doctor has decided to take back his referral to the endocrinologist for me. Therefore, my appointment that I have been looking forward to since last week has been cancelled!

I am so pissed off for a number of reasons; the first being that I feel my ENT surgeon doesn't believe me and/or my symptoms. That just plain hurts my entire being, as someone that I trust, doesn't believe me. I KNOW that something was very wrong with me last week and it is so invalidating to have someone tell you that they don't believe you, or at least, won't help me. I can't remember the last time I was at the ER for something, so it was serious that I ended up there last week.

The other thing that pisses me off is that someone once again, has control over "my life". Because this doctor doesn't feel I need to see someone else, then that's the end of that, no matter what I think. That is bullshit and the fact that I have no control in this is burning me up. I am so upset about everything that is going on, that I feel the need to "shut down" everything and regroup. I really need to figure out what is going on with my health and so that is what I'm going to totally concentrate on for a while.

February 26, 2009 (Thursday)

It's been a while since I've written as nothing with the case is really happening and emotionally and physically I've been trying to pull it back together. I've been feeling a bit better, so Danny and I went up north last week snowmobiling and as usual it was fun, refreshing and peaceful. We stayed at the Indian casino up there and I won about $350 although I put back in about $150. Still not bad as I went up with $16 in my pocket!! It paid for the trip as well as having some left over for home.

Danny is currently back up north with his brother-in-law Charlie and a couple of other guys to celebrate Charlie's 65th birthday. I can't go because I don't have a "certain male organ"!! Not fair and of course I cried when he left because I wanted to go so badly. We will go back up in a couple of weeks, but still, I would have liked to go with them.

March 7, 2009 (Saturday)

Survived another week, but of course not without drama. In getting control back over my health, I have at least discovered that some of the pain in my neck and throat area is because of an infected abscess located on the root of a tooth that I have already had 2 root canals on!! As a result, I had to have surgery on Monday to cut out the infection as well as the root of the tooth. See, I KNEW that something was going on.

This is just insane and once again, I am blaming my deteriorating health on all of the stress that I am under. Of course this could have been the result of the lame dentist that performed the first root canal and did it wrong. Whatever. I did call both of my doctors at the clinic to inform them that I had a seriously infected tooth so they would know that I am not crazy or psychosomatic. I also wanted them to hopefully get the message that I am pissed at all of them. They never suggested that I see a dentist for this pain, but rather suggested physical therapy. Give me a break! As you can tell I am still angry about this whole thing and actually have made an appointment with a new primary doctor who specializes in multiple disorders with women. I hope that she will be better than my last primary physician, but I'm already afraid that they will think I'm some sort of hypochondriac or something. But I

KNOW that there are still some other things going on with me besides this infected tooth and I really need to know at this point.

I also find that I'm getting dysregulated by the upcoming trial, which is now only 7 weeks away. On one hand I want it to come quicker, but then again, I don't want it to come at all…another dialectic. I am now getting scared that they will somehow manipulate or twist whatever I say and therefore we will lose the case. I am also astonished at how few subpoenas DA Koss sent out for the trial. The only people I have heard that received a subpoena were my parents, my brother David, Janet, Mr. F. and the P.'s.

I also found out that I will be first up and everyone else who got subpoenaed will be sequestered until they speak. That means that neither of my parents, David nor Janet will be able to hear the trial. On one hand that gives me comfort but at the same time I wonder if they will be ok sequestered together; especially my mother. I worry that she "needs" to be at the trial, but then again I don't want her or my Dad to have to hear all of the embarrassing things that are going to be said.

Conversely, I don't want her to go insane waiting in a little room with other people that she doesn't really want to be around. I don't know what to think, but I did discuss my concerns with my parents and Dad said that they would figure things out once they had their meeting with DA Koss.

My Mom is also becoming nervous that she is going to "mess up" while on the stand, but I don't know how she could. DA Koss will review with them the questions he will ask them on the stand when they meet with him on April 2, so that is the next date that I am focusing on. This is so difficult and I am exhausted. I'm not sure if it's just because of the infection right now, the stitches in my mouth or being tired of dealing with my clients, but the obvious answer would be all three are doing it to me.

I would like to watch a movie today, but since television has changed over to that DTV thing, I can't figure out how to tape or for that matter, how to watch a tape on the DTV television we have. That has been extremely frustrating as I can't tape ANY of my programs and not seeing some of them is very upsetting to me. For example, I can't tape "Survivor" and for people who know me, I HAVE to watch that program. I could watch it on the Internet as I have speakers that work now, but it's not the same, so I don't/won't do it.

That's enough for now, but I just wanted to get you up to date on the continuing drama. I hope and pray that when this case is over and I'm done being a therapist that the drama in my life will quiet down to a manageable level. That is all I ask for because as of right now, I'm done with needy people.

CHAPTER 43

Getting Closer

March 16, 2009 (Monday)

We just got back from our last snowmobiling trip up north as the season is now basically over and I thank God that we made it through another season without any injuries!

It was really good to get away from things down here and have that peace and tranquility that I find while in the northern woods. Snowmobiling this time wasn't as calming as usual as I kept thinking about the upcoming trial as well as the fact that it was three years ago almost to the day that I was riding up north wondering if the DA was going to take the case. Here it was three years later and not only did the DA take the case, but the trial is now in 5 weeks. It was amazing to see how things have evolved over the last three years!

Unfortunately as the trial draws near, I am finding that I am thinking about it endlessly and am beginning to have that "nervous energy" that I have experienced in the past. I find that I'm once again having a difficult time focusing on the here and now and therefore I am making stupid mistakes because I'm not paying attention to what I'm doing. For example, I was cutting something and sliced my finger pretty deep. I've been spilling drinks in cars, hitting my finger with a hammer, dropping things and losing things. I'm beginning to be afraid about driving again as I'm just not paying attention to what I'm doing!

The good news is that at least my tooth and hence my neck isn't hurting anymore due to the surgery that was needed. I still have issues, but I'm seeing a new physician tomorrow, so maybe she will be able to help me find some answers. I'm just worried that she might think that I'm being psychosomatic or a hypochondriac or something, but that's only because that's the way my current physicians make me feel.

For the next 5 weeks though, I'm going to try and keep my stress levels down to a minimum by trying to keep the drama in my life to a minimum. I also plan on using this nervous energy to my benefit by getting spring-cleaning done as well as cleaning up my gardens. I might even paint a room in the house!!

Happy birthday Grammy!! Happy Anniversary to Gram and Pop as well!! I sure do miss them, but did stop by the cemetery last week to make sure that the cherub was still there for them, and it was! I am so thankful that no one stole her as I really feel like she is protecting them.

As the trial is getting closer, I am getting more and more nervous and I finally had a meltdown yesterday. Danny took one look at my face in the morning and asked what was wrong and of course I burst into tears. I just feel so overwhelmed by everything and am finding it difficult to focus on thinking about one thing at a time. There is so much on my mind as far as work, finances, my clients, my health, Mom and Dad's health, the trial, what I'm going to do in the future, that it finally all hit me yesterday.

Of course I called Mom and Dad and started crying with them as well. They are so wonderful to me in so many ways and they are doing the best they can to help me not get so upset about things.

The newest thing that is pushing me over the edge is that I did decide to look for a new primary physician and I finally met with her on Tuesday of this week. She seems to be an attentive doctor and spent over an hour with me. She was also already very well versed in my past health issues as she had taken the time to read my medical records.

The most important thing is that she did notice that there is a "fullness" in my groin area, so of course I'm off tomorrow to have an abdominal and pelvic CT scan. The doctor also had me set up an appointment with a surgeon before coming back to see her, so I'm thinking that she thinks that I will most likely need some type of surgery. I'm just praying that it's nothing serious.

The worst thing is the timing because the trial is just around the corner. So now I'm worried about not only the trial, but what they are going to find in my groin as well. What also makes me angry is that I've been complaining about this pain for years to my previous doctors and they have felt the area a number of times, but didn't find this "fullness". It was validation in that this new doctor immediately knew that something was in there. If I had gone to her a year ago, then it would have already been diagnosed and fixed. As it is now, all this is happening right before the trial.

Another thing that has me upset is that Tucker has another lump by his private part so he has to go to the vet today. I don't think that I can go with as I get too upset by what happens to him when he goes to the vet, so I think I will take a Lorazepam and try to relax. Tucker got his "chill pill" at 7 a.m., so hopefully he'll be so drugged when he gets there, he won't fight the vet. Still, he is better than my old dog Riley who Dr. Thayer labeled a NATE dog…Not Able To Examine!!

On top of all of this, I am trying to figure out logistics for the trial and where Janet and maybe I should stay. Dad offered to put us up at the Abbey, but it's $159 a night, so forget that. Kirsten and Sarah have offered their cottages, but I just found out from DA Koss yesterday that he doesn't want Janet and I to really "meet" before and during the trial. DA Koss said that the county would put Janet up at the AmericInn in Elkhorn, so I guess Janet will have to go with that. If I can't really talk to her until after the trial, then I might as well go home every night. Since I live so close, the county doesn't want to pay for my lodging, which is perfectly fine with me. I don't want them to spend any more money than they have to as a result of this trial. Not only that, but I think that I will "need" the comfort and safety of my home and dog.

I will have to call Janet and talk with her about what she wants to do as far as wanting to stay in a hotel or at my friend's cottage. I did call her yesterday morning, because I got the feeling while driving home from work the night before, that she needed to hear from me. When I called, she was busy with workmen moving her furniture back into her house and she was terribly sick with a cold. She sounded terrible on the phone and so we agreed to talk later in the week. Maybe I'll try her today. She hasn't gotten her ticket yet, but that's ok because right now airfares are way down, so she should be able to get a flight at a reasonable price. Then if her hotel is paid for, hopefully this won't cost her a fortune to come.

It's funny in that while it seems like time is just creeping towards the date of the trial, it also feels like it is coming up really fast. That is another dialectic for those of you who are interested in DBT. How can one thing be true, but yet another be true at the same time?! It is also amazing to me that Lesser hasn't accepted the plea bargain. I am trying to find some comfort in the fact that as nervous and anxious as I am, he has got to be worse.

I've been finding myself thinking again about if it were me facing years in prison, what would I do? I think that I would rather kill myself than live in prison for the rest of my life. Therefore I'm wondering if he is thinking the same thing. Most importantly and interesting to me, is that I'm not thinking about him or nervous about him, but rather I'm thinking about my parents, Janet and myself. It feels like he is more of a "concept" to me than a "real person" right now. I think more about his attorney and what he is going to try and do, but I don't think too much about Lesser.

This journey is a strange and eerie "trip" and I can't wait for it to be over. It's also hard waiting to see the surgeon because I'd rather just get on with the things that have to be done. I feel like my life is in a "holding pattern" right now and that I really have no footing or anchor so to speak. I'm emotionally fragile, have little or no energy for anyone let alone patience. I feel scattered and just feel "adrift" and I don't like these feelings at all.

I have worked hard through the years to develop a "starting base" for myself...something that I can rely on. I'm not really sure what I mean by that, but my life was fairly predictable is I guess what I'm trying to say. That predictability brought me a sense of peace in that I was safe and knew "where I was going". Now there is nothing predictable about my life at all and that is so dysregulating. It feels like I am simply "existing" and floating from one thing to another. Just like I did when I used to use drugs in the past. Back then I didn't think about the day ahead because I didn't want to think about what the next day might bring. Now I find comfort in knowing what is happening in my life from day to day, but I don't feel that right now. No wonder I used drugs to mask this feeling. I even thought about buying a bottle of Schnapps yesterday after work, but I was strong enough not to.

Later in the morning:

Just got done with a lot of phone calls and wanted to report what happened. I had called Janet to tell her that we wouldn't be allowed to get together before the trial or even during the trial, so therefore the idea of using my friend's cottages is out the window. Janet told me that Evelyn has already called her and that the county is going to pay for her airfare, her hotel, a rental car and give her a daily allowance to live on. She is very excited about that as it was going to cost her anywhere from $600 - $700 for everything and though she can pay it, it's better if she didn't have to. I am so very thankful to the county for taking care of her expenses.

I then called Evelyn to ask some questions, and it turns out that there are 10 people on my side that were subpoenaed. I knew about most of them except for Peter S., an old friend of mine who was involved in this sordid ordeal. Peter had been served a subpoena while he was at work and I feel so badly for him as I know that this whole thing has caused him some pain. That was evidenced when I called him so long ago and told him that this was going forward. I then wrote him a letter, as he wouldn't return any more of my phone calls but I still haven't heard from him since the first time we talked.

Evelyn also told me that Jeannie (Lesser's ex-wife) was excused from the trial due to health issues. I know that when I previously talked with her, she told me that she had been fighting colon cancer for 6 years. The sense that I got from Evelyn is that unfortunately I think Jeanne's time left in this world is very limited. I feel badly for her, but then she is such a religious person that I know she will be going to heaven where she will finally meet her God. That is the only comfort I find in this news. I must admit that I am at the same time selfishly wondering if this is going to hurt my case or not. Evelyn said that DA Koss doesn't feel that this will hurt our side and I pray that that is true.

We also talked about my fears concerning my mother and that I am afraid that she is going to go "wiggy" as a result of testifying. Mom wants to testify and I think that it is important for her own mental health to do so, but at the same time I'm afraid that she is going to have a stroke or something. I also asked her if there was any way that we could get Lesser's attorney to go easy on her. Evelyn replied that she will document all of this in the case file and that since DA Koss and Lesser's attorney are on friendly terms, that maybe DA Koss will mention something to him about it. Evelyn also said that it wouldn't look good to the jury if his attorney "beat up" on an elderly woman, which is true. Evelyn further reminded me that there is still the possibility that Lesser would accept the plea bargain and he has the option to do that right up until the trial starts on Monday.

This whole thing is such a nightmare and it feels like we are coordinating a play or something. It's really weird, but I feel better about things being under control after talking with Evelyn as well as Janet. I wanted Janet to know once again that I feel badly about dragging her into this whole mess, but she assured me that this was healing for her and that she is thankful for the opportunity to try and resolve this once and for all.

Now all I'm waiting for is news about Tucker as he is in his appointment as I'm writing this. It was a good way to keep my mind off of him as well as to get down on paper all that has transpired this morning. I've decided to take a Lorazepam as I can feel the anxiety beginning to build inside my body. Tucker will be too "loaded" after his appointment to play outside as he got his chill pill and looked pretty buzzed on the way out the door. Please God; don't let anything be wrong with my dog.

March 21, 2009 (Saturday)

It's been a rather hectic couple of days, but I'll begin with the report on Tucker. He has two fatty tissues by his privates and the biopsy showed no cancer or anything!! He won't have to have them removed unless they start interfering with his private parts. The sense of relief I feel is overwhelming.

Yesterday was spent doing paperwork and then I had the CT scan done on my abdomen and pelvic area. I won't get the results from that until Monday, but at least that part is over. When I got home, I checked my e-mails and there was one from DA Koss answering my e-mail about whether or not he could send me Lesser's list of people but also to report that Lesser's attorney had said that he was "in discussions" with Lesser and that he would have "some answer" for DA Koss on Monday. DA Koss wonders if this means that Lesser is thinking about pleading guilty. With 4 weeks until the trial starts, Lesser might be rethinking things, but I'm not going to hold my breath.

On one hand I would be grateful if we didn't have to go through the trial and everything, as it would be so difficult for everyone involved. On the other hand, I might feel a little gyped in regards to being able to tell my side of the story as well as to have his despicable face be spewed all over the newspapers. So right now I have mixed feelings as to what is going to happen. Once again, hurry up and wait for Monday.

March 23, 2009 (Monday)

It's finally Monday and I'm still exhausted from the events of last week and the weekend. I'm anxious this morning and have been awake since about 5:30 a.m. thinking about everything. There are so many things going through my mind that it was nice to have the calm of the morning and the house to try and figure out what to focus on first. Things are just so up in the air today as I'm waiting to find out about two very important matters. One is what Lesser has decided to do and the other is to get the results of my CT scan.

It's now 11:05 a.m. and DA Koss just called to inform me that Lesser is currently having more "family meetings" for the next couple of days to "discuss things" and therefore won't have an answer for us until Wednesday! Now I am going to have to agonize for another couple of days wondering what he is going to decide to do. I suppose their "family meetings" will involve whether he should just plead guilty or go through with the trial.

The other news is that I do have a fibroid tumor that might need to be removed. That's not bad, but there is some evidence of some blockage in one of the arteries in my leg, so that is a little scarier. At least there was some good news mixed with the bad this time. I am exhausted by all of this to say the least.

March 25, 2009 (Wednesday)

Last night I didn't sleep very well at all and just remember tossing and turning all night. Waiting for DA Koss to call me today with what Lesser has decided to do is killing me. I am so nervous, anxious, my stomach hurts and I threw up already this morning. As a result, I've decided to stay home from work today and wait for his call. It is now 1:30 and though I have gotten a ton of paperwork done and bills paid, I haven't heard yet from DA Koss. I think Lesser is just "messing" with my head and actually he's doing a really good job as I'm dysregulated today.

On a lighter side, I have to tell you journal about this image I got in my head while driving home from work last night that made me feel surprisingly good. The image is of me being this big black spider and Lesser is caught in this vast web that he had begun to spin so long ago. I could visualize Lesser entangled in the web and the more that he tried to fight his way out, the more he became entwined in the web.

The spider (me) is just waiting patiently, watching as the prey is losing energy and hope as it struggles in vain to escape the web.

Anyone who has watched a spider do this to their prey can understand what I am saying. This is how I feel right now and though I don't consider myself a vindictive person, I am enjoying this visual. It is his turn to be terrified and trapped! This visual has given me some comfort during this agonizing wait to see what he will do.

It is now the end of the day and DA Koss reported to me that he hasn't heard a thing from them. Those bastards!

March 26, 2009 (Thursday)

What a day it was today. I finally got an e-mail from DA Koss early in the morning saying that Lesser's attorney wanted to meet with him tomorrow, Friday, at 8:30 a.m. DA Koss isn't sure what he wants, but they will be meeting tomorrow! Finally we might have an answer!

After thinking about this news for a while, I began to wonder if they might be trying to pull some crap tomorrow and I am not going to stand for that. As a result of these thoughts, I sent DA Koss another e-mail stating my "wish list" in regards to their meeting tomorrow, as I am sick of them "jacking us around".

One thing on my "wish list" is that I don't want any more delays with this case, whether Jeannie passes or not. Another thing is I don't want him to plead to anything less than the second charge with a maximum of 15 years. I also don't want him to be able to have "time" to get his affairs in order if he is convicted. I wanted DA Koss to know that I have just about run out of patience with this jerk and his tactics and fortunately he agreed with all of my "wishes" or demands if you will.

Finally, I called Janet about 11:00 a.m. to tell her that there is going to be a meeting tomorrow and she was sicker than hell when she answered her cell phone. She said that she was so sick to her stomach and that she was parked alongside the road to try and throw up, hoping that it would make her feel better. She was about 15 miles from home, and was too sick to drive the rest of the way. I called her back an hour later to see if she had made it home, and she was still sitting there! I was so afraid that she might be having a heart attack or something and even suggested that maybe she needed to call an ambulance. I told her that I was even tempted to start driving down to help her and I meant it, but she said she would just keep sitting there until she felt better.

I called her again immediately when I got home from the doctors' and thank God she was now at home. She said she sat there for 2 hours before she felt good enough to drive home and that she was feeling better. She sure scared the hell out of me!

I've had enough for today, although I just checked my e-mail and DA Koss had answered my question about what happens next if he pleads guilty. Does he automatically get the 15 years or what? DA Koss said that he wouldn't automatically get the 15 year sentence if he pleads guilty but rather that Lesser is taking a chance on what type of sentence he might get. DA Koss is so faithful about returning my e-mails and I can't thank him enough for keeping me in the loop and being available when I need him!! I am so lucky to have gotten such a wonderful DA!!!

March 27, 2009 (Friday)

It seemed like it took FOREVER for this day to come and it's ½ hour until the meeting between DA Koss and Lesser's attorney. I've already thrown up 3 times and taken a Lorazepam. I am so scared that they are going to try and pull something this morning and I just can't take any more delay tactics or bullshit. I am at the end of my rope physically, emotionally and almost mentally. Of course I don't want them to know that I'm getting "fried", but that's the way I feel.
I don't trust either Lesser or his attorney and it's going to be "interesting" to see what he wants to talk about. I know it isn't productive to obsess about their meeting this morning, but it's just weird to me that his attorney requested this. Another fear I thought of this morning is what if Lesser's attorney quits or gets fired, then what? Is the trial then delayed longer or what?

I have tried to pray about all of this this morning, but found that my thoughts would wander and I would end up thinking about other things and totally forgetting that I was praying. Of course God knows what is going to happen and I really do have to leave it in His hands, like it has been this entire time. But I still worry about this "next move" in this "game" and how "damaging" that "move" might or could be to me.

It's hard to believe that this has been going on for 3 years now, although I feel every day of those 3 years in regards to my emotional, physical and mental state. It has been an absolutely exhausting endeavor and I couldn't have done it without the support of my parents, Danny, Richard, David and Janet just to name the primary ones. It's kind-of hard to imagine what my life will be like once this is over. This case is all I have lived and breathed for the entire 3 years and I'm beginning to yearn for a time when this wasn't in my life anymore. There have been so many "false starts" and delays with this process, that it doesn't seem like it will ever really be over and maybe that is what is so upsetting to me this morning. I just want it over but I can't help but feel like they are going to try and keep it going, and I can't handle that.

Finally checked my e-mail at 9:45 and of course DA Koss had e-mailed me saying that he wanted me to call. Basically what happened is there was no agreement between the two of them! It appears that Lesser's attorney has been recommending to Lesser that he accept the plea most likely because we have a pretty good case, but he won't. My understanding of their conversation is that Lesser is "in denial"! He actually thinks that he has done nothing wrong! Like my mother said, the "hubris" of this guy is incredible.

At any rate, the trial is back on for now and the last day for Lesser to be able to accept the plea bargain is April 14th. If he doesn't accept it by that date he will have to go to trial. After hearing that he is in "denial" it won't surprise me if he follows through all the way to the trial. Bring it on…but having said that, I just hope and pray that we will win.

DA Koss also sent me Lesser's witness list, and I don't know a soul on it. He has some men that he has worked with in the past, his two stepdaughters and two of his own children. Interesting that there isn't anyone from Campus Life to provide a "character witness" for this idiot. In fact, there are very few people on it and they are mostly from his "new wife's" family. This should be interesting. Enough for today!

March 28, 2009 (Saturday)

Late yesterday afternoon, I decided to go up north with Danny, as he has to meet with a client. I cleaned the house, got the outside work done and even packed, but this morning, I woke up and don't want to go. The mood shifts and indecision that I have must be bugging the heck out of Danny. He was a good sport though and said that he just thought that I might like to get out of town for a couple of days, but me staying home was fine with him. Tucker was of course happy because he got a reprieve from having to go to "Doggy Day Camp". He knows when he is going and he understood by our words and actions today, that he wouldn't be going. In fact, he and Danny went to town for breakfast and to do some errands for his mother. Therefore the house is nice and quiet!!

David also contacted me this morning asking to read this memoir, but in actuality, he felt it was now time for him to begin to participate in the game. He has been on the sidelines this entire time (per his choice and mine) and now with the trial 3 weeks away, he feels that he better start thinking about things. Rather than send him this memoir, which wouldn't be of any help, I sent him all the information that I had compiled and sent to DA Koss. That's the only bummer about going to trial is that everyone has to testify. Danny mentioned to me yesterday that I seemed to be happy about the trial being on and upon reflecting on my attitude; I would have to agree with him.

I feel that even if the jury doesn't convict him, his ugly ass face will be spread all over and people will know what a predator he really is. His "denial" as to the situation that he is currently in, is just evidence to me that he doesn't feel any remorse or guilt for his actions. He doesn't feel that he did anything wrong. Well, I hope that a jury of his peers disagrees with him and finds him guilty. Maybe that will rock his world.

I am also beginning to be afraid for my personal safety again as his refusal to accept the situation further solidifies in my mind that this guy could be dangerous. For a while I've backed off on that worry, but it is creeping back in. I am getting nervous about being alone and with Danny heading up north tomorrow afternoon, I'm wondering how I'm going to handle it. I hear all sorts of noises at night anyhow, but with this situation, those nighttime noises become "people in the night".

Tucker certainly doesn't help at night because the coyotes are howling again and Tucker will wake you from a dead sleep howling back at them at the top of his lungs. It is such an eerie howl that he lets out as well. It sounds more like the coyotes than a dog and sometimes the coyotes will actually shut-up when they hear him. It's always hard to fall back to sleep after that as your adrenaline is just pumping like crazy because of being woken up like that. There is still a loaded gun in the back room, but I have it barricaded and am terrified to even pick it up. I prefer my pepper spray; although it's so old it probably won't work anyhow!

April 1, 2009 (Wednesday)

Obviously I made it through the other night just fine, but on Monday I did e-mail Detective Sharp and DA Koss about being scared again. Detective Sharp got right back to me and said that he would call the Green County Sheriff's Department to "keep an eye on me" so to speak. Detective A. from the Green County Sheriff's Department called me right away yesterday about the situation. He was very nice and familiar with our "house" because we of course had the hunter shoot through our house a couple of years ago. There was also that accidental 911 call that I had made last fall that resulted in having an officer come out. What an airhead I was that time!

I also finally had my appointment with the surgeon in Madison and though I loved her, she can't do anything because she doesn't perform gynecological surgery so now I have to see a gynecologist. I feel that things are finally on the right track with my health and that I do have good professionals looking out for me, so that has been calming to me. I am/was tired of having to figure everything out so to speak, so it is nice to have someone taking care of me for a change.

I can't believe that the trial is now 19 days away!! I am still "coordinating" everything on my side, even sending my family an e-mail reminding them to get their "suites" dry cleaned for court. When I talked with Richard this morning, he good-naturedly gave me a hard time about it, asking me if I thought they were 10 year-olds. I had to laugh and told Richard that Mom had made a comment to me too on how I was managing things right down to the last detail. Like she said to me earlier, this is like a big production that we are putting on, except that it isn't for entertainment. It's about my life as well as other people's lives and that is serious. I want to make sure that we "win" this case and if that means micromanaging the whole thing, then so be it. I have in fact been micromanaging this thing from the start, so it just makes sense to continue to do that until this is over. I bet this micromanaging has been bugging the daylights out of Detective Sharp and DA Koss! Ha Ha.

I also received a wonderful e-mail from David in regards to him reading all of the information that I had provided to Detective Sharp and DA Koss over these past 3 years. David said that the information I had put together was "extremely well laid-out"!! To get a compliment from David like that is rare, so I saved it to savor! He is being such a good sport about having to go through this and I can't tell you how much I appreciate his love and support.

I have put a lot of thought, planning and work into this whole process and it was nice to have David validate that I have been doing a good job. Of course I've been telling him this whole time that I had everything under control, but I know he didn't know what a good job I have done until he saw my work. It's difficult for me to understand how Lesser thinks that he is going to "win" with all of the ammunition that I have to throw at him.

I still find it upsetting hearing that Lesser is in "denial" about all of this. The fact that he feels he didn't do anything wrong, just makes me that much more angry!

Later:

Just got an e-mail from Scott F. that Mr. F. is in the hospital and they don't know what is wrong with him! I feel so badly about this as I think that the stress from having this trial could be affecting his health. Mrs. F. just died last summer and now their dad is sick, so I feel awful about it.

I immediately e-mailed back that Mr. F. is to take care of himself and that he shouldn't worry about the trial. I also said that we probably don't even need him as we have plenty of other evidence against Lesser. I forwarded on Scott's e-mail to DA Koss and fortunately he told me the same thing about not necessarily needing him. Good thing as I had already told Scott that without conversing with DA Koss! I hope and pray that he is ok as it would be awful for the kids to lose their dad so quickly after losing their mom.

April 4, 2009 (Saturday)

Thank God it's the weekend! There were some good things that happened this week and I'll begin with my medical report. Went to a new gynecologist yesterday to check the fibroid tumor and he thinks the pain I'm having isn't the fibroid, but rather scar tissue from my old appendectomy scar is growing around my fallopian tubes and right ovary. He said those female organs are as sensitive as a guy's gonads and that they hurt us just as bad as if we kneed a guy in the privates! Interesting diagnosis and I will talk with my new doctor next week.

It was very upsetting however going to this male gynecologist who I have never met in my life and yet he was going to perform a pelvic exam on me! I said something to the nurse about my feeling uncomfortable with someone I don't even know, doing that, so she actually came into the room when he did it. That was really nice of her and I thanked her for that.

After my appointment, Danny and I took off for a counselor education reunion at the UW-Whitewater. It was a reunion for all of the people who have graduated from the Counselor Education Master's program and there were about 100 people there. The chancellor and the dean of the college were in attendance and it turned out to be a great time.

Granted I didn't know many people there, but it turns out that I was one of 9 who were recognized for our contributions to the field since we graduated from the program! What an honor and truly a big surprise. Dr. O'Beirne had asked me to write an article about myself and send it to her, but I thought it was going to be put in some booklet like they do for class reunions. Little did I know that she was going to read it in front of everyone. If I had known that, I might have made it bit more "interesting". Ha Ha. It was so nice to be recognized by my peers and it really gave me a shot of confidence, something that I really need right now.

April 8, 2009 (Wednesday)

Yesterday is the day that I finally was able to see the artery surgeon and my new doctor and it actually turned out to be a good day in regards to health issues. First up was the artery doctor and though I now have PAD, Peripheral Artery Disease, it is minor and I don't need any medication as of right now! That was great news!

Then up was my new doctor and because we have ruled out any serious illnesses, we are going to take a "wait and see" attitude with how to proceed next. It's really a relief to know that there isn't anything seriously wrong and that I have checked out pretty well. Granted there are issues, but I'm also getting older. Not only that, but I am fairly hard on my body and always have been.

What a huge sense of relief knowing that I don't have to have some type of major surgery in the immediate future! I can once again focus all of my energy and attention on nailing Lesser!!

CHAPTER 44

The Home Stretch

April 9, 2009 (Thursday)

Janet called this morning while she was driving to see her mother and while we at first discussed her upcoming fears about the trial, she also needed to tell me some terrible news. Janet is currently being tested to see if she has the cancer – Myeloma. It is so unfair that just when it seems like things are going to get better in her life, she gets this devastating information. She is supposed to meet with her doctor to find out the news the week of the trial, but she is going to put it off until the week after.

I am sick about the news and now I'm feeling badly again about dragging Janet into this whole mess so I once again apologized. Janet, bless her heart, continues to think completely the opposite; she is thankful that I found her and that she can participate in this process for her own healing. Janet said that this process has enabled her to finally talk about it with her husband and with her family. Janet says that this has been a "good experience" and not to worry about the anxiety that she is feeling. She says that it is a "good" anxiety in a way as there is finally going to be something done about what happened to us when we were just innocent young girls. But now she has to deal with this new "fight" and it just doesn't seem fair at all.

Then when I got home from work last night, I found that DA Koss had left me an e-mail saying that he had talked with Janet as well as my brother David to prep for court. DA Koss also informed me that Mr. F. most likely wouldn't be able to make it to the trial, as he was too ill, but that Mr. F. had really wanted to be here to help. Maybe that is "why" he came to the preliminary hearing...so he could see for himself justice being done, as now he won't be able to. Maybe God knew what was in store for Mr. F. and that it was important for Mr. F. to "have a hand in this", so I'm thankful that he was there that day.

Finally and most importantly is that DA Koss also mentioned that he had heard from Lesser's attorney who said that Lesser has had a "seismic shift" in his attitude. His attorney once again assured us that Lesser was going to be in the area on Monday, although he didn't say why. We do have a motion hearing on Tuesday regarding Janet's testimony, but I don't think he has to be there for it, so why is he coming?! Maybe it has something to do with Tuesday also being the last day that he can take the plea bargain. Just knowing that he is going to be in the area makes me sick to my stomach and I puked.

I then called my parents to tell them about the e-mail from DA Koss and while we were on the phone, Dad asked if I had gotten the e-mail about Mr. F. being very very ill. I hadn't so I went back on and it turns out that Mr. F. has an aggressive form of Leukemia and that they are looking for hospice for him!

That is so very sad and I couldn't stop crying for a while. He was so supportive of me through this process and that meant a lot to me. He was also a good father and husband as well as a devout Christian. Mrs. F. just passed away sometime last fall so for the kids to lose both of their parents in such a short period of time isn't fair.

I'm not sure what is going to happen with Lesser coming here on Monday, but I hope that I don't end up like last time "holding my breathe" and being very dysregulated. I am determined to remain calm, however Danny and I are already arguing about whether or not people can come out here this weekend. I just can't handle it, but he doesn't seem to understand that we are almost there and to bear with me for a while longer. It just might be a Lorazepam weekend!

Both DA Koss and Janet think that Lesser will take the plea agreement, but I don't. I think that he would rather "go out with a bang" so to speak, and I would actually like him to go out with a bang! There is so much evidence pointing to him doing this though that he might just take his chances on a sentence. I don't know and it's fruitless to spend any energy worrying about that bastard anymore. The thing is though I need to be "ready" with my "next move" in this "game".

April 11, 2009 (Saturday)

Janet called last night to tell me that she had gotten a call from a private investigator! She wasn't home, but her husband Jerry took the message and I guess he wasn't very nice to the investigator. Janet wasn't quite sure what to do about speaking with her, but didn't really want to talk with her, so she has decided she won't.

The fact that she got a call from an investigator is interesting to me because if he were going to possibly plead guilty, why would he hire a private investigator and why would he do it 4 days before the last day he can take the plea? It makes me wonder, but there is also that motion hearing this Tuesday about whether or not Janet's testimony can be used, so maybe the investigator is fishing for information before the motion hearing.

Janet gave me the investigators phone number and of course I went on the Internet to see if I could find this number. I can, but it will cost $4.95 to see whom it belongs to. I don't feel like doing all of that right now, but if I get bored later today, I just might.

Yesterday I also heard from Deanna about this journal and she was quite positive about it. She was however extremely worried about my mental and emotional state. I tried to reassure her that since January, I've had a shift in attitude as well as in the severity of my anxiety and nervousness. I wish she had the next part of the journal that reflects this new "strength" if you will. I'm not sure what caused that shift, but maybe it was the fact that we finally got a date for the trial. I guess that indicated to me that there was an end to this whole process.

She also thought that I should wrap this journal up with some positives, as Americans love a good ending! I certainly hope that this journal will end on a good note, but I have a feeling that it will.

Another thing that Deanna stressed is that I should put in here that it is important for people to seek professional help when faced with the issues and events that I have expressed here. I totally agree with her on that and definitely believe that someone should seek therapy for whatever their issues are. I hope that people who read this memoir realize that the only reason I was able to do this is without a therapist is because of my therapeutic knowledge, skills and tools as well as a wonderful support group.

People must remember that I have had extensive "therapy" simply going through my master's program. I found going through the program that it was important for me to "face my demons" as how could I help others if I didn't have my "stuff" together, so that is what I had to do. A "normal" person would have no clue about "what is happening to them" and that is why it is imperative that a person seeks out a counselor that they feel comfortable with and that can be effective in helping them.

April 12, 2009 (Easter Sunday)

Happy Easter!! It's a gorgeous day in Wisconsin!

Watched church, which wasn't too inspirational actually, but still enjoyed seeing all of the flowers and hearing the music.

After church, I checked my e-mail and there were two e-mails from Janet. One was this YouTube video where all of these people in a train station, start dancing and singing to the song "Do, Re, Mi" from the "Sound of Music". It was really cool as it looked like people just started joining in out of the blue, but it had to be orchestrated. I love "The Sound of Music" and once again, it is interesting how much Janet and I am alike.

The other e-mail was her sending me this weird e-mail that she had gotten from someone she didn't even know. This guy wrote to her "If you saw me walking on the street, would you know who I was? It's been a long time". That is just too weird and Janet e-mailed back that she didn't know this guy and he replied that he was sorry and he would take her off of his contact list!! What's up with that?

She was also freaking out because she thought that she saw Lesser at the garden center where she works. Remember journal that she only lives about 3 hours away from him, so it wouldn't be a problem for him to get there. There is also no restraining order keeping him from Janet that I am aware of, however I remember telling DA Koss that I didn't want him to be able to contact her either. Janet isn't sure if it was him as this guy's build was a little different, but it still freaked her out. She said that she is beginning to get "the willies" like I am and that it's just creepy. You're not sure if someone is watching you or what. Janet is more afraid that he will confront her rather than hurt her. I am just the opposite as I feel he would hurt me because once again, if I "disappear", so does this case. They also had a different "relationship" if you can call it that, but it seems like he really created something with her while I was just a "piece of ass" to him. In thinking about that, I would rather be a "piece of ass" to him because the betrayal that Janet must feel is probably a gazillion times worse than I will ever feel. That's why I said before that she is "more screwed up" than I am because of that sense of betrayal she must feel.

Tomorrow is the "big day" because according to his attorney, Lesser will be in town tomorrow. For what I'm not sure, but I'm going to shower right away in the morning in case I have to run over there. There is no sense worrying about it and I'm really not. It's not that I'm not thinking about his "next move" constantly, but rather I'm not going to get so upset because I know that the noose is getting tighter and that feels good. I still would like this to go to trial though, so I'm actually worried that he might take the plea.

I do have some nervous energy, but it's not the incapacitating anxiety thankfully. It's hard to sit still because then my mind wanders, but I found that I could let it go for a while. I actually took a nap after working in the yard yesterday! In the past I wouldn't have been able to take a nap for the life of me. To me, this is a sign that I am not necessarily healing, but more that everything might finally be falling into place to nail Lesser.

April 13, 2009 (Monday)

Today is the day that allegedly Lesser is in Wisconsin so I immediately left an e-mail for DA Koss to call me if anything happens. It will be interesting to see what unfolds over the next couple of days, as tomorrow is the last day that he can take the plea deal.

Mom and Dad hope that he takes the plea bargain, as I don't think they want to testify. I can't blame them for that, but I personally hope that it will go to trial. I've said that before and I'll say it again…I want it to go to trial. I want 12 people who don't even know me to say that he did what he did. To me, that would be validation. I'm just afraid that if he pleads guilty, then people won't take it as seriously as if a jury had found him guilty. Mom and Dad think that if he takes the deal that will be total vindication that he did what he did. I have mixed feelings about it, but all I have to do is wait two more days and I will know for sure what is going on!!

I take that back because until the trial actually starts, I wouldn't put anything past this jerk. I feel anxious today, but also extremely tired. I dreamt about Janet a lot last night and though I can't remember the specifics, I know that in my dream, she was in danger and I was trying to save her. It's amazing how dreams can seem so real when you are dreaming them. It's also amazing how exhausted a person can be upon waking! There must have been a lot of action in my dream.

It's currently 11:00 a.m. and no word yet from DA Koss. I wonder if I'll hear anything today!!

Later:

DA Koss called at 4:00 to tell me that Lesser never showed up today like his attorney said he was going to, so therefore nothing has happened. Instead, he is allegedly supposed to show up tomorrow, so we talked about the plea bargain and how that would happen if he decided to do that. DA Koss said that if he is going to plead guilty, he's going to make Lesser do it at the 2:30 motion hearing pertaining to Janet's testimony.

Regardless to me, tomorrow is the day that I have been waiting for in regards to finally knowing whether this thing is going to go to trial, or is he going to plead guilty.

I also asked DA Koss if he could wait on interviewing Mom and Dad until after we find out what might happen tomorrow. If Lesser pleads guilty, then they don't have to go talk to DA Koss and I would prefer for them not to. Mom is getting more and more confused about what is happening when, and I don't want to further stress her out by having her talk to DA Koss if she doesn't have to. Fortunately DA Koss agreed to that, so we'll just wait and see what happens.

I quickly called Janet to tell her what had happened, or in this case that nothing had happened. She brought up the idea of whether or not he is going to "bolt", and I can't say that I didn't think about that as well. He allegedly took off when he found out that there was a warrant for his arrest, so he might take off now. I think that I might take off if I was facing spending quite a bit of time in prison. I promised that I would call her if ANYTHING happens tomorrow.

Now it's wait until tomorrow, but that's ok as I can handle one more day. I don't know what I will do or how I will feel if he does "take off" and become a fugitive. I guess I'll have to deal with that if it happens. Right now it's day by day, but then again it seems like it's been that way for a long time.

I also have to say that I was able to take 2 naps today!! I fell asleep only to have a friend call me and wake me up. I was able to fall asleep again after that and slept until DA Koss woke me up. All that without any medication to help me fall asleep!! It felt so good to take that nap and obviously I must not be too upset or I wouldn't have been able to fall asleep!

I also received other bad news in that Mr. F. died last night. That was certainly "quick" as he just went into the hospital about a week ago and at that time they didn't even know what was wrong with him. I cried for quite a while because I feel so badly for the kids. They have now lost both of their parents in less than a year. That is just too sad.

April 14, 2009 (Tuesday)

I wanted to quickly write some things down before I head off to court for the motion hearing. There is still no word from DA Koss about whether or not he is going to plead guilty, but I guess he might not do that until 2:30.

I am a bit anxious today and my "routine" for court is all screwed up because Danny is home. I like being alone on days that I have to go to court and having him around is annoying me to say the least. He wanted breakfast and since I had a little nervous energy, I made breakfast for him, but grumbled about it the whole time. I never make breakfast and I don't want to "take care" of anyone right now.

I was able to eat a little bit, but now I have a terrible stomachache. Then to top it all off, he invited Charlie to come out here this morning to look at his "cement slab"! It's what's left of the old chicken coop and why Charlie would want to look at an old stupid slab of concrete is beyond me, but Danny is excited about him coming out. I on the other hand am upset that I have to have someone out here while I'm trying to get physically, mentally and emotionally ready for court.

I'm finding it so hard to believe that today is the day that I have been waiting for since hearing that this is the last day that he can plead guilty. I have no idea what is going to happen today and I'm not sure that I will have the energy to write in this journal when I get home, but the next time that I do write in here, we will know!!

CHAPTER 45

"GOTCHA"!

April 15, 2009 (Wednesday)

CHECK---CHECKMATE---GAME OVER!!!

While I was getting ready to go yesterday, I got a call from DA Koss telling me that Lesser was going to plead guilty!!! Upon hearing those words, I physically felt like I had been punched in the stomach, but surprisingly I didn't cry or scream or really do anything. A person would think that I would be jumping up and down and screaming at the top of my lungs, but I didn't feel like that at all. Rather I told DA Koss that I'll believe it when I see it and that I was on my way over to court. DA Koss also told me what an excellent job I have done on this case and though I was a bit surprised that he said that, it felt very good to hear, as I knew that I had put A LOT of work into this whole ordeal.

After hanging up with DA Koss, I immediately called my parents, my brothers and Janet to tell them that DA Koss had just called to tell me he was going to plead guilty. Janet screamed in the phone and Mom started crying! Again, I didn't really feel anything for myself, but it felt "good" that Janet and Mom were so happy. I had to leave David a message and Richard of course was very happy for me. I finally got a hold of Dad on his cell phone and he was thrilled to say the least! Danny and Charlie were outside and I had yelled the news out to them so of course they were happy for me as well.

As I wrote yesterday, my usual routine was out the window, so it seemed "different" this time. I felt scattered, unsure and surprisingly, numb. I did take the time to stop and buy DA Koss one of those Blue Mountain Art greeting cards thanking him for all that he did. I also didn't listen to any music on the way over, but rather listened to all of my thoughts instead. I wondered why he pled guilty; although I knew in my heart it was because he knew he couldn't beat us. I wondered what the process would be like in court today; I wondered why I wasn't having more of a response to this and that surprisingly, I felt badly for Lesser. I wondered if he knew how his life was going to change as a result of him pleading guilty. I was also thinking about this whole journey these past 3 years and that this is finally the end. I also profusely thanked God and marveled at how He had pulled this all together 35+ years later.

I got to the courthouse and went up to the DA's office and immediately saw Lesser's attorney sitting in the waiting room. I didn't really want to sit near him, but since it is tiny, we had to acknowledge each other. He was in fact very nice and asked if I had talked to DA Koss yet about what was to happen and I said no. I asked him if Lesser was here and he said that he was and again, my stomach dropped. Mr. K. further added that he and DA Koss were trying to get some paperwork together that they needed in order to be able to accept his guilty plea. He said that they were hoping we could finish this all today so that I wouldn't have to come back the next day. I replied that I would be glad to come back tomorrow if I had to, and his response was "I know you will"! He said it in a way indicating that he KNEW I would come as I had already proved my formidability to him. Ha Ha.

Mr. K. was being very nice and I actually thanked him but added that I wasn't sure why I was thanking him. I also felt this urge to acknowledge to him the fact that we both know Prisoner Pete, so I said to him "It's certainly a small world" and he just laughed and said it certainly was. Thankfully DA Koss then came out to get me, as he didn't want me to have to sit in the waiting room with Mr. K, because it really was uncomfortable.

This was the first time I had been in DA Koss office and it was big and beautiful. He had pictures of his family around, so I felt like I was in on some "inner sanctum" of his and that felt weird. The whole day was feeling "weird" to me. Detective Sharp joined us and we talked about how the whole case had played out. Both Detective Sharp and DA Koss complimented me on a job well done and Detective Sharp even complimented me on being the one to find Lesser as he couldn't. I'm sure he could have found him if he tried as it really wasn't that hard.

I still wasn't jumping up and down and I think that DA Koss and Detective Sharp were a little surprised that I wasn't more emotional or reactive to him pleading guilty. I've honestly felt like I was a "bump on a log" since hearing the news. DA Koss asked if I was a bit disappointed that it hadn't gone to trial and I said that I was and explained why. DA Koss is so wonderful as he validated my disappointment, while at the same time stressed that Lesser pleading guilty was the best scenario possible. I guess it's just that I have had to psych myself up so much for this whole ordeal, that it's hard to "let the air out" immediately. I told DA Koss and Detective Sharp what Richard had said about my lack of reaction or thoughts to this twist of events as it was perfect. Richard said it's similar to a person who is totally psyched up to "go hunting for bear", and then the bear drops dead in front of you. That analogy describes my feelings exactly!!

DA Koss explained that a huge advantage to him pleading guilty is that he can't ever file any appeals or come back to court for any reason (or almost any reason), therefore this thing is now OVER. DA Koss also stressed that a trial is not a pleasant ordeal and though that is all well and good, I still feel a little let down. I do appreciate how this "has ended" and as I sat there and we talked further about it, it is much better that he pled guilty no matter what I had wanted or thought I wanted. It's a good thing if for no other reason than my loved ones won't have to testify and that is huge for me!

DA Koss also informed me that when he had called Dr. Hadley to question her, her daughter informed him that she had Alzheimer's disease now and therefore wouldn't be able to testify. Our witness list was dwindling because now we have lost Jeannie, Mr. F. and now Dr. Hadley, so that is another reason I should be grateful he pled guilty. I do know in my heart that this is the perfect way to end it all, but still... DA Koss told me that Lesser's wife is most likely the one who encouraged him to plead guilty. I think she just wants to get this matter resolved and move on, but who knows. I thank her if she did indeed encourage him to plead guilty.

DA Koss, Detective Sharp, Evelyn and I then went up to court and Lesser was there with who I assume was his wife. She looked so "worn out" that I felt sorry for her, but most definitely not for him! It was all I could do to look at him, but he never once looked my way. I also thought it was disgusting in that when he was called up to the defense table, he slapped his wife on the butt.

The judge asked him a bunch of questions as far as did he understand what he was pleading guilty to as well as all of the ramifications that came with pleading guilty to a felony. Lesser told him that he knew it all and after what seemed an eternity, he pled guilty to the second felony charge of sexual intercourse with a 15 year-old. I've waited 35+ years to hear those words and know that I finally have justice! That moment was really the only time that I have ever got teary in court but I was determined not to let them fall! Throughout this process I have wanted to show no weakness whatsoever to anyone and I still felt that way for some reason. Evelyn did pat me on the back when he pled guilty and that was my first congratulations on winning! All I felt was a huge sense of relief and satisfaction that this was finally over and that we had won!

The court proceeding was over in about 15 minutes and it was anticlimactic to say the least. Lesser didn't get handcuffed and hauled out of court as I had expected, but rather walked out of the courthouse, got into his car and drove off. No one was in the courtroom but Evelyn, Lesser's wife, some other lady and myself. When it was over, Evelyn, DA Koss and I walked down to the DA's office where I hugged them and thanked them numerous times. I still wasn't jumping up and down or crying, but I did tear up a little when I hugged DA Koss. The clerical staff seemed happy too as they were all smiles. It makes me wonder if this must be a kind of coup, for someone to plead guilty, but in my mind, that is the way that it should be. He knew what he did was wrong and I feel that it's only RIGHT that he should confess and be held accountable. In my childlike mind, I feel that if more people admitted their mistakes and tried to make repairs, this world would be a much better place.

Driving home I called everyone to tell them what had happened and Janet said that she feels like an enormous weight has been taken off of her shoulders. She said that she didn't think that she would feel any different, but she said after my first phone call telling her that he was going to plead guilty she did feel different. I'm glad that this process has been such a healing event for her as that is something that I had wanted to accomplish. She seems like such a good person and she deserves to have some peace in her life.

David was a joy to talk with, as he was full of accolades and praise for his little sister! He is amazed that I was able to single-handedly bring this jerk down. He kept saying that no one pleads guilty to a felony offense as they will usually go down denying that they ever committed the crime, but Lesser didn't. I had produced such a good case against him, that he knew he had no chance to beat me. So as difficult as it was to do all the things that I did, it proved to be what nailed him in the end. That I feel terrific about. This was a nice birthday present for David as it is his birthday today!!

It is now the next morning and I still haven't celebrated or jumped up and down ecstatically as I just don't feel like it. It isn't over completely as he still has to get his punishment, but I must admit the hard part is over. I haven't even cried for goodness sake and I can't really figure out why. I still feel "numb" for lack of a better word.

The only "feeling" that I can immediately identify is that I have a deep sense of satisfaction. I feel like something that was done a long time ago and that was really really wrong, has finally been "righted" and so there is a sense of relief.

The last thing I did today was I sent out an e-mail to everyone telling them that he had pled guilty and that it was over! The other thing I wanted people to know when responding to me is not to ask if this brings me "closure" or even to use the word. To be honest, I hate that word and I didn't want to get pissed off reading messages about "closure"! There is never going to be closure for me because the effects the molestation had on me will never go away. That's what people have to understand, that this will NEVER go away. Hopefully by reading my Victim Impact Statement, people will realize how this crime and its effects will always be a part of who I am.

I think that I will close for the day as I am exhausted, but I wanted to at least tell you the good news!!

April 16, 2009 (Thursday)

It's about 6:00 in the morning and I've been awake since about 5:00 knowing that it is over!! For the first time in 3 years I can wake up and not worry about this case and to be honest, I don't know quite how to handle this. Once again, I find that I keep replaying in my mind what happened in court as well as this whole journey. I found myself rereading all of the information that I provided to Detective Sharp and DA Koss over the years to see what a strong case we did have against him. I'm also a little amazed that it really was me who brought him down. I am most proud of that.

Yesterday I spent most of the day trying to make contact with area newspapers. I have decided to use my name for a couple of reasons and therefore I needed to contact the newspapers before they came out with the story, so I could give them permission to do that.

I first talked to "The Lake Geneva Regional News", the ones who "outed" me by saying that I lived in Iran. I talked with the news editor for quite a while and explained to her why I wanted to use my name. I found it hard to articulate exactly why, but one of my main reasons was that I wanted to try and help others. I also mentioned that I had written a journal about this whole experience with the hopes of it being of help to others. She said that maybe the paper would do a story on it in a couple of months!! I'll take her up on that.

I then called the "Janesville Gazette" and managed to reach the editor. We discussed the reasons why I had called the paper to tell about my story and again I was having a very difficult time articulating why an article about this case was important. All I know is that for some reason, I want/need for them to print my name. I explained to the editor that I was fairly well known in the area and that as a professional in the business, I thought it was important to use my name. He sounded interested and told me that he would have his new reporter who covers the Walworth area give me a call.

That is why I have been up since 5:00!! To think of what I want to say to the reporters about this whole thing. It is important to get the article "right" so to speak as hopefully this article will help other victims. I think my story has already helped at least one person who works with Danny. She told him to thank me for doing what I did as I spoke for many of the victims who have always wanted to do something, but didn't for some reason or another. Obviously something happened to her and she wanted to thank me. THAT'S WHAT I'M TALKING ABOUT!!!

This whole ordeal has been to help not only myself, but my family as well. It was to try and make something good happen for all of us and help us to heal from so long ago. This journal is an attempt to hopefully help many different people in different ways, from victims to family members to students.

I have been trying to pull my thoughts together so that I am able to effectively articulate to him and their readers, what I want to say, and I think I've done it. It's important to me to get this right, as again, my goal by using my name is to help others. I have decided that what I'm trying to accomplish by using my name, is to take away the stigma that sexual abuse victims seem to have. Society has a tendency to view sexual abuse victims as being low-class, ignorant and from poor families. People think that sexual abuse is something that "happens to other people", but certainly not in their world or in their circles. Society also views victims as "tainted" or "dirty" and that somehow they got what they were asking for. I want society to understand that bad things happen to good people, but that doesn't make us bad. We were the victims of an insidious crime that already makes us feel "tainted or dirty" and to have some people in society treat us that way, makes the shame that we already feel that much worse.

I want others to know that there is nothing to be ashamed about and I'm doing that by proudly saying my name, as I know many people in many different communities. We were the ones who were terribly hurt and had our lives forever altered and there is no shame in that. Fortunately Lesser ADMITTED that what he did was wrong, but that most likely won't happen for others.

April 17, 2009 (Friday)

I think today is going to be a tough day. Yesterday I talked with Pedro who is a reporter for the "Janesville Gazette", and Rob who is with "The Lake Geneva Regional News". I spent an hour talking to both of them and I just pray that what I said isn't stupid or taken out of context. I am sooooooo worried about how these articles are going to turn out and therefore, my stomach is in knots. I thought that feeling was over!!

I just hope that by giving them my name, and even a picture for the Janesville Gazette (!), others will find comfort, healing or at least a little less shame about being a victim themselves. I am afraid that I talked too much, so I'm really nervous as to what they will end up printing. I have already been in tears thinking about ALL of the people who are going to read about it. I know so many people personally and professionally and I think many of these people are going to be in shock to discover that this happened to me. And that's my point! That if it can happen to me, a nice person from a nice family, then it can happen to anyone. Not only that, but also to "show" people that someone as nice as me, had a "dirty little secret".

I also realized this morning that maybe some people won't "like" me anymore or might "look" at me differently now and I'm in tears about that possibility happening. People might now apply that "tainted" or "dirty" label to me where they haven't in the past. I'm sure that I'll be writing in here again, especially after the story comes out.

April 20, 2009 (Monday) Day of the trial that wasn't!!!

Today is a beautiful day!! I should have been sitting in a courtroom right now, but instead I'm sitting at home with a smile on my face. It really is a blessing that he pled guilty, as I don't know if we all could have held up during the trial. Mom has been sick to her stomach since last Sunday so as a result, we had to cancel our celebratory lunch because she was now throwing up. The fact that she is physically throwing up is upsetting to me because she NEVER throws up. The last time she threw up was when we lived in Iran and she accidentally drank some watered down bleach that she had cleaned the vegetables in. Hopefully she has the flu but it easily could be all of the "stress and ickiness" finally coming out. Mom has been emotionally "paralyzed" for the past 35+ years so it's only natural that she has to "purge" all of that crap.

I have always known that the fact I was molested had affected my parents. They were literally devastated that they hadn't "protected" their daughter as well as the fact that we never "went after him". Therefore I had to ask them if they felt vindicated as parents for finally getting justice. Dad said that he felt vindicated as this whole ordeal with Lesser has been "nagging" at him all of these years. He had also felt badly that we hadn't prosecuted Lesser years ago, but since we have already gone over the reasons why we didn't he hopefully can let that go.

I don't think I have put that part in here, so here are some of the reasons why "my family/parents" never did anything legally after I told:

1. We were halfway around the world and my parents wouldn't be back to the states for any long period of time for at least 3 years.
2. I never brought it up to them again after telling, as I didn't want to bring them any more pain than I knew they already felt.
3. They never brought the idea up to me because since I hadn't said anything more to them about it, they didn't want to bring it up and upset me again.
4. Dad didn't want me to go through with a trial that most likely would have been nasty.

These "reasons" made perfect sense to us back then even though we never voiced them out loud to each other! It was the old proverbial "white elephant" that no one talked about.

I know that Mom feels vindicated because "nailing" Lesser was something that she has always wanted to have happen, but to hear how happy she was, meant the world to me.

I shared with them how important it was for me to hear that they felt vindication as that is probably the most important thing that I wanted to have happen as a result of going through this whole process. I felt like I couldn't let them go to their graves with any regrets in their lives as they were the most wonderful parents I could have ever hoped or dreamed for. I want them to have a clear conscious knowing that they did nothing wrong and that they did indeed protect their daughter in the end. I know that they will never get over their guilt, but hopefully this will be of tremendous help to them.

Personally, I've been feeling really "weird" since this whole thing went down and I'm trying to figure out why. I should be bouncing off the walls, but I'm not. I am extremely exhausted, physically, mentally and emotionally. It's hard to concentrate on getting things done, but I've had to for numerous reasons and it's just so difficult.

I know that I have to get back to work as I need the money, but I also clinically realize that I need some time to "process" this whole thing. David had sent me an e-mail suggesting that I seek counseling now as most likely I will be experiencing PTSD. I had to laugh as I've been experiencing PTSD on a daily basis for the past three years! I'm now hopefully nearing the end of it. I do appreciate his concern and it does make me think about "what happens next", so to speak.

I don't feel like this is "over" as we still have the sentencing to deal with and that is over 2 months away. I think the best way to describe how I'm feeling right now is like a "wounded bird". I feel it is important to surround myself with things that provide me comfort and to "nurse my wounds". I feel in some ways like I'm 14 again and trying to understand why this all had to happen in the first place. He admitted guilt, but he didn't say, "why he did it". Therefore I can only assume it was "because he wanted to" and that hurts more than anything. To have a person take your entire life away from you just "because they wanted to" is too hard to comprehend. His "pleasure" resulted in my life being eternally a struggle on so many levels and I really want him to pay by going to hell when he dies.

It is also so difficult because I feel like people think I should be able to immediately transition back into work and life, and I'm finding that not only invalidating, but upsetting. This has been such a long and exhausting challenge, that it's going to take a while to figure "things" out. I'm not really sure what I even mean by "things" and that's what I need some time for.

I know the newspaper articles haven't come out yet and that is one "thing" that is making me nervous. I'm not sure what they are going to say and I'm just praying that they were able to relay to their readers, what I was trying to say to them. After the articles come out, then I have to see what happens, if anything. All I do know is that this isn't over yet...not by a long shot.

I find that I have to keep reminding myself that the most difficult part of this journey is over and that was getting a guilty plea. The more I think about that whole thing, the more I am so THANKFUL that it didn't go to court. God played this "game" absolutely perfectly as things couldn't have gone better. In fact, I never even considered that Lesser pleading guilty would be a miracle unto itself. God knew what He was doing and all of the glory goes to Him!!

April 22, 2009 (Wednesday)

Today is the day that the trial would have been over had we had it!! I think it has finally been sinking in how miraculous it was that he pled guilty last week!! I am just sooooooo thankful that it didn't come to a trial as I do feel it would have been so upsetting to everyone.

The newspaper article from the "Janesville Gazette" came out on Monday and though my picture looks terrible, I'm pleased with the article. There has already been a few people who have put positive blogs on their website. One person even put how sexual abuse affects a person's life much better than I did. There was also a Nun who is a victim advocate in New Castle DE who wrote a rather long statement about the United States having different statutes in all the different states. That got me thinking that maybe that is something that I should do next...advocate for getting the statute of limitations higher for all of the states. God, where is that "open window" as I feel I need some guidance on what to do next with my life.

As far as how I'm feeling about this whole thing now, I'm still feeling kind-of weird to be honest. It's like I'm still waiting for the other shoe to drop or something. I'm exhausted and not wanting to think too much about anything, which is actually ok because my thinking is still a "bit off". I don't feel that I can think straight enough to see my clients or to take their problems back on. I am too exhausted to care to be honest. We are thinking about going to Florida next week and possibly even going to meet Janet, but even that seems too monumental to handle. I go back and forth as to whether I want to go or not, but I truly think I need the break as does Danny.

Now that I've had a chance to sit and reflect on things, I can now recognize how "depressed" I have been for these past 3 years and that it was just getting worse towards the end. How could I not be depressed dealing with this situation with all of its ups and downs? I realize that maybe the way I'm currently feeling and acting is in reality me coming out of this "state" that I have been in. I saw Ruth yesterday and told her that I was feeling "weird" and not sure what was happening with me. She validated that it was perfectly ok to be exhausted and feeling "weird" and that it was important for me to take care of myself right now. It felt so good to hear that as it seemed like I have been given "permission" for feeling whatever I was feeling.

What is clinically interesting to me is that I am beginning to do "small things" once again such as cooking. Even though I've cooked meals over the past couple of months, they usually turned out to be terrible. Meals were over-cooked, dry or just plain awful. Since I wasn't hungry anyhow I'd pretty much given up on cooking. But last weekend I had the urge for 7-Layer Salad, so I did make that and boy did it taste good. That's about all I've done, but still, it's a start.

I also find that I am finally feeling the energy to do some things that need to be done not only around the house, but as far as paperwork too. I have let so many things "slide", especially these past couple of months, and I'm just beginning to see what needs to be done. Cleaning has been haphazard at best, so there is some cleaning that needs to be done in the house. There are bills and other paperwork that needs to be accomplished, and I'm just beginning to think about working on that. It's like I'm slowly coming back to life, although I still don't want to be around crowds of people.

April 29, 2009 (Wednesday)

There has been a lot going on these past couple of days, but I wanted to jot down some things before I forgot them.

Today is really the first day that I have started to have a "meltdown" since the guilty plea. It started with a call from Richard who I felt was rather insistent that I go for therapy. I realize that he is also concerned about his little sister, but it felt invalidating to me for some reason.

I don't think he realizes all of the clinical work that has occurred in my life these past 3 years. The more I tried to explain things to Richard, the more I realized that I was finally explaining things to myself! I tried to convey to Richard that this whole process has been therapeutic and that my healing began when the Fontana Police Department believed me and brought my case to DA Koss. From then on, everything that has happened over these past 3 years as a result of this case has been my therapy. From the very beginning to the very end, this whole thing has been a long therapeutic process for me.

I told him about Mom's words to me, that through this process, I have been untying all of the knots or problems that have occurred over my lifetime and that's been healing. I also reminded him that this whole journey has been documented in this journal and that if he reads it, he will be able to see how therapeutic this whole process was for me in the end.

What I also realized from talking with Richard is that I am most likely grieving for that "little girl" that was hurt so long ago. I have in the past grieved for all of the things that were lost to me in this world as a result of the molestation, but I think that I have to go through that process again. To cry and mourn for the loss of innocence and purity I once had as a little girl. What is interesting is that in some ways I feel like a 14 year-old.

I think another thing that caused my meltdown is that Janet does indeed have Myeloma. I didn't cry on the phone when she told me as I wanted to remain strong for her, but when we hung up, I cried and cried and then threw up. It is so unfair and I wonder why God allowed that to happen. I know in my heart and mind he didn't cause her to have cancer and in thinking about it, maybe that is why we had to do this thing with Lesser at this time. God knew that Janet had cancer and he wanted her to get justice and peace before she left this earth. I am sick about it and blame Lesser for this as well.

The good news is that Danny and I are taking off for Daytona Beach tomorrow morning for a little R & R as well as an AA – Attitude Adjustment! I really need to get away from everything and everyone for a while and Daytona Beach just seemed the way to go. I have been imagining going to lay on a beach somewhere when this is over, and now it is coming to fruition! Not only that, but we won!!

We had gone down there three years ago to display and sell my greeting card line, L.A. Cards, at the Foster Parent Conference. What seems crazy to me is that when we were down there before, I know that I was dysregulated as this whole thing had just started. Of course nothing had happened as this was May of 2006, but still, I knew at that time that the investigation was going to go forward. I just didn't know when and I remember being very "off" at that time. I also remember that despite how upset I was while down there, I was able to achieve a sense of peace and calm spending time on the beach. I remember telling Danny and my parents that the time on the beach was the most peace I have felt in my life since I was 12 years-old or younger. I want to go back there and try to find that peace once again since my spirit and soul desperately need it.

The other good news is that I finally got to see my parents since this whole thing has been over, as Mom was finally feeling well enough to venture out of the house. It was so good to see them and I think they needed to see me, especially Mom. She continues to be physically ill and even though she might have a touch of the flu, I believe that it is all of the "poison" coming out of her. I could tell that she is also emotionally fragile right now as she was very teary-eyed during lunch and that's not like Mom either. It seems like her emotions are totally at the surface, something that I understand as I'm finding myself more emotional and sensitive than usual.

CHAPTER 46

3,000 Miles of Therapy

April 30, 2009 (Thursday)

Finally we are off!!! Talked with Danny non-stop for the first hour as I felt a need to review my entire life and the experiences that came along with my life. I don't know why I had to do that, but I did. Maybe it was because I needed to reassure myself that I was "going to be ok".

For the rest of the drive down to Florida, I'm going to try to be mindless yet mindful. Mindful of all of the sights, sounds and smells on the road, yet mindless in regards to all of the thoughts and worries that have occupied my mind for these past 3 years. Having said that, I also realize that riding in a car has ALWAYS been helpful in that I am able to better process things and think things through. Hopefully I won't do too much of that as I only want peace in my head!!

May 3, 2009 (Sunday)

It is absolutely paradise to be in Florida!!! We were sunburned from yesterday, so we spent the morning going for breakfast and then shopping. Neither of us really brought enough T-shirts, so we did some power shopping. Today is also the day that we met with Danny and Kevin K., friends of mine from Tehran. It was weird in that a week before we left for Florida, I got an e-mail from Danny K., a friend I hadn't heard from in over 30 years. A mutual friend of ours had given him my e-mail but most importantly is that he and Kevin live in Daytona Beach, so we made plans to meet up while Danny and I were here.

I was so nervous about how we were all going to react towards each other after not seeing each other for 32+ years, but then again, they were such good friends that I was more excited than nervous.

When they walked in with their wives, I knew in a heartbeat that it was them. They hadn't really changed in all of these years and we had a wonderful time!! We had so much fun that Danny and Kevin invited us to a Cinco de Mayo party on Tuesday.

It felt so good to see them today and they just made me feel so "comfortable". I don't know why, but it felt like I was seeing "family" and the total sense of comfort and peace that I felt being with them was surprising to me. We really only knew each other for about a year while in Iran, yet our bond with each other feels so strong. Of course that's probably because we were together 24/7 for that year. It was great to see them!!

May 5, 2009 (Tuesday)

Yesterday was back to the beach for most of the day. There had been some stingrays all along the beach on Saturday and Sunday, but there weren't any around yesterday, so we were able to go swimming in the ocean. We body surfed for quite a while, and then had lunch and cocktails on the beach. What a life!! We also saw a dolphin feeding up and down the beach right in front of us while eating dinner outdoors at the bar called Snack Jack's. How incredible and relaxing it was to watch this dolphin swimming back and forth right in front of us for about 15 minutes before disappearing.

We laid on the beach again today before heading off to meet Danny and Kevin again for the Cinco de Mayo party. It was just as good to see them the second time and I shared with them how good it made me feel to see them and that that somewhat surprised me. I had been wondering if I was different while in Tehran but they assured me that I am the same person today that I was back then. That made me feel really good, but they haven't changed either. Danny K. made the comment that most people really don't change whom they are and fortunately for all of us, we didn't change. We just picked up right where we left off.

This close feeling that I have for them had me wondering why being around Danny and Kevin was so wonderful and calming to me and I think I finally figured it out!!

When we first went to Tehran and I told my family about Lesser, I think that I was depressed about everything. I was stuck halfway around the world in a third world country and when my brothers left to go to school in England, I was completely alone. Tehran was fine and I made the most of it while I was there, but when the Keeler boys showed up, they made it so much better.

I figured out that Danny and Kevin were like my brothers while in Tehran. They are almost exactly like David and Richard in regards to their respective personalities and the love that they have as brothers. They made me feel safe in Iran, as I knew that no one would mess with me because Danny and Kevin wouldn't have allowed it. They also made life in Tehran more fun and as a result of all this, I think they pulled me out of the depression and funk that I was in!

After figuring this out, I have to laugh at the power and intelligence of God, as He is the one who put them in my life when I needed them most. God was taking care of me back then as well and I am so thankful. This was a wonderful light bulb moment for me!

Today we take off for South Carolina to meet Janet and I am a nervous wreck for many reasons. One is that there is road construction all through Georgia and all the traffic is totally dysregulating to me. My nerves are on edge and I am scared to death of everything, which in turn was frustrating to Danny. I recognized that my PTSD is still around and I ended up explaining to Danny about how thoughts trigger physiological reactions in a person and that a person can't help that their bodies are reacting to their thoughts.

For example, I was terrified of this guy who was driving all over the road and I kept thinking that he was going to cause an accident. As a result of that thought process, I was anxious, trembling, my heart was racing and I was sick to my stomach, all physical reactions to the thoughts that I was having. Danny suggested that I change my thoughts in order to alleviate the physical reactions I was experiencing and that made me laugh as that is what I do with my clients. But as my clients and others know, that is easier said than done, but I assured him that I was trying to implement my DBT skills!

I am also nervous to meet Janet. In all honesty journal, I don't have a BURNING desire to meet her in person right now and I'm not sure why. I really do care for her and want to meet her, but for some reason this seems "too soon" or something. For me, the relationship and bond that we have developed over the telephone "seems safe", but she wants to meet me before she gets "sick" and it's perfect as we aren't far away from her at all being in Daytona Beach. My wise mind tells me that it is the right thing to do and it seems providential that we do meet now as we are close to where they live. I don't know why I am feeling this way, I just am and for some reason I felt it was important to share this.

I'm also upset because I am not ready to leave Daytona Beach. For some reason I find complete and total peace while on a beach, but this time I don't feel like my emotional energy and soul have been replenished. There is still too much to "accomplish" on this trip, but at least I was able to find that peace for a couple of days. I don't know how anyone who lives in Daytona Beach gets anything done because the whole atmosphere down there is one of being on vacation!!

I have been able to do quite a bit of thinking about EVERYTHING while lying on the beach and here are some of the things that I have figured out.

1. I don't want worry or hassles anymore;
2. The Keeler boys were a huge factor in helping me to begin healing while in Tehran;
3. I've had a fortunate and marvelous life being able to travel the world;

4. I have made some wonderful intimate friends all over the world who love me;
5. I have made a positive impact on this world and continue to do so on a daily basis;
6. That I've always been kind, fun and considerate of others and that it is something that I do unconsciously and impulsively;
7. My life as I know it is going to change somehow;
8. How this whole journey these past 3 years has been healing for me as well as others;
9. The realization that while I was trying to help others heal through this process, God was taking care of me and my mental health;
10. I realize I don't want any more negativity in my life. This might not be realistic, but I'm going to eliminate as much as I can;
11. I realize that I want to continue helping others, maybe just not one-on-one anymore;
12. I realized that I deserve to be happy and calm the rest of my days;
13. I can't and won't tolerate injustices any longer and will now speak up more often when I see it. I even confronted some guy in FL who I saw kick his pit bull while walking down the street;
14. The realization that God has used me all of my life to help others. All of my daily impulsive moves have hopefully brought joy, hopefulness and comfort to others;
15. I am not going to be anyone's emotional garbage dump anymore;
16. How thankful I am for my wonderful parents and family;
17. How thankful I am for having Danny in my life!! God knew that I needed him.

May 7, 2009 (Thursday)

I finally met Janet…my partner in crime!!! We ended up checking into the motel last night in order to clean up before going to Jerry and Janet's for dinner and boy was I nervous! I even threw up before leaving!

We found their house fairly easily and both of us were surprised to find that it was in a very expensive neighborhood. I'm not sure what I had been expecting, but I didn't expect a home that could have been featured in "Better Homes and Gardens". It was absolutely beautiful!

Janet came flying out of the house and we immediately embraced. She was this warm, generous, classy and open spirit who I felt I had known forever, but then again, not. It was a weird feeling, but then again it was another dialectic.

Jerry was still at work, so we poured ourselves some wine and went out onto their enclosed patio to smoke, drink and pet the dogs. It was interesting in that we really didn't engage in any "small talk" to get acquainted, but rather just started right off with "the important things".

We discussed the case as well as talked about how wonderful DA Koss and Detective Sharp were. We talked about the sentencing and what did both of us want for him. We both feel that 3-4 years of being IN PRISON will be enough for us, but it isn't up to us what he will receive.

We both talked about God and how He had been such a powerful influence in this whole thing. We discussed the people that were supportive to us as well as the people that weren't. Janet wanted to share some pictures she had of her and Lesser and I had to point out the body language in those pictures as that alone said a thousand words.

Jerry came home and we ended up drinking and smoking a lot more before he grilled some steaks. Jerry is a wonderful man who loves Janet very very much. Jerry has a southern charm and style to him that is endearing and reminds me of James Carville. Jerry did talk with Danny and I about how the experience with Lesser totally screwed Janet up. I think Danny would totally agree on the fact that he screwed me up as well.

We had a wonderful dinner, took some pictures and we could tell they were tired, so we took off for the motel. I was so happy to have met her and Jerry face to face and to put a new face on Janet, as all I remembered was what she looked like back in 1976. It was a wonderful time and I'm so thankful that we went. See, the wise mind knows best!

We are now driving to Nashville to see my niece Kayln graduate from Vanderbilt and of course, Danny and I processed what happened last night as I "felt off" today for some reason.

I am having a difficult time this morning processing and reconciling the "life scenario" I had created of Janet prior to meeting her with the one I have now. What I hadn't expected was for her to have such a beautiful home, perfect manners and to be a classy entertainer with the perfectly laid dinner table right down to the gorgeous napkin holders. I guess I hadn't expected her to have it "so together" in life even though I knew that she had come from a wonderful and loving upper middle class family, like I did. I think that I had been expecting Janet to be "damaged" somehow and that "damage" would be visible from the "outside". That somehow I would be able to "tell" that she had been a victim of child abuse, but that isn't what I found at all and I don't know why that is "throwing me".

I've spent a lot of time thinking about why I feel so "off" and the only analysis I can come up with and that I am ashamed to admit is that maybe I hold the same "beliefs" and "stigmas" about victims that society does. The very thing I was trying to combat by using my name in the newspaper articles!

I think that everything about Janet challenged my "unconscious" and until now my unknown belief system that most sexual abuse victims are "lower class" individuals; that the victims parents were neglectful; that victims aren't intelligent; that victims can't do well for themselves in life. What I find so difficult to understand though is that I already KNEW from talking with her all of these months that she came from a loving Christian family, that she was well-raised and well-educated, so the question was why did meeting her throw me for such a loop? I'm not sure if that is the correct analysis of why I'm having difficulty with this but it sounds right. I'm now wondering if that is why I intuitively felt that I needed to include my Life Experiences essay in this journal. I knew in my "wise mind" that I had to put it in, but wasn't quite sure why until maybe now. Maybe I unconsciously felt that I needed to "show" readers that I came from a wonderful, loving, protective, nurturing, upper middle class Christian family. To try and trump societies stereotypes before they even began reading this journal by proving to people that I wasn't some neglected child who nobody cared about but rather cherished from day one.

Finally, I want to say that Janet felt like a big sister to me. She is older and even taller than I am and I "felt" like she was trying to take care of me. Her interactions with me felt warm and fuzzy but then again, she is really the only one who totally knows and understands my thoughts, feelings and issues in life. She is most certainly a kindred spirit and I am so thankful that God not only put her in my life but worked it so that we could meet as well!

After all of this revelation this morning, I still had more "mental work" to do on myself as we were going to be driving RIGHT PAST the exit to Lesser's resort in the Smoky Mountains. He has a resort on a lake that caters, I would imagine to families, and I must say that the area he chose for his resort is absolutely gorgeous! As we neared his city, I started to get very upset at him for what he did to Janet. She is such a wonderful soul and spirit and I wanted to go to his resort and confront him. Of course Danny said there was no way in hell that we were going anywhere near his place, and though he was perfectly right, that statement of course made me even madder. What right does he have to tell me whether or not I can confront Lesser, but as we neared the exit, I of course had a change of heart as then I became scared to do it.

What I had really wanted to convey to Lesser by showing up at his resort, was that no matter where he was, I was going to find him and hound him. I know that confronting him wouldn't be the smartest thing for me to do for many reasons, but I felt like he needed to know how pissed off I am at him. I want him to suffer for what he did to Janet and I and who knows whom else.

Even though I didn't get the chance to confront him directly, God with all of His humor, did reveal to me how Lesser is going to suffer and that revelation came through some orange signs that were placed alongside the highway in North Carolina. These orange signs inform drivers that there are "inmates working" and the thought of Lesser working as a prisoner alongside the highway cracked me up!

I also started wondering about what he must be thinking while driving on this very same road when he heads to Wisconsin for all of the court hearings. The beauty and serenity of the Smoky Mountains is so prevailing that it must be difficult for him driving through God's gorgeous scenery knowing that where he is headed only holds hell for him. He must dread coming to Wisconsin and I wonder how he is going to deal with not being able to see this beautiful scenery, maybe for the rest of his life. Too bad, so sad!

Next up is Nashville and my niece's graduation from Vanderbilt. We are also looking forward to experiencing the country music scene as neither Danny nor I have ever really been to Nashville. Then it's homeward bound!!

CHAPTER 47

What Do I Do Now?

May 10, 2009 (Sunday)

We got home yesterday and though it was great to see Tucker, I'm finding that I'm nowhere near ready to be home. It was wonderful to get away from everything for a while, but it wasn't the type of trip that replenished my emotional energy. I still feel like I have more "work" to do on myself and that I'm not ready to put back on my "therapist hat" right now.

Rather I feel like I am trying to "find myself" and to determine what I want to happen next in life. I'm finding out that I am still obsessing about "things" and one of those things is this journal. I REALLY want this journal to help people from all sectors of life understand how sexual abuse affects an individual for life. I want educators to be able to use it as a guide to helping future counselors understand the ramifications of this crime. I want significant others to understand why their partner is screwed up. I want other victims to be able to identify that they aren't the only ones who feel this way or think this way. I want family members to understand how abuse affects the core dynamics of a family and I want "regular" people who have never been exposed to this before, to understand. In order to accomplish all of this, I have to make sure that this journal is the best it can be, so I'm beginning to worry about that. I will have to self-publish, as there was never any interest from the traditional publishers. That means that this whole "book" is now on me and I want it perfect.

I also want to do something in regards to lobbying for tougher legislation against sexual offenders as well as making the process easier for victims. I feel that I can do this because I have made contacts in the past with Wisconsin Congresswoman Tammy Baldwin and Wisconsin Senator Jon Erpenbach. Maybe that is why God put them in my path so long ago. I have always told Congresswoman Tammy Baldwin that I needed to keep "my face in front of her" for some reason. Well, maybe this is the reason.

I feel that these aspirations aren't unrealistic as I now can see my whole life might have been in preparation for this next stage in my life.

If I hadn't become a therapist, I would never have had the knowledge to go through this criminal process. Being a therapist has also helped me to understand the dynamics of sexual abuse as well as to be able to articulate that to my clients so that they also can "get better". My credentials are impressive and if I want to get people to listen to me, I have to know what I am doing and saying. That is why this book is so important to me and why I have put all of my blood, guts and tears into it.

The columns that I wrote for the National Foster Parent Association's quarterly magazine; being trained in DBT and training others in WI to utilize it; the greeting card company that I started and all of the contacts that I have made through that. All of these things give me the credibility that I need for not only this journal, but for helping other's as well.

I'm not sure what my future path will be, but I am confident in the fact that God knows what it will be, and for right now, that is good enough for me.

May 12, 2009 (Wednesday)

I thought that the vacation to FL would be relaxing and calming enough that I would be able to leave some "nervousness" there on the beach, but unfortunately that didn't happen. It's right back to it and I can't seem to find the energy to do anything right now except to work on this journal.

I finally got the strength to call Mr. and Mrs. P. as I didn't have the opportunity or in all honesty, the strength, to talk with them since Lesser pled guilty. To be totally truthful, there was something that Mr. P. had said to my parents when he called them after the guilty plea that really cut me to the core. I don't really want to put what he said in here, as I don't think Mr. P. meant to hurt me, but I think that it is important for people to understand how certain comments make victims feel. Mr. P. had told my parents that Lesser pleading guilty "clinched" it for him. To me that said that he still had some doubt and that hurt me more than anything. I didn't have the courage to bring it up to Mr. P. when I talked with him, so I wasn't able to check this theory for sure, so in all fairness, maybe that wasn't really what he was thinking and I apologize that he had to read it here.

I knew that they had many unanswered questions about this whole thing and that it was going to be a difficult call. Unfortunately I wasn't able to talk with them both at once as I had hoped, but Mrs. P. and I talked for about an hour. Most of the discussion I spent explaining basically what is in this entire book. The how's, they why's and the what-ifs. Needless to say, this was a difficult conversation and I was dreading that I was going to have to do it all over again with Mr. P.

Today I finally mustered the energy to talk with Mr. P. and that lasted about an hour as well. They both had many questions that were valid questions, but still difficult for me to rehash. We talked about so many things from why I didn't tell, to how he was able to "get me". We discussed the ramifications Lesser's actions had on all of us as well as the fact that they were terribly sorry about not protecting me.

Mr. P. and I talked about the betrayal that he feels with Lesser as they continued to be friends long after he left the Lake Geneva area. I tried to answer all of the questions that he had, but it was still difficult. I realize however that since I made the decision to use my name and to write this book, I have to be open and honest with people when they have questions. No matter how embarrassing or humiliating their questions or my reactions to them might be, if it will help explain things to others, then I will gladly do it.

Another question that he had that I found interesting was why I was entitling this journal "Justice Before Mercy". I explained to him the constant dilemma (dialectic) that both Janet and I had about wanting him to fry, while at the same time feeling badly that we were destroying someone's life. I told him about Hans e-mailing me that statement to remind me that mercy was okay, but justice needed to come first. Mr. P. asked what my "mercy" was to Lesser and that was easy to answer. One is that I agreed to the plea bargain, (even though I didn't know it at the time) thereby lowering the sentence he could have got. Secondly, I have asked for him to receive 4 years in prison versus the 15 that many people seem to want him to receive. Finally I have decided that I'm not going to try and sue him to take away everything that he has. I believe that those things constitute the "mercy" part.

Mr. and Mrs. P. were the last "knots" that I had to address since the ending of this phase of the process. I have already sent out a ton of thank-you notes to those who supported me as well as a letter to Peter S., but I still hadn't talked with the P.'s, so I'm grateful that piece is over.

I'm just getting so tired of rehashing all of this not only for people that I know and love, but also for this journal. It is very difficult to experience all of this stuff firsthand and then have to re-experience it all over again writing it down. It's like some of my more difficult client sessions where I have to regurgitate into my notes what happened. It was hard enough going through it in the first place, but then to have to relive it for the notes is just doubly anxiety producing.

Friday is the memorial service for Mr. F. and I'm afraid that it will be just horrible. It wasn't even a year ago that we were at Mrs. F.'s memorial service. I will also have to face the Lake Geneva community and many of our friends who now know what is happening with me as a result of the newspaper articles. I feel that what little emotional energy I do have left this week, I have to leave for finishing this book as well as for Mr. F. and his family.

I also found it was interesting in that Mr. F's daughter, Deb, who is not only a "friend" of mine, but was also in Campus Life, didn't know a thing about the criminal trial. I don't know why Mr. F. didn't tell her about this as it's been going on for 3 years, but unfortunately I'll never know why now. I can only think that he was trying to protect her somehow.

CHAPTER 48

Tying Up The Loose Strings

May 21, 2009 (Thursday)

I called Janet this morning, as I haven't heard from her since she saw the doctor in Atlanta and she actually had some good news. Since she isn't presenting with any of the symptoms right now, this doctor wants to wait in regards to treating the cancer. Some people go for 5-10 years before experiencing the symptoms of Myeloma, so we are going to pray for the best.

We also finally had a chance to process what seeing and meeting each other had done for us, and we both agreed that it had been a meaningful and extraordinary experience. I even shared with her my difficulty processing and understanding why I feel so "off" after meeting her. That led to my shameful revelations about the "stigma's" that I hold in my head, but still don't understand as I KNEW all the positives about her and her family. We discussed our preconceptions of each other, what it meant to have a kindred spirit in this fight and how comfortable we both felt with each other. She will truly be a friend forever.

May 30, 2009 (Saturday)

It's been a while since I have written but a lot of things have been happening.

First off is that I did sign with a self-publishing company since no traditional publishers showed interest in publishing this journal. That fact however hasn't diminished my hopes for this journal to help others, so I took a leap of faith and signed with a company. This step is so exciting while at the same time I'm terrified that it will be a big bomb. I'm so tired of dialectics!!

There has also been some wonderful things that have happened since Lesser pled guilty and the most important is the change that has happened within my parents. My mother finally pulled out of her "sickness" that lasted for a good 3 weeks! Even though she was ecstatic about the news, physically she wasn't doing very well and that was of concern to all of us.

Having said that however, in the last couple of weeks, she has done a remarkable turnaround emotionally. When I talk with my mother now, it seems like she is "a little girl again". She sounds happy, full of energy, carefree and willing to go places with Dad again. She has also quit smoking, which is truly amazing and possibly why she isn't feeling well, as she is withdrawing. Mom has been smoking incessantly since she was forty-years-old and she is now 77, so she definitely had an addiction to cigarettes. The last couple of weeks however, she is smoking at the most 1-2 cigarettes a day and doesn't even miss it. Mom believes the reason she doesn't "need" to smoke anymore is because she doesn't need to "worry about me anymore". I honestly can't remember the last time I heard my mother so happy and carefree in life and to be a witness to that was worth the entire 3 years of agony.

Another wonderful thing that happened is that Mom had also been wanting to thank Mr. Sweet, our family attorney, for providing them with the legal information necessary to run Lesser out of town so many years ago, but found that she was having a difficult time putting her thoughts down on paper. She wanted to personally talk with him, not just write him a note. Leave it to God to finish up with all of the loose strings because lo and behold, Mom and Dad ran into him while at lunch at Moy's in Elkhorn. As a result, she was able to personally thank him for all that he did for our family and that was the last thing that she "needed" to do before she could "put this down". I am as thrilled for her as she is for having been able to tell him in person! I had already sent him a note thanking him from the bottom of my heart.

As far as I'm concerned, I really haven't given Lesser another thought since coming back. I did have to talk to the person conducting the pre-sentence investigation, but besides that, I feel my work is done. I am not obsessing at all about June 25th, the day that he gets sentenced and in reality I keep forgetting about it. I don't want to spare one more minute of my life thinking about that bastard. I feel that I have done my job and now it's over.

June 2, 2009 (Tuesday)

Lesser is supposedly in the Elkhorn area today as he has to be interviewed for the pre-sentence investigation. I get the "creeps" knowing that he is in my state!

I'm trying to get back to "normal", but find that I still want to stay home. I have been working on this journal these past couple of weeks and it is difficult to relive this whole thing even though we won!! What I have found while rereading it is that I most likely was in full-blown PTSD for the entire three years. No wonder I was such a mess!

I also find that I am still emotional about things and crying about the littlest things. My emotions are still at the surface and I'm not sure when they are going to "be manageable again". Maybe life will go back to "normal" after the sentencing, but I'm not sure about anything right now. I feel like I am just "existing". Some things are better, but some aren't. I feel like a racehorse that is being walked to "cool down" after going full board in a race and though I keep walking and walking, I'm not "cooling down".

June 10, 2009 (Wednesday)

It is now a little over two weeks before the sentencing hearing and though I'm not obsessing over it, I am finding that I'm thinking more about it as it nears. I can't help but wonder what Lesser is thinking as it gets closer.

Janet called this morning to catch up on things and fortunately she still isn't feeling any symptoms of her Myeloma yet. She is rather finding herself enjoying life, spending time with loved ones and is now the proud owner of a convertible car! She said that she has always wanted one, so her blessed husband Jerry bought one for her.

We also talked further about my "problem" reconciling the feelings and thoughts that I have had since meeting her. I told her I can't figure out what is bothering me. I keep coming back to the belief that I would be able to "tell" that she had been abused, but I couldn't from looking at her. We discussed how maybe as victims we try to portray an "outer image" of things being fine and that we have our "heads on straight" when in reality, our insides are a complete mess. The reality is that a person can't "tell" if another person has been molested, unless the victim shares it with them. It's seems like we victims are in "a secret society" of some kind. The whole thing is weird to me but a thought came to me. I would like for everyone who has been sexually abused, to put a big "A" on his or her forehead for one day, so that the whole world could see how many human beings this happens to. I think that society would be shocked to not only see the vast number of people that have been a victim of this insidious crime, but I think they would also be shocked at "who" has been abused. They would see that friends, acquaintances, co-workers, normal every day people as well as famous people have all been abused and they didn't even know it. Wouldn't that be an eye-opener for society!

Another thing is that I have e-mailed DA Koss a couple of times to ask some questions and one of them was to ask if Lesser will have to go immediately to jail after being sentenced. His response was "I assume so"!!

June 11, 2009 (Thursday)

This morning has been rough for a couple of reasons. While I was driving home from work last night, I started thinking about having to write something to say at the sentencing hearing. I had been thinking about whether or not I even wanted to say anything, but after thinking about everything, I believe that it is important that I do say something.

Since that decision has been made, I now have to write something and that is upsetting me. All I know at this point is that I want it to be a powerful statement and in order to do that, I will have to go to that private place inside of me where the pain comes from and knowing that is making me profoundly sad. As a result, I finally sobbed this morning about the whole ordeal!

I am also finding myself sad that in 2 weeks, his life, as he knows it, is going to be over. While I want him to join me "in hell", I can't help but feel sorry for him, so once again this dialectic is throwing me for a loop.

June 12, 2009 (Friday)

I had e-mailed DA Koss about the PSI report and this morning he had e-mailed back that he saw the report and that the recommendation is for 9-11 years in prison and what did I think?! My immediate reaction was shock as well as a sense of sadness to see that he might be receiving that long of a sentence. I truly was shocked seeing that long of a time, but I trust that the PSI investigator knows what he is doing. He has worked with sexual offenders for over 17 years so he KNOWS how to read them and I will defer to his judgment.

This deep sense of sadness is a result of a couple of things I think. First I am sad that he is going to have to spend maybe the rest of his life in prison, so his life is over. Knowing that I am the one, who has done this to another person, makes me feel badly as I don't like to hurt anything.

I am also sad in that this long sentence shows me that the PSI thinks that he is obviously "devious in nature" or possibly a sociopath. The fact that I was targeted and destroyed by such a twisted person makes me literally sick to my stomach and of course I puked. The fact that I was touched by pure evil just plain hurts down to the core of my soul.

Lately, I've also been thinking a lot about the traumatic effects that this case continues to have on me. I recognize that I am "coming out of PTSD" so to speak, but I still am anxious, emotional and "scattered". I had to go see the young man who was actually the impetus of my greeting card business as he has been struggling with life lately. It was a 3½ hour drive each way and I was a nervous wreck the whole way. During the drive, I realized that this is the farthest that I have driven alone in a year. I am still "scared" to venture too far from home, but it did feel comforting to me that I made it. I can't believe that it is difficult for me to drive 4 hours from home when I have traveled not only around the world twice, but moved to Switzerland by myself and without knowing a soul. Of course I had no choice as I HAD to make this drive, but that forced me to do something I haven't felt able to do in a long time.

Another thing that is interesting to me is how I'm reacting since the guilty plea in regards to my "physical space". In many ways I feel like a rape victim and I would know what that feels like, as that is another tragedy that has happened to me. I don't want other's to touch me or invade my "bubble" which is my personal space. I am feeling very vulnerable and therefore, feel like staying in my house once again.

While driving to see my client up north, I had to drive on this road where there weren't many people or other cars, and that had me terrified. I was afraid that there were "bad people" along that road and that if I broke down, I would be in big trouble. I can't help these thoughts and feelings no matter how ridiculous some of those thoughts are. Normally I LOVE driving in the woods, so the fact that it scared me so, tells me that I'm not out of the woods yet myself. Now I'm beginning to wonder if these awful thoughts and feelings of mine will ever end.

June 15, 2009 (Monday)

I was able to talk with the PSI investigator today and after speaking with him, I am so angry that I can't see straight.

The investigator told me some of what had transpired between him and Lesser and that in the beginning, Lesser denied that he had ever touched me. Of course as the questioning went on, he admitted to touching more "parts" of my body, but couldn't remember whether or not we had "intercourse". I am so angry that he is still denying that he did this, that I fired off an e-mail to DA Koss asking how I can put this last "nail" in his coffin so deep, that he won't be able to ever see the light of day.

The investigator also said that the reason Lesser says he pled guilty was to spare his family the embarrassment of a trial. That is such bullshit and it makes me furious to think that he might con his way out of this by having people believe that ridiculous statement. What about the embarrassment that I have had to endure by trying to bring him to justice?

The next move in my game will be to make a plea to the judge to lock his ass up. Maybe I will have to change the name of this book to "Justice With No Mercy" because now I really don't care what happens to him. I have mentioned in the past that the last thing a person wants to do is piss me off and right now, I feel nothing but disgust and hatred for this man. Jeannie made that comment to both Janet and I about hoping that the road he was going to have to go down would bring him back to God. Obviously that didn't happen, but he better start rethinking that concept as he is going to need God where he is going.

Now my statement during the sentencing is more important than ever, as I want to make sure that the judge gives him plenty of time. This is most likely the last thing that I will have to do in this criminal case and now I want to make sure that everyone knows what a rotten liar he is. He reminds me of the emperor in the fable "The Emperor's New Clothes". Everyone can see him for the sick, evil person he is, except for him and for those of them who believe in him. I hope they read this journal. That should dispel any "questions" that they might have about whether this really happened or not. He might be able to "explain me away", but there is no way in hell he could "explain" Janet away.

I just received some of the most tragic news that has got me heartbroken. This young man I know was crossing the street with his seeing eye dog, when a car hit him and the dog. Adam is currently in critical condition in the ICU trauma center in Janesville and if he lives, he will most likely be a vegetable for the rest of his life.

What makes this even more tragic is that it was only a few weeks ago, that his sister passed away, so this is a double whammy for their parents Mark and Kim. I met this family when I had to "practice" on a family for one of my graduate classes. I had met them before and what was unique and special about this family, was that three of them have the disease, Neurofibromatosis (a.k.a. Elephant Man Disease). The father Mark unknowingly had the gene for this disease and passed it on to his two younger children, Adam and Jessica. Melissa, the oldest, was spared this tragedy.

Adam's tumors grew inside of his body and as a result, they were pressing on his brain as well as his optical nerve, causing him to go totally blind later in life. His sister Jessica was worse off than Adam as her tumors grew on the outside of her body. To say that this family faced numerous challenges doesn't even begin to describe what this family has faced, but I thought they would be a great family to "practice" on and as wonderful as they are, they agreed to be my "guinea pigs". I thought for sure that this family would have "issues" as Adam was going totally blind and Jessica wasn't able to do anything at that time and really ever. She couldn't speak, couldn't feed herself, and at that time, couldn't sit in a chair. Mark and especially Kim spent almost everyday of Jessica's 26 years of life taking care of her total needs. She had to pick her up out of bed everyday, dress her, feed her, bathe her and take care of her multiple medical issues. What is further remarkable is that NEVER ONCE have I heard any family members complain about their lot in life.

Despite all of these challenges, I found this to be the most wonderful family in the whole world with few if any issues and my admiration for this family was unparalleled. They are the most fun, loving, caring, compassionate, open minded and openhearted families I have ever met, professionally or personally. We have continued to stay in touch over the years and it was only a few weeks ago that Jessica finally gave in to this horrible disease. She was 2 days shy of turning 26 and it is absolutely a miracle that she lived as long as she did considering her vast and constant medical challenges. Everyone who knows this family knows that it was the incredible love and dedication of Mark, Kim, Melissa and Adam that kept her alive all of these years. They have just lost Jessica and now they are going to lose Adam as Kim told me that even if he does live, his brain damage is so severe that he will never be "cognizant" again.

Jessica's funeral was heartbreaking enough and now to have this tragedy occur doesn't seem fair. Why do such bad things happen to good people when there are jerks like Lesser that trot through life without any cares or worry? What can a person say to Mark, Kim and Melissa as there is nothing that anyone can do or say to take away their pain. The world seems so unfair and cruel right now, it's no wonder that people sometimes just want to "get out of it".

June 18, 2009 (Thursday)

7 days and counting! It was an exciting day because today I got my hair done and then had my picture taken for the cover of this book. I wanted the cover of the book to have "psychological" meaning and one of the things I wanted to portray were the colors of black and white. To me, that symbolizes that the substance of this case was very clear. There were no "gray areas", but rather it was black and white. Lesser intentionally groomed and molested Janet and I and that's it. The white scarf around my neck symbolizes to me the role of a judge, so I am in effect the judge, jury and executioner.

June 23, 2009 (Tuesday)

Two days and counting until the last move in this "game" and needless to say, I am nervous, scared and sad. Yes, sad. While most people are expressing their wishes that he fry in prison, I do not feel that way right now. I mean yes I want him to go to prison for quite a while, but I am not finding any pleasure whatsoever in his demise.

I am sad that I have had to ruin other people's lives, as I'm sure his family is having a difficult time with this. I am sad that he will have to go to prison and who knows what he will have to endure there. I am sad for myself and Janet and how are lives were forever altered as a result of this man. And finally, I am sad that this ever had to happen in the first place. If he hadn't have put his dirty hands on us in the first place, none of this would be happening and he wouldn't be going to prison.

I find that I am also sad because this is going to be the end of this journal and right now, I can't imagine not having "you" in my life. You have been such a support throughout this whole ordeal and I couldn't have done it without you. I am actually crying right now as I've come to think of this journal as a confidante and friend. I know that it is an inanimate object, but to me, this journal is an extension of myself and the thought of closing it down feels like I am "losing" a piece of myself. We know how much I hate to lose a "piece of myself" and so I honestly feel like I am "shutting down" part of who I am.

Maybe that sounds crazy, but to have something that was always there for me, never judgmental, willing to listen at any time of the morning or night and never complained about my whining and bitching, saved my sanity. The other thought I just had is maybe this journal really is "me" as it seems that it talks back to me and reveals answers to questions and confusion from so long ago. It's "me" talking to "me" in what seems at times like a real conversation. I am really going to miss you journal, so I think that I am beginning to mourn "your loss". Maybe I'll simply have to write a sequel to this so I don't lose you entirely!!

Another thing that I found myself thinking about over the weekend is that this would be the last weekend of freedom for Lesser and I found myself wondering what he was thinking and feeling. I think the emotion that I am feeling towards him is "pity": the definition of pity being compassion and compassion meaning "mercy". Isn't that weird how it comes down to me feeling exactly what is in the title of this book?! I know that he did something terrible to Janet and I and I know that he deserves prison. But still, he is a human being and most likely going to have it very rough in prison, so I feel pity for him.

I found that while writing my sentencing statement, I don't want to suggest a specific period of time that he should receive. I have felt since he pled guilty that whatever he received for a sentence would be what God determined he would receive, not me. That takes the pressure off so to speak because for some reason, I don't want to be responsible for how long he gets. I feel that I have done my job in this process and it is no longer up to me.

Janet feels the same way. I called her yesterday to see if she had written a letter to the court commenting on what he did to her, and to my dismay, she hasn't as of yet. She said that she was having a difficult time pulling her words together and therefore hasn't gotten anything down on paper yet. Janet said that she has a thousand ideas floating around in her head all of the time, but when she sits down to put them to paper, it doesn't work. Janet also expressed the same "hesitation" I feel in regards to suggesting a sentence. She also doesn't want to be "responsible" for whatever sentence he is going to get. I shared with her that I felt the same way and didn't suggest a specific "length" in my statement. Isn't that weird that we have these thoughts and feelings? I wonder why?

It's not like I "like" him or anything. In fact, I can't stand to even look at him. The only thing that I can think of is that I am not a vindictive, vengeful person and it honestly "hurts" me when someone or something else is suffering, and it is my belief that he is going to suffer immensely in prison. I try to rationalize and justify it by telling myself that he deserves it after what he did to Janet and I and who knows whom else, but there is still a part of my soul that is sad. What I do find comforting feeling mercy for him, is that at least I now know that I am a kind-hearted individual through and through and that is a part of my personality that Lesser didn't destroy. Fortunately God continued to nurture that kind-heartedness no matter what befell me during my life and I'm thankful for that.

Today I go to preview the picture for the cover of this book and though I am excited about this next step for the journal, it is another indication to me that this journal is almost over. It seems only appropriate that here is yet another dialectic that

I am presented with even though this process is ending. It's been astonishing to me to see the vast number of dialectics that I felt throughout this journey and since dialectics are "dysregulating" maybe that was why I was so dysregulated these past three years.

Fortunately I will be able to come out of it, while some people never do. I found out first-hand how difficult a life of dialectics is and I will never look at them the same way. I think that it was providential that God put learning DBT in my life so long ago, because without it, I honestly think I would have gone crazy 2 years ago. Just another example of His grand design! I am so grateful to Him for not only helping me through this traumatic criminal process, but for planning it so beautifully as well.

That is something else that I wanted to document with this journal; how God's fingers were in this process from the beginning. I know that I can see how He masterminded this whole thing, but I wonder if others can. For those of little faith, I want you to know that there is a God and that He is a wonderful God. He isn't the one who "allows" bad things to happen, but rather He is the one who brings good out of that bad. God gave Man the ability to make choices in life and therefore it is my belief that mankind does bad things to others, not God.

Later:

Oh, journal today is sooo hard and I don't know why. I have been crying on and off all morning and throwing up again. I know that it is nerves, sadness, grief, anger, frustration, hurt as well as some other things thrown in. I also just read Janet's letter to the judge and it is so upsetting to hear the pain and anguish in her words. She was really a trooper and did a great job.

I'm trying to pull it together before calling her, as I really don't want anyone to see me in this much emotional pain. Danny is working, the dog is sleeping and so I am letting out all of the pain that I currently feel. I am so not looking forward to Thursday and I can only pray that I will be able to keep it together enough to say what God wants me to say.

June 24, 2009 (Wednesday)

It is the day before the sentencing hearing and surprisingly, I'm not that upset. I haven't even had to take a Lorazepam, although I probably will before bed.

I'm not sure why I'm not upset because yesterday was horrible. Maybe it is because I have kept busy all day long and am now tired from all of my endeavors. Whatever the reason is, I'm glad that I'm not as upset as yesterday. I did puke when I got up, but that's par for the course.

The great thing that happened today is that I sent Janet my book yesterday and she called to tell me that she has been reading it and LOVES, LOVES, LOVES it. She also said that she feels that it could be her story as well. I am so excited that she likes the book so far and that it has brought her comfort!! That gives me hope that my "leap of faith" in publishing this might have indeed been a "God Whisper".

Another wonderful thing happened in that I received the foreword that Dr. O'Beirne wrote and not only it is inspiring, her message is heartfelt. I told you journal she had a huge heart!! Dr. O'Beirne couldn't have put it more eloquently describing what this book is about as well as my hopes and dreams for it helping others. Again, I am thankful that God had her be a part of this journey!!

I think I will try and finish up my sentencing statement and try and relax for the rest of the day. Tonight is the finale of "I'm A Celebrity, Get Me Out Of Here" and though it was cheesy in ways, I loved watching it. What I wouldn't do to escape to a jungle for a while!

CHAPTER 49

Justice Is Delivered

June 25, 2009 (Thursday)

It is finally over! I am so tired and have such a headache, that I will write more tomorrow, but I simply had to tell you journal what he got for a sentence. What I think is most interesting journal is that I haven't called a soul (although I did e-mail quick), but I HAD TO TELL YOU! You have been with me through thick and thin and I want to thank you too for being with me every step of the way. I honestly couldn't have done this without you and I truly thank you from the bottom of my heart.

Oh, by the way, he got 10 YEARS!!!

June 26, 2009 (Friday)

I can't believe that it is over but of course when I woke up this morning, I threw up. This is still upsetting on some level but I will now tell what happened yesterday.

Danny and I left for court and unfortunately for him, the ride over was spent playing my music loud and telling him not to say a word to me. It was dysregulating having him along as he "threw me off" my routine. I felt badly for the way I was treating him, but he was a good sport and I was thankful that he was with me.

When we got there, David and Julie were just pulling in to the parking lot, so we waited and walked in with them. I immediately had to go to the bathroom and throw up I was so nervous. We went up to the DA's office to wait and Evelyn had a nice room we could sit in. Richard and Deanna were already there and then Mom and Dad showed up. Blessed Richard was such a help to Mom as she could barely walk she was shaking so badly.

I introduced my family to DA Koss and Detective Sharp when he came in and DA Koss briefed us on what was going to happen. He said that anyone who wanted to speak on my behalf could speak in court. He also shared that there had been rumblings from the other side about this whole thing. It appears that some of Lesser's "side" were saying that this whole thing was rigged, that DA Koss and I were friends, that my ex-husband was in prison, and that DA Koss, Sharp and I were all laughing about "things" one day in the hall. One of his advocates even said that this whole thing "didn't pass the smell test". Turns out he was a police officer for 35 years. He might have been the reason that we had such "difficulty" with the police in NC. Remember journal that we thought that "something fishy" was going on down there after the arrest warrant was sent to them.

At any rate, we all then went up to court but the previous case wasn't over yet, so both "sides" had to wait in the hallway. It was awkward to say the least as they kept looking at us and we kept looking at them. Amy and Doug, who are life long friends, were there despite the fact that it was their 32nd anniversary. It was so nice to see them and have their support as they had also been involved with Campus Life and were part of my "core friends".

We finally got called in and I thought it was interesting in that Evelyn insisted on sitting on the aisle. Julie had decided to make a statement to the court, so she went first saying how they have over 800 children in programs at the church where she works. She said that not only were they "children" who thought like children, but to work his agenda in the name of God was the worst thing a person could do.

Next up was David and he was full of raw emotion, which is rare for him. He started to yell at Lesser and call him a liar, con man and I think a piece of shit (!) but the judge and DA Koss stopped him. He was supposed to address his statement to the judge! He pulled it together and gave a statement about what a liar and jerk he was. I felt badly he was so upset and really don't remember all that he said.

I was last and though I had prepared a statement, I really didn't look at it because I was so nervous. I started by thanking DA Koss for even taking this case and that he was a "hero among hero's" for victims. I thanked Detective Sharp because if it hadn't have been for him, this would probably still be in the investigation stage! I also thanked the judge for believing me enough to send it to trial and look what had happened. He had pled guilty!

I then addressed some of the statements that they "had said" such as the fact that I didn't know DA Koss before this case started. I think I also said this was the hardest thing to do but it's hard to remember what I said to be honest. I told Lesser that I had the opportunity to meet Janet last month and that she was a wonderful person. I think I said "how dare you do that to her". I said for those that still believe Lesser, read my book "Justice Before Mercy" and then see if you still believe him. I also made some comment to Lesser that he reminded me of the Emperor in the fable "The Emperor's New Clothes" in that everyone could see what he was but him. Finally I told him that I had talked with Jeannie and that Jeannie had made the comment to me that she hoped "this road that you were going to have to go down will lead you back to God", but it was obvious that that hadn't happened. I suggested that he rethink that suggestion as he was going to need Him where he was going.

I then directed my comments to the judge because he was the one I really wanted to speak with. I had a couple of pictures of me when I was 13 years-old (going on 14) and 15 years-old and I gave those to him. I told him that the one picture with me looking adoringly at my grandfather is not the same person sitting in front of him today. That girl ceased to exist the day that Lesser put his hands on me. The other picture was of me on my 15ᵗʰ birthday at which time, I was already being groomed by Lesser.

I reminded him that he has read my Victim Impact Statement as well as the PSI. I told him that he has seen a lot of criminals come through his courtroom, so I trust that he knows what he is doing and that he will give him the sentence he feels he deserves. Though I didn't cry as in having actual tears come down my face, my voice was breaking while I was talking.

There was a reason why I didn't suggest a sentence and that is because I don't want to be responsible for whatever he gets. As I said earlier, my job was to get him convicted and then it was up to God to decide the rest of it. Another reason why I didn't suggest a sentence is that I wanted the judge to know that I TRUSTED him to make the right decision. Since trust is a HUGE factor for victims, I was hoping that he knew how much I was depending on him to do the right thing.

DA Koss then spoke and addressed some of the issues such as "we knew each other", that I didn't have an ex-husband in prison (we of course know they're referring to Prisoner Pete) and that this most definitely wasn't rigged. He reminded Judge Carlson that I had reached out 25 years ago to Mr. Sweet as well as other attorneys as evidenced by his letter. He was very soft-spoken and not confrontational to the "other side". He reminded the judge that this is a serious matter and that sexual molestation isn't a crime that a person ever recovers from as evidenced by other cases that they have tried in Walworth County. He did a wonderful job!

Next up was Lesser's side and I did feel sorry for his stepdaughter and wife. Both of them spoke as to how this situation had been affecting Lesser, his health, his wife's health and their business. They brought pictures of how he looked before this case started, and then after this case started so that the judge could see his weight loss. They said that they have never seen any indication that Lesser could do anything like this and how he had been a loving husband and father. They both asked that he receive probation since he obviously wasn't this horrible man that I was claiming he was. I did feel sorry for them as they didn't ask for this whole situation and I'm sure it's going to be difficult for them. But more importantly, I felt sorry for them in that they couldn't see this man for what he truly is.

The last person speaking for his side was his brother-in-law who had been a police officer or something for about 35 years. He said that he was the one who mentioned that this didn't pass the "smell test" and that if this had happened anywhere else, it wouldn't have even come this far in court. He said some other things too that I really don't think helped Lesser whatsoever. They all should have thought more about what they were going to say and how they were going to say it. It seemed like they were trying to say that he shouldn't have to pay for something that was done so long ago. That as well as the fact that he has been nothing but a loving presence in their family.

Then Lesser decided to speak, which also didn't help his case. He tried to show "remorse" and said that he was sorry that he had done this. He said that he wished he could take this one-year out of his life. He stated that when he moved to Indiana after "getting kicked out of Wisconsin" that he had realized his mistake and decided to "turn his life around". He talked about what a good guy he was and that he had forgiven some huge debt I think to his son. Blah, Blah, Blah. As I listened to him speak, I could visualize him getting himself more and more entangled in his own web of deceit. The spider was closing in for the kill.

The reality is that he kept coming back to Wisconsin to see me for almost 8 months AND he was still "seeing" Janet. It is also my understanding, although I'm not sure, that this might be when he began an affair with his current wife. As he was talking about his "turn around", I don't think that he realized that he was only digging his hole deeper because were all catching him in his lies. I was just praying that the judge was "catching" his deceit too as his timeline about "turning his life around" didn't add up to what the evidence was. It appeared that he still wasn't taking responsibility for this even though he had pled guilty. It was unreal and it was all that I could do to keep my mouth shut. I think that it is so UNFAIR that I can't speak last as he had the last word and they were all lies. I was soooo afraid that the judge was going to believe him.

The last person to speak was his attorney and the poor guy had a lot to say, but nothing to say. As my family said later, how can you defend a man who pled guilty? There was really nothing that he could say as Lesser had only made it worse by what he and the man before him had said. To me, his words to the judge only reinforced that he is still trying to be a "master manipulator". Unfortunately for him, we were all too smart for him.

The judge then said he had to go do something and left the courtroom. I had to run to the bathroom and I thought that it was interesting that once again, Evelyn said that she would go with me.

The judge then came back in and talked about all sorts of things. He talked about previous cases like this one and what length of sentence that those offenders had received. He read in court EXACTLY what happened between us sexually and how it had progressed to touching my "who who", but he used the real word. The judge read about how in the PSI Lesser claimed that it was ME who asked him to touch me and that it was ME who asked if I could give him oral sex "under the dashboard of the car". It was soooo embarrassing to have my parents hear that, but I trusted that the judge knew what he was doing. Or at least I was praying fervently at this point that he did! The judge reviewed the psychological reports from Lesser's own "doctor" that said that he was minimizing what had happened and that he needed to work on his "perception" of the actual events. I watched Lesser as the judge spoke and his head kept hanging down further and further as time went on.

I don't think that I have ever anticipated anything more in my life than hearing what his sentence was going to be. I had noticed that the courtroom was filling up with a number of sheriff deputies and though it was scary, it also felt very very good as I knew that we were nearing the end and it wasn't going to be good for Lesser.

And then it started, the part in the television programs where the judge begins the language of imposing a sentence. My heart was literally in my throat and when he said he sentenced him to 10 years, I felt such relief and joy that the judge "had gotten it". He "had gotten it"!!! He knew that this man was a sexual predator who continues to manipulate people to this day. I am so grateful to the judge for the perfect and just verdict.

Right after the sentence was read, Evelyn wanted all of my "side" to get out quickly so then we all went down to the family room. I didn't even get a chance to see his family, but I was able to see that Lesser was being "rushed" out of the courtroom by at least two rather large Sheriff deputies. Having that vision in my mind is going to remind me for the rest of my life that we finally got justice and that he is now beginning to pay for what he did to Janet and I. I had also sworn to that girl in Williams Bay that I would get him for her too and I did. I might have to try and find where she is buried so that I can bring some flowers to her grave. I'm not sure for a fact that he molested her, but I know in my wise mind that he did, so I hope that she is smiling from heaven. As I say that, I'm thinking that she probably had a hand in one of the many miracles that happened during this epic journey.

We all sat in the "family room" in the DA's office decompressing from all that had just transpired. We were hugging and Mom was sobbing with happiness. We talked about our feelings and thoughts and gave David a hard time for his behavior in court. He had been "talking" during the sentencing hearing and at one point, the court officer came over and took him out of the courtroom. He told David that "he (the officer) was sitting on a powder keg and he didn't need David to ignite it"! Therefore, David had better be quiet in the courtroom. David was glad that he was allowed back in as he said he would have missed the best part…and that was hearing the sentence and seeing him being ushered out of the courtroom to go to jail. DA Koss also said that Lesser's attorney is going to file an appeal in regards to what he considers the severity of the sentence. I think that the sentence is perfect. He has the opportunity to be released after 25% of his sentence is served, so if he is a "good boy", he could be out in 2½ years.

As far as Lesser's family, I didn't get a chance to see them either right after the sentence was read or ever again. I now know that the reason Evelyn was by my side is because of the possible "things" that I guess could happen during something like this. Doug said that he had been watching "the other side" during the hearing and that as time went on, they seem to "deflate". I think that the judge read all of that stuff so that "his side" could see how he groomed me and totally manipulated me. To prove that his actions weren't some "youthful" indiscretion on his part as they were trying to assert.

I'm not sure who all of the people were on his side, but Doug said that they appeared to be shocked by what just happened in court and one guy was crying. Doug also said that someone said, "What the hell just happened"? I do feel badly for them, but Lesser isn't the guy that they think he is.

After thanking DA Koss, Detective Sharp and Evelyn profusely, my family along with Doug and Amy all went to Abbey Springs for lunch where we further decompressed by talking about what happened in court. Everyone was surprised by the "high drama" and that experiencing it in person is much different than watching it on television. We talked about how both Danny and David wanted to beat the crap out of him when they saw him for the first time. I guess that Danny was literally shaking so badly, that Deanna and Julie had to go and calm him down. This has been so difficult for him as well and I appreciated the fact that he would have beaten the crap out of him for me. David too!

I also took this opportunity to thank Mom and Dad for ALL that they have done for me not only during this process, but in life as well. They have always been a constant source of support and love. I thanked Richard for his support and for taking my numerous phone calls over the past 3 years. He was ALWAYS willing to listen and help me in any way that he could. I thanked Deanna for reading my journal because that was huge right there. I thanked David and Julie for their statements and their support. I thanked Amy and Doug for their presence and support at the hearing today. And last but certainly not least, I thanked Danny for all that he has done for me these past 3½ years because as he shared in his letter to the judge, this ordeal has been one of the toughest times of his life. He also got a round of applause from everyone, as they know how difficult it must have been for him as well.

Last, but not least, I had to call Janet and tell her the news that he had received 10 years. I believe that she is also satisfied that he got the sentence that he did. Both of us have always said that the sentence part would be up to God and we both accept what He had decided. I also thanked her for her support and encouragement, as she was a big part of this process as well.

It's been quite an endeavor and I'm thankful for so many things. I was able to process this a little bit yesterday as I had to for the newspaper reporters and here is an analogy of how I feel.

I believe as a therapist that it is important to reconstruct a person's life so that they can see how their issues emerged. I refer to their life as a jigsaw puzzle and that it is my job to identify all the pieces of the puzzle and then begin putting it back together.

I sincerely feel and can now see, that the jigsaw puzzle of my life was missing a HUGE piece right in the middle. There are of course other missing pieces and there always will be, but as a result of this criminal case and its outcome, that big piece has been put back into place. It feels like that piece of my soul that was ripped out so long ago is finally back. Maybe that's why I hate losing parts of my body so much, because I had "lost" that big puzzle piece. I was only able to find that "piece" once again because of the courage and dedication of the Walworth County judicial system and I can't thank them enough.

Another "positive outcome" that I have been able to identify is that the length of sentence validates to ME that others also feel what he did to me was wrong. Judge Carlson even said "It would seriously depreciate the nature of the offense and impact it had on the victim if I didn't sentence the defendant to prison". I am so thankful that the judge understood how much this crime affected my life. Even though we as victims are forever tethered to our perpetrators, I now have the satisfaction of knowing that he is paying for his crime.

June 27, 2009 (Saturday)

This will be the last entry as I need to get this to the publishing company and if I can see through my tears, I wanted to share a few observations before closing this chapter in my life. I felt that it was important to share that while I'm continuing to feel satisfaction that justice has been served, I can't help feeling a little sorrow for what Lesser must be going through right now being in jail. I must admit that I have been thinking about how scared he must be and how his whole life has been turned upside down. That was something that I wanted to have happen from the beginning, but now that it is happening, it doesn't feel as good as I thought it would. I don't understand how anyone can get any pleasure from destroying another human being, as that wasn't God's intent for man.

But maybe that is what has always separated Lesser and I; the fact that I have a heart and a conscience and he doesn't. I feel badly for what has now happened to his life, while he never gave a thought of how he had destroyed mine. I'll bet that right about now, he is definitely VERY SORRY for what he did, because now he is experiencing what hell is like.

I'm sure that this whole endeavor will take a while to process and I have no idea what is in store for my future. I am confident however that God will provide a "whisper" as to what path he would like me to follow next. I only hope that it is a "smoother" journey than the one I have taken so far in life.

I feel like I should "wrap this up" with some profound statement or "light bulb moment", but to be honest, I don't have one right now. This whole journey has been filled with miracles, lessons to be learned, light bulb moments and profound realizations. I hope and pray that by my sharing these personal revelations with you, they can now serve others as well.

It is now time to close and I feel that it is only appropriate that I end with something I learned while talking with Mom and Dad yesterday. I guess they had felt the need to go look at my baby book after the emotional state of the sentencing hearing and they found something that they thought was prophetic and so do I.

The name Laurie means "little victorious one".

APPENDIX
VICTIM IMPACT STATEMENT
LAURIE ASPLUND
JULY 22, 2008

I find it very difficult to put into words the impact that this crime had on me because the devastation of my life was so invasive. Sexual molestation isn't just a crime that people "can get over with and move on" from, but rather it is a crime that rips apart a person's core being and forever changes the trajectory of a normal development.

In an effort to try and convey to the court the devastation that this crime had on me, I decided to send you the following; something that I actually wrote months ago when someone asked me how this crime had affected me. When they asked me that question, I suddenly found it overwhelming to identify all of the ramifications that the sexual molestation had on me. I also realized that because much of the resulting trauma is "internal" and therefore not something people could "see", I had to figure out how to convey the mass destruction it caused in my life. It meant that I had to rip open all of the wounds and share my most intimate and personal thoughts and beliefs.

What I wrote was/is unscripted and expressed with a raw emotion from a place so private, that I'm afraid of what people will think. Some of the effects might seem redundant but I found that many of my issues can be analogous to a plate of spaghetti in that it is difficult to know where one strand ends and another begins. They become all entwined together. But as difficult and painful as it was to identify all the ways that this affected me, it's been even more difficult living with it.

VICTIM IMPACT STATEMENT
(LAURIE ASPLUND)

PERSONAL ISSUES:

1. A piece of my soul was ripped out as a result of this. Everything I thought the world was, was no longer that. I lost my self-confidence, my dignity and felt like I was no better than dirt in this world;

2. Lost my own identity for a long time;

3. Was on a death wish for many years and in actuality, I still am;

4. Felt like I had no power in this world and no control over my destiny;

5. Ended up drowning who I was in alcohol and drugs and was never really able to figure out what I could have been in life; I feel that I could have been much more of a person and could have been more successful and happier if I didn't end up dealing with this thing for most of my life;

6. Was a doormat for many people and let them take advantage of me because I didn't care about myself or feel that I was worthy of anything;

7. Don't care about my appearance and in fact, have always downplayed my femininity, don't ever wear make-up or style my hair...In fact, I really wish that I wasn't a female as life would be a lot easier;

8. Really haven't been able to grow up and be responsible for myself;

9. Don't even really see myself as an adult, but rather still a child. It's like it stunted my entire healthy growth of any kind and I yearn for a time when the world and life was a safe place. I think I am still trying to find that, yet never will be able to and that alone terrifies me;

10. Never want to get married again as that means that someone else has control over me;

11. I also think this affected my intentions of whether to have children or not. I can't/don't want to bring anything into this world that could be hurt so badly and since I can't control what would happen, it's better off that I don't even have them;

12. Major control issues on EVERYTHING, most specifically sex;

13. I felt such shame, humiliation, stupidity, total betrayal, worthlessness, anger, frustration, hurt, disbelief but the most debilitating emotions were the shame and even guilt that I felt over it even happening. These feelings have NEVER gone away and they are constantly resurfacing;

14. For years as a result of this, I tried to hide all of my more painful and negative emotions by blunting them with alcohol and drugs;

15. I can't even lie down on my chiropractor's table as I begin to feel like I could be taken advantage of while in that physical position. Once again, he has the power over me due to me being vulnerable;

16. Despite having to have control, that for many years I put myself in vulnerable positions and as a result had bad things happen. That could be connected to my feelings of low self-worth and a type of death wish desire;

17. Whenever I see injustice to anything or anyone that is defenseless, I re-experience all of the emotions such as anger, helplessness, a sense of doom, unfairness. Do you know how many things people are exposed to on a daily basis about the injustice in this world? Not just daily, but numerous times a day they show things on television and on the Internet just to name a few;

18. I don't dance. To me dancing can be provocative and once again, I don't want anyone looking at me in a sexual manner;

19. When I herniated my lower disc and had to have massage therapy, I couldn't let her even work on me without all of my clothes on, as I didn't feel comfortable without them. I still hated getting the massages as someone was touching me all over and I don't like that feeling at all;

20. The same was true of my physical therapist;

21. The only people in this whole world I totally trust are my parents, and maybe that is why I rely on them so much;

22. When my parents die, I really don't want to keep living, as then there will be no one that I can totally trust and rely on;

23. I have had nightmares throughout my life that usually revolve around someone hurting me;

24. I have no bedroom door so that if someone is coming after me, I can see them;

25. I ALWAYS have the doors locked no matter where I am at;

26. I don't like people at my house, as it is my safe haven so to speak. I am very private that way and it's difficult for family and friends, as they aren't ever invited out.

FAMILY:

1. The effect that this had on my parents which was devastating to say the least. They didn't protect their child and the guilt that they feel will never go away;
2. My brother being resentful and angry towards my parents for not protecting me;
3. They can answer better than I about what this has done to them;
4. I can't even go swimming with my nephews as I feel very uncomfortable about them maybe looking at me in a sexual manner. They tease me about not swimming with them on our Ely vacations, and I can't even be truthful about why I can't. I think they've seen me in a swimsuit a handful of times in their lives. That is just not fair;
5. Due to me being on alcohol and drugs, I didn't interact with my nieces and nephews, as I didn't want to expose them to me. As a result, I don't have a very close relationship with them, which hurts me to this day. I have better relationships and know more personal things with some of my kid clients than I do with my own family;
6. The financial woes that I have caused my parents over the years as a result of my drug/alcohol addictions, inability to work at times and medical bills just to name a few;
7. This also has greatly affected Danny's life in that he has to deal with all of my issues.

WORLD VIEW/BELIEF SYSTEM:

1. I learned that the world is an unsafe place;
2. I learned that people aren't to be trusted...especially religious people;
3. That all men really care about in this world is sex and that drives them more than anything. There are many examples that reinforce this belief. Ex. Bill Clinton...Everything in this world is driven by sex;
4. That true evil exists in this world and therefore I might be touched by evil again;
5. That I am constantly looked at and assessed by men in a sexual manner, whether that is true or not;
6. That no one can truly love me solely for who I am, but rather there will always be the sexual element involved;
7. Scared to grow old and be dependent on others for my safety. I would rather be dead than have someone take advantage of me again...especially if I'm old, feeble and senile;

8. I was even afraid having surgery, as I would be out of it and not aware if someone took advantage of me or whatever. I even asked the nurse who all would be in there and would I be exposed in any way;

9. Wouldn't take any pain medication in the hospital as I don't like to be not aware of things anymore;

10. Couldn't even get a soothing massage in the hospital as I don't like people touching me; I even freaked out the nurse's aide due to my adamancy in her not touching me;

11. I learned that people will take whatever they want from you and will do anything in order to achieve what their desires or perceived wants and needs are;

12. I learned that when people are like that, another person has no defenses to make it not happen;

13. I learned not to talk about it or reveal it to others as I believed it was in some way my fault and why did it ever happen;

14. I learned fear in that I was afraid of what others could do to me and the power that others have to literally destroy someone or something;

15. It is also my belief that there will never be anyone who loves me unconditionally as there is always some ulterior motive of why they are with me and what they want from me;

16. That the thought of unconditional love from anyone but my parents isn't possible in life;

17. People aren't necessarily what they appear to be. What are they really like…client who was the drug dealer in IL, Halloween, People who act like they're good people, but really aren't. Catholic Priests. Their duplicity.

SEXUAL DEVELOPMENT/BELIEFS:

1. Unhealthy view of sex…I don't equate sex with loving someone or having them love me, but rather an "animal instinct" and all that men care about;

2. I still feel like a spittoon;

3. Felt like that was all that I was good for in life…to satisfy men's desires;

4. Miss out forever on what the true meaning and feelings behind sex should be;

5. Don't really enjoy sex and don't like to do certain things especially foreplay as it reminds me of Lesser pawing at me all of the time;

6. Hate being looked at as a "female" as I don't want to draw attention to my sexuality;

7. Am constantly reminded about Lesser and the effect that it had on me due to television programs and society in general;

8. Can't look at other relationships as healthy in that I freak out when I see a child sitting on someone's lap…even if it is a father and son or something. I get physiologically and emotionally dysregulated;

9. Can't listen to any dirty jokes, watch sex on T.V. or anywhere, get physically and emotionally upset reading anything that surrounds sex…especially with children;

10. Don't like my boyfriend to see me naked at all, or even playfully grab my privates at any time. I will explode. I don't like him "ogling" me as that once again reinforces my belief that men are only interested in me in a sexual manner;

11. My beliefs about sex make it very difficult for my boyfriend and I worry that he might leave me someday due to my hang-ups about sex. Again, that is a reinforcer that men really only do care about one thing;

12. Always had to have sex either high or drunk;

13. Since quitting drinking, sex has to be the same every time. There can be no deviation from the routine or in the way he touches me or I literally freak out;

14. Intimacy is imperative to have with your partner and that can't happen with us. How I have gained intimacy is through how he takes care of me when things are bad.

I hope that these intensely private revelations have been helpful in providing the court with a better understanding of the insidious nature of this type of crime.

www.ingramcontent.com/pod-product-compliance
Lightning Source LLC
Chambersburg PA
CBHW060839280326
41934CB00007B/851